# The Toughest Fighting in the World

# The
# Toughest
# Fighting

## IN THE

# World

The Australian and American Campaign
for New Guinea in World War II

## George H. Johnston

WESTHOLME
Yardley

Frontispiece: Australian troops following a Stuart light tank through a New Guinea forest in 1942. (*Library of Congress*)

Originally published in 1943 by Duell, Sloan and Pearce
This edition © 2011 Westholme Publishing

Westholme Publishing, LLC
904 Edgewood Road
Yardley, Pennsylvania 19067
Visit our Web site at www.westholmepublishing.com

First Printing September 2011
10  9  8  7  6  5  4  3  2  1

ISBN: 978-1-59416-151-3

Also available as an eBook.


Printed in the United States of America.

*This Book is Dedicated to*
COMRADES-IN-ARMS, BOTH
AMERICAN AND AUSTRALIAN,
WHO FOUGHT IN NEW GUINEA
FOR THE WAY OF LIFE THEY
LOVED; WHO IN FIGHTING
GAVE THE LIE TO AXIS PROPA-
GANDISTS WHO SAID THAT
DEMOCRACY WAS DECADENT;
WHO IN DYING LEVIED A TOLL
ON THE REST OF MANKIND—
THE PROMISE THAT THESE
MEN SHALL NOT HAVE DIED
IN VAIN

# NOTE

THE author spent the period covered in this book as war correspondent in the Southwest Pacific Area officially credited to the Australian Army and Royal Australian Air Force, to the United States Army, and, for a period, to the Royal Australian Navy. For most of the time he was in New Guinea, and for the balance of the time was either at General Headquarters or advanced operational bases. In that time he represented the *Argus*, Melbourne; the *Advertiser*, Adelaide; the *West Australian*, Perth; the *Mercury*, Hobart; the *Examiner*, Launceston; and Australian United Press. For a period in the early months he was war correspondent in New Guinea for the *Sydney Morning Herald*, the Melbourne *Age*, and the *Daily Telegraph*, London. In recent months he has also been war correspondent for the New York magazines, *Time* and *Life*. The author points out that no attempt is made in this book to give a detailed day-by-day account of events, but rather to paint a general picture of the campaign in the tropics.

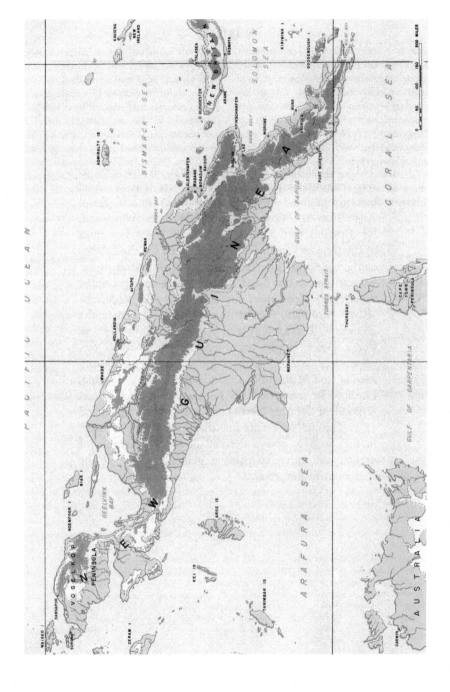

# INTRODUCTION

by the Right Honorable Herbert Evatt, K.C., M.P.,
Australian Foreign Minister

IN New Guinea, one of the largest islands in the world, including
territories of enormous strategic importance to Australia and the
United Nations, one of the greatest struggles in all military history
has been waged; the facts of the campaign make an epic story. The
difficulties faced by Australians and Americans were amongst the
greatest ever experienced in military operations—thick jungle,
treacherous swamp, tropical rain, moist heat, high mountains,
malaria-infested areas, and a powerful and insidious enemy including specially trained Japanese jungle fighters.

For a lengthy period incapacity caused by tropical disease was
four or five times as heavy as losses through actual combat. The
type of fighting was new. For the most part air transport and
transport by natives were the means of carrying our supplies and
moving our wounded. Many generals who won battle fame with
the Australian Imperial Forces in the last war and also in Libya,
Greece, Crete, and Egypt during the present war considered the
New Guinea fighting by far the most arduous they had ever
experienced.

The jungle conditions must be seen to be appreciated. A few
excellent films have been shown which illustrate the type of country
in which operations were conducted and the wounded had to be
carried. But even these films fall short of the reality. In the early
stages of the Battle for New Guinea—which was also the Battle
for Australia—we had little to fight with. We were in much the
same position as Britain was in after the rapid collapse of France.
Gradually the situation improved, and the efforts of the Australian
Government and the Australian people have helped to transform the

situation from one of deepest gloom to one of justified optimism.

In the air fighting, Americans were numerically stronger than the Australians. But in the ground fighting the great bulk of the forces were Australian. Supreme difficulties and hardships always draw brave men together. The American land forces have generously honored and praised the fighting qualities of the Australians—A.I.F. and Militia alike—who carried the whole burden of the campaign for some time, and who rapidly became experts in the art and science of jungle warfare.

This book—"The Toughest Fighting in the World"—will help us all to understand better what Australian and American servicemen have suffered and sacrificed in the war against the Axis in the Pacific. It has been written by one who was an eyewitness, and its intimate detail and its stories of heroism, hardship and comradeship paint a vivid and stark picture. It will help to end any last traces of complacency.

One of the most encouraging features of the New Guinea campaign was the help given to the Australian and American fighting men by the natives of the territories of New Guinea. Road transport being impossible, the wounded had to be carried by stretcher over the mountains or through the jungle, or along tracks which had to be specially cut for the purpose. No soldier will ever be stinting in his praise for the way in which these natives succored the wounded with loving care. They assisted us in many other ways.

The territories of Papua and New Guinea have long been administered by the Australian Government. Surely the active co-operation of its native peoples with our armies is a measure of the success with which Australian administrators have carried out their obligations to protect and care for the native population. Moreover, we should remember with undying gratitude the pioneer work of the great missionaries and churchmen who, facing incredible hardships, carried the torch of Christianity to these Melanesian islands. After this war the gratitude of our soldiers must be reflected in an even greater concern for the welfare of the New Guinea "Fuzzy-Wuzzy."

One of the best auguries of the future is the practical spirit of comradeship and mateship between the Australians and Americans under the leadership of men like General Douglas MacArthur and General Sir Thomas Blamey. Australians and Americans fought well together in 1918. They are still fighting together wherever British and American air forces are hammering the Axis. In New Guinea their comradeship was the basis of military successes which have proved to be of strategic and general and not merely of tactical and local significance.

Mr. Johnston is well qualified for the task of authorship. He is a distinguished writer and newspaperman. His experiences in the New Guinea campaign were reflected in vivid day-by-day despatches. He and other Australian and American observers have performed magnificent service for Australia and for the common cause and I am glad to have this opportunity of paying my tribute to them all.

The New Guinea campaign emphasises our duty to those who fought. At the very least we must resolve to avoid the reappearance of the curse of unemployment and poverty which plagued the youth of all countries between the two great wars. I think it is possible to achieve this objective of full employment without that harsh regimentation which is alien to our traditions of civil liberty.

But our recent successes should not be allowed to mislead us as we move toward even greater Pacific offensives. Those offensives may be costly. They will certainly involve a heavy draft on our courage, patience, and fortitude. They will also call forth all the wisdom and leadership of the United Nations. Overconfidence and complacency can no longer lose us this war. But they can certainly prolong it. Humanity and common sense both demand that we bring the war to a victorious conclusion at the earliest possible moment—not only in Europe and in Asia, but in the Pacific. The objective everywhere is not only victory. It is speedy victory. Time is now of the essence of the contract.

# CONTENTS

# CONTENTS

## III. CHECKMATE

## IV. RETREAT TO VICTORY

## V. THE CLEANSING

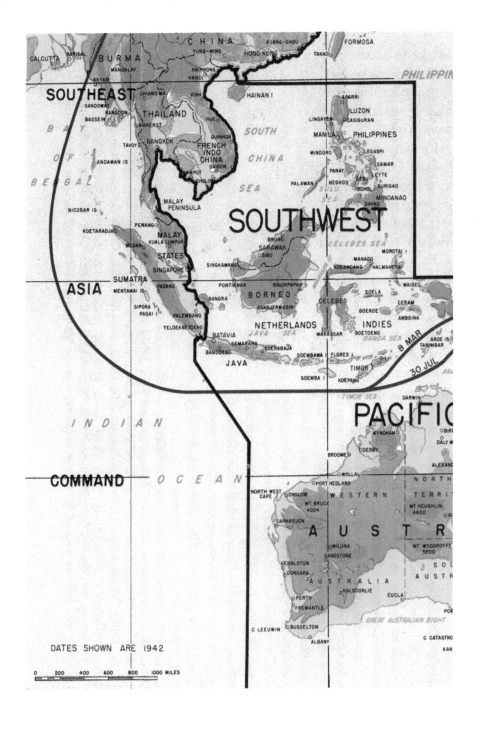

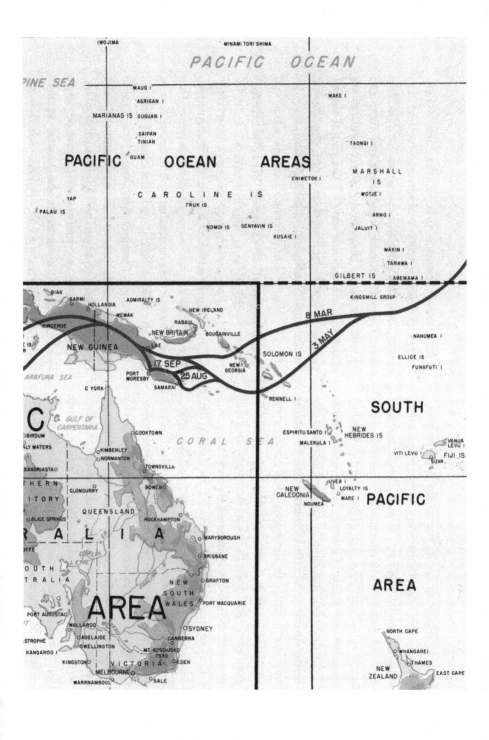

# I. TROPIC SIDESHOW

*January 23, 1942—March 14, 1942*

---

*Overture*

THE Battle for New Guinea has begun. It is January 23, 1942. It seems strange. They're still fighting in Malaya. Why are the Japs striking also at this little tropical outpost less than five degrees below the equator? That's only one of the questions. There are a lot of loose threads to be tied together on this story.

The communiqué doesn't say very much. Radio communication with Rabaul ceased at 4 P.M. A strong Japanese invasion force landed somewhere about dawn and drove our little garrison of 1400 men from their fixed defense positions. It was believed that the Australians were continuing resistance in the hills.

So Rabaul had fallen and the invader has at last gained a foothold in Australian mandated territory. Looking back over the last fortnight or so it is easy to see how the show has been building up.

A small force of Japanese bombers came over Rabaul on 4 January. No doubt the enemy was vitally interested in this cornerstone in the defense strategy of Australia's outlying island barrier. Controlling St. George's Channel, main gateway to the scattered islands of the Bismarck Archipelago, Rabaul's magnificent harbor, cupped within the 1400-foot girdle of mountains and smouldering volcanoes, could hold a large naval force; its twin airfields could base many bombers and fighters. Now bombs have fallen among the coconut palms and Casuarinas of this little tropic port which was once the capital of German New Guinea (where Australians first went into action against Germany in 1914), and capital of British New Guinea until the torrent of lava and ash and pumice from erupting Matupi drove the administration to a new capital at Lae only a few years ago.

3

By the beginning of this week it was pretty evident that the preliminary shadow-sparring had ended. On Monday between 100 and 130 Japanese fighters, bombers and dive-bombers were over Rabaul showering high-explosive bombs and incendiary bullets on the ash-covered buildings. The freighter *Hersteen* was blown up at the wharf with eleven men killed, others wounded. The air was filled with planes, only five of which were Australian—five slow Wirraways that went up to give battle to more than 100 enemy aircraft each of which was faster, larger and better armed. All five were shot down. But three Japanese planes came down. One crashed on the lava-hardened slopes of Matupi and in the cockpit were found the bodies of two Japanese. In each man's hand was clutched a little cotton bag filled with sand from some picturesque little town back in the Japanese islands. They were a long, long way from home. There were bodies of Australians and bodies of Japanese to be buried in the quiet little cemetery behind the town where Australia's first dead of the last war rested side by side with some of their enemies.

Next day Japanese cruisers were steaming off the coast of New Ireland, hurling shells into the pretty little tropical town of Kavieng. Funny thing that the Japanese Navy operated in these same waters in the last war—as our allies! The naval guns swung inboard and, in wave after wave, 40 bombers and 20 fighters swept in to plaster almost undefended Kavieng. Not until the town was a shambles of rubble and shattered lath and plaster did the Imperial Japanese Marines make the landing that conquered the town. Two hundred and fifty miles to the westward, Lorengau, capital of the Admiralty Islands, was being raided, and at noon the Japanese bombers struck at the New Guinea mainland, dropping high explosive on Madang, formerly Kaiser Wilhelmshaven, "capital" of the wild Sepik district. Rabaul, this Tuesday, had a quiet day in which to bury its dead, its first dead of the Second World War, of the first war in the Pacific. Wednesday came and Japan continued to introduce its New Order to the tropic towns with a heavy hand. Over Lae, undefended capital of British New Guinea, 60 bombers and fighters had a field day and in less than an hour property worth almost $1,000,000 was ravaged by bombs or destroyed by flames. Keith Parer, famous goldfields pilot, met swift death in the cockpit of his plane as he tried to get it off the drome to safety. Some of the Chinese and natives, assisted by the "low whites," looted and plundered the town, half mad with the whisky they had stolen from the shattered hotels. Through blinding tropical rain the civilian population streamed inland to the terrible swamps and jungles that meant discomfort, hunger and disease—but also meant safety. Up in the mountains Bulolo, also, was bombed.

The events of yesterday foretold what would happen today. The Japanese Air Force went where it wanted to go. In Malaya we had a few Brewster Buffalo fighters. Not much good, but something. Out here, we had nothing. Bombs fell on Kieta, in the North Solomons; on Tulagi, in the South Solomons; on Bulolo, in New Guinea; on Rabaul, in New Britain. Some of this was diversion, some preparation. Early in the day we pondered the question as to where the blow would fall. The answer must have been clear to the handful of men charged with the defense of Rabaul. From 9 A.M. the sky was filled with aircraft—all Japanese. For almost an hour the coastal fort at Praed Point was bombed and dive-bombed until the guns were blown out of the ground and half a dozen young Australian gunners were buried beneath the shattered concrete and twisted steel.

Later came a report that a Japanese invasion fleet was sheltering in the lee of Watom Island, off the coast to the north of the town, a fleet of five big transports, three heavy cruisers, three destroyers—with an aircraft carrier out to sea and other ships heading south from Truk. In Rabaul there was the roar and thunder of explosions as engineers carried out essential demolition work. Why is our defense so much a policy of scorching the earth, of only token resistance, of strategic withdrawals? A battalion of the A.I.F. and a few small units of the Australian Militia and Permanent Forces moved in to prepared positions. But what could they do against this overwhelming force sheltering behind Watom?

Today has provided the answer to that: Nothing beyond fighting a beachhead defense for a few short hours and then retiring "according to plan." Tonight there is only a grim silence from Rabaul. Japan has, for the first time, advanced and conquered south of the equator. She has, in a few vital hours, captured one of the greatest natural defense points and naval bases of the South Pacific. Only one Australian base stands between Rabaul and the

Australian mainland—the little garrison of Port Moresby, on the south coast of Papua. And how long can Moresby hold?

### Friday The Thirteenth

New Guinea was somewhere in the blue-gray haze ahead. The camouflaged airliner was droning evenly northward. Below was the dazzling emerald green of the Great Barrier Reef. It was warm in the cabin and I was half dozing, half thinking.

It was Friday, February the thirteenth. Although Australia had yet to receive the definite news for which it was being prepared by half-hints and solemn warnings, Singapore had already fallen to the Japanese. The black stain of Japan's co-prosperity sphere in East Asia was running southward rapidly. Since the day, little more than two months before, when Japan had dropped her twin masks of hypocrisy and suave politeness and had struck devastating blows at Pearl Harbor, Singapore and Manila, the new enemy had moved swiftly. Armchair prophets who had written smugly about "Japan's fourth-rate air force, third-rate army, and navy that has yet to be proved even second rate" were scratching away with their pens to prove that Nippon had gained victory by treachery, not by skill at arms. They refused, even then, to concede that it might have been something of both.

Now they had crushed the "impregnable" fortress of Singapore— the fortress whose guns had faced the wrong way. They were investing the Philippines. They had struck at Sarawak, at Borneo, at the Celebes. They were simply taking no notice of the experts who told them that they were stretching their supply lines far beyond the limits of safety. They had thrown great tentacles across the western and southwestern Pacific, and the extreme end of their longest tentacle was about 3000 miles from Tokyo. They had gained a foothold in New Guinea and were less than 1000 miles from the continent of Australia. But between their new base at Rabaul and the green seaboard of North Queensland stood the Australian garrison of Port Moresby, already bombed by Kawanisi flying boats based on Rabaul. And I was going to Port Moresby.

That was where we all were going. A military captain with the Staff Corps badges on his tunic, a young cipher officer of the Royal Australian Navy, a party of naval ratings hot as the very devil in their thick blue uniforms, another war correspondent beside my-self—Osmar White, of the Melbourne *Sun*. There were no un-uni-formed persons in the plane. All civilians were leaving Papua and New Guinea.

It seemed hard to believe that war had come to Australian terri-tory after all these years of talk of Japanese ambitions, of White Australia, of the Yellow Peril. But in the pocket of my uniform was the army license for "Accredited War Correspondents accompany-ing a force in the field in Australia or its territories." And at the top was the endorsement "License No. 1;" the first license ever issued in Australian history for a newspaper man to cover war in Australia. The plane droned on across the incredible peacock blue of the Coral Sea. It seemed strange that the army should want to send war correspondents to cover this little campaign in New Guinea, a tropic sideshow that seemed so pathetically unimportant when one saw the searing headlines that told of the last grim days of the Malayan campaign, of bloody battles on the frozen Russian front, of the continuing resistance of MacArthur's men on Bataan Peninsula.

None of us knew what was going to happen. Mainland farewells had been rather frighteningly final. People had shaken hands with an air of "Well, it's been pleasant knowing you. . . ." All Austral-ians seemed to be quite certain that Moresby would exist as an Aus-tralian base only for as long as the Japanese refrained from attack-ing it. And that happens to be pretty well my own state of mind, too. We have been shaken by Singapore, and defeatism is in the air. But yesterday after leaving Sydney we had turned back again after having crossed the harbor. Something wrong with the port engine. We waited by the hangar. We were yarning together, Clive Bernard, the second pilot; Scotty Cameron, who had flown me down from Darwin six months before; and myself. There was a roar in the sky and a squadron of sixteen P-40 fighters came diving in to make perfect landings. Beneath slim wings they bore the star emblems of the United States Army Air Corps. It was a novelty to see modern fighter planes in Australia. It was a comforting novelty. It seemed, after all, that we were not to be left to fight out our little war alone.

"I was up in Darwin when one of these Kittyhawk squadrons was flying north to Koepang," recalled Cameron. "There were 16 of 'em. Fifteen flew right up top. One was down on its own, 6000 feet below the main formation. The Japs sighted the lonely little fighter and three of the Zeros jumped it. They were just getting ready to shoot hell out of it when down came the other 15 Kittyhawks right on the tails of the three Japs. They didn't shoot 'em down. They just blew 'em to pieces."

On a northern airfield was an old three-motored monoplane, held together with pieces of wire, a plane that had pioneered, 12 years before, the airmail service to New Guinea. Decrepit in her hastily daubed camouflage, and laden to the staggering point with refugees, she had lumbered from New Guinea across the Coral Sea to Cairns, where she finished her amazing career with a perfect three-point landing and had been immediately condemned as unairworthy and unfit for further service. This morning on Cairns airfield a young mechanic was reverently wiping down her ancient engines with a chunk of greasy cloth.

But hundreds of men, women and children in New Guinea owe their lives to old planes like this. In the evacuation of these people from Rabaul and the Solomons and the North New Guinea coast every machine that would take the air was pressed into service. All the laws of civil aviation authorities were flouted. Planes built to carry five passengers staggered across the Coral Sea with twenty. Planes built to carry sixteen carried thirty-five. These planes were still coming out after Japanese bombs and bullets had smashed into Rabaul, so there was no time for regulations. Personal belongings were tossed away, even excessive clothing, to permit another passenger or two being packed into tightly jammed fuselages. Day after day the crazy rescue fleet of battered old transport planes that had freighted the mining dredges up to Edie Creek and Bulolo; of unwieldy old Ford monoplanes; of sleek, modern airliners; of two-seater Moths, and shabby, fabric-covered biplanes, joined with camouflaged bombers of the Royal Australian Air Force in ferrying backward and forward between Australia and the newest battle zone of the Pacific. They came south with people who had been forced to sacrifice a lifetime of bitter pioneering in a few hours.

Veteran prospectors, one with his white hair worn in a long "bob" like a Navajo Indian, came down with women who had slaved for years to keep some trader's home neat in the sweltering equatorial heat of the north coast. They clutched meagre handfuls of baggage. The miner who looked like a Navajo walked the dusty streets of Moresby with a long wooden staff in his hand looking for a soldier to whom he could present the trusted prismatic compass that had guided him in his lonely wanderings along the Snake and Bulolo valleys. He wouldn't need his compass any more. The Japanese had declared the destiny of the jungle country for a long time to come. They had smashed and conquered Rabaul and now they were hurling tons of high explosives on the gold towns and native villages, on copra ports and administrative stations. In the swamps and in hidden caches of the northern jungles tough miners had locked away their finds. It was said that more than $2,000,000 worth of gold had been hidden by these men in secret places north of the ranges. They weren't allowed to take it with them. Very well, they told me, they'd "come back when this silly business is over."

And they came down by air, all of them. They had to. There was no other sane way of crossing the dreadful swamps and crocodile-infested rivers and fearful jungles of the hinterland. Planes returned from one trip crammed with refugees. Ten minutes for refueling and they were off again, back across the blue mountains or away across Dampier Strait to New Britain. There was no time for overhaul, no time even to check defects. With spluttering engines they did a job that nobody had believed was possible and when that job was done these heroic civilian pilots—the unsung heroes of the New Guinea war—had the satisfaction of knowing that they had rescued more than 2000 men, women and children in the craziest rescue fleet that New Guinea had ever seen—and they had done it with the loss of only one suitcase!

We were approaching the Gulf of Papua. Lookouts were posted to watch for Japanese planes. What we should have done had we seen any nobody seemed to know! The total armament of the plane was a Colt .45 carried by the pilot. Down below we could see the flying fish skimming from whitecap to whitecap. And there ahead of us, a faint purple darkness in the heat haze, the mountains of New Guinea.

As we circled the coral reef, the town of Port Moresby lay below us, flimsily built white houses with almost every roof of corrugated iron, a sleepy wharf, dust rising brownly from the quiet streets, hills of brown and ochre and olive rising from the blue-green waters of the harbor. No sign of any bombing. No evidence of any excitement. A sleepy, dusty, dilapidated port of the tropics and a white-painted schooner moving out from the shore. We skimmed in over the stunted hills. The landing wheels thumped the tarmac and scrunched along through the dust. Men in shorts and khaki shirts and dust-caked steel helmets ran out to the plane. There was a hurried consultation with the pilots. I overheard the phrase, "Air raid expected." Men raced up with a mobile petrol pump; others herded refugees. In five minutes the airliner was roaring over the hills heading back for Cairns, laden with a crowd of women and children brought down from Wau. The squat brown hills around the aerodrome shimmered in the noonday heat. I had the smell of dust in my nostrils. There was dust caked on the broad leaves of the trees, dust eddying along the runway. Over to one side an air force ambulance stood alongside a Lockheed Hudson bomber of the R.A.A.F. I could see holes ripped in the fuselage, and the glass cupola of the gun turret was shattered. Nearby was a battered Gannet monoplane and in the shade cast by its starboard wing a young man reclined wearily. His face was caked with dust and furrowed by tiredness.

"Got to go back to Bulolo in ten minutes to get some miners," he said with a grin. "God, if the Japs come over again I hope they get this bloody plane. Then I won't have to go up there again. This'll be my twentieth trip in three days."

A grimy saloon car, impressed from some evacuated civilian, lurched through the dust. Two suntanned men, covered with dust and wearing nothing but tattered, stained khaki shorts, came toward us. They looked like tramps. Later I found that one was a major of Royal Australian Engineers, the other was chief signal officer of the Port Moresby garrison.

"Nice day to arrive," grinned the major. "Friday the thirteenth! I'll run you out to headquarters. And we'd better get cracking. There's some vague buzz about the Japs coming over. I think it's wrong, but just to be on the safe side we'd better get off this airfield. It's likely to be number one target."

As our car climbed over a brown hill I looked back to the aerodrome. The battered Gannet was taking off and circling to gain height for the climb over the mountains to Bulolo, piloted by the weary young man making his twentieth trip in three days.

### The Land of Wait a While

It's not long since they called New Guinea the "Land of Dehori." The most frequently used word in the Motu language probably was *dehori*, which is to the Papuan what *mañana* is to the Spaniard, what *ti d'apa* is to the Malay, what *maskee* is to the Chinese. For *dehori* means "wait a while." And that word had been, to a very large degree, the design for Papuan living. Anything that demanded more than ordinary exertion—and in the tropics even thinking is sometimes arduous—could be put off until tomorrow in this Land of Wait a While. It usually *was* put off until tomorrow—unless it happened to be a cocktail party or a golf foursome or a game of bridge or a dance with a pretty girl. Now the cocktails and the pretty girls have gone, and the golf links have pandanus palms sprouting from the bunkers and kunai grass a foot deep over the fairways, and, if what I've seen today is any criterion, you'll find the bridge tables scattered in army tents and native huts throughout the garrison of Port Moresby.

Well, the current owners of the bridge tables—khaki-clad Australian troops—were the people who really began to sweep the cult of *dehori* out of Papua. Startled white men who had lived for years in the tropics were rather horrified to see Australian soldiers sweating with picks and shovels in the blazing sun, working harder even than the "coons" when, by all the laws of tropical behavior, they should have been lolling back in cane chairs, sipping long drinks and discussing hangovers of the night before. Generally speaking, although there were exceptions, the men in white linen suits vaguely disapproved. But they saw pot-holed tracks take on the semblance of military roads. They saw great gray-painted transports coming and going through the emerald reef, camps rising from the brown, stunted, dust-covered scrub, white men working from dawn to dusk to prepare Moresby for at least some share in the Pacific War.

Even that couldn't shake their smug self-satisfaction. Nothing, they thought, could sweep away the measured, leisured, slightly dissolute life of this Australian outpost ten degrees below the line.

They even began to absorb some of the military personnel into their little social circles.

Then came the night of 3 February, when the whining drone of Japanese aircraft was heard overhead for the first time, the whistle of bombs descending through the humid blackness of the night, the sullen thunder of high explosive falling along the waterfront. And the artificial, slothful, rather pleasant life that had been built upon a decades-old tradition of *dehori* was swept away by that first running salvo of high explosive.

The life that had never existed for most of the men in khaki no longer existed for the men in white linen. All women left the territory, and with them went most of the gaiety and pseudo-sophistication of the tropics. Men who were unfit for military service, or over age, were bundled off to the mainland, where quite a few of them managed to get their names among columns of hair-raising stories in the daily newspapers. To read them one would imagine that Moresby was a constant target for an incessant hail of Japanese bombs. One man went to great pains to describe the Japanese fragmentation bomb, or "daisycutter," which, he said, was filled with scrap metal, and showered old razor blades, broken glass, discarded hacksaws, and rusted pairs of scissors over the target area! About this time, too, the story began to circulate about the bomb fragment dropped by a Japanese plane which carried the legend "New South Wales Government Railways" stamped on it. I don't doubt that a good deal of the scrap metal we exported to Japan for many years will come back to us in the form of munitions—but I don't think we'll be able to find the words "Made in Australia" on them.

A number of New Guinea's civilians, however, have gone into khaki. And they have gone to work in the tropic sun just as the troops have been doing for many weeks. There's a new word to be used in place of *dehori*. Previously it was used only by the white men to make the natives work a little harder. Now they are having it used against themselves—and used with a new urgency. The word is *karaharaga*. It means "hurry up!"

Yesterday all Papua and New Guinea officially came under military control. Civil administration ended. Even now, down at the government printing office, the old flatbed press is churning out the proclamation. Now, under the direct command of Major-General Basil Morris, G.O.C. of the New Guinea Force, is an area of 185,000 square miles with a population of something like 2,000,000 natives, whites and Chinese.

Yesterday, too, Singapore, the impregnable fortress, fell to the Japanese.

We spoke about these things today as we stood in the hot sun with General Morris. As he spoke he swished flies with quite the most elaborate fly swatter (Bombay variety) I have ever seen.

It was clear he knew the gravity of Singapore's fall in its relation to his own command. It was simple for any person to see how Singapore's fall would release a flood of additional enemy strength along the straddled Japanese supply lines that were reaching south beyond the equator.

"There's no doubt," he said, "that the significance of Port Moresby to Australia and the allied defense lines has increased enormously. I suppose the Japs will try to capture Port Moresby, because it would give them a marvelous striking base for air blows against the Australian mainland. Australia's outer defenses are falling and our inner defenses are naturally becoming more and more important. Whoever holds Port Moresby holds Torres Strait. If it becomes necessary we must be prepared to make Port Moresby the Tobruk of the Pacific, because while it remains an Australian stronghold it is a direct barrier to any Japanese advance southward."

Southward—only 150 minutes' flying time away—was the fertile green mainland of Australia's rich east coast. This little garrison was its last outlying citadel against attack from the northeast. General Morris's words expressed determination, but the bare facts of defense are less encouraging. The total air support, I have discovered, is a handful of slow Catalina flying boats and Lockheed Hudson reconnaissance bombers, and a Wirraway (minus one wing) which is propped up behind a clump of trees on the airfield.

And tonight we were talking to the commander of Moresby's one anti-aircraft battery. Three sentences are still running through my mind:

"We've been told our job is to hold Port Moresby for thirty-six hours to give them time to prepare the mainland defenses. We've been testing the guns and find that by depressing them to minimum elevation we can use them for beach defense as well as anti-aircraft.

Rabaul only held out for four hours when the invasion came, but I think we'll be able to keep 'em off for thirty-six!"

## The Refugees

Refugees are pouring south from the towns devastated by the Japanese in northern New Guinea, telling for the first time the full story of the evacuation of Lae and Salamaua. The attacks on Salamaua began about noon on 21 January, when Japanese Zero fighters skimmed in over the tree-tops with engines cut and raked the whole Salamaua isthmus with machine gun fire. "It sounded as if somebody was rubbing a huge file along an iron roof," said one woman refugee.

Behind the fighters came dive-bombers and light bombers, and when they had finished their hammering of the defenseless town heavy bombers dropped high explosive from 2000 feet. Fifty-four planes pummeled the little seaport for 40 minutes and in the crash and thunder of high explosive the natives panicked and went bush.

It was some time about midnight on 23 January that the local authorities decided to evacuate the town. There was some rumor of a Japanese invasion. One woman and 132 men left in a blinding rainstorm for an evacuation camp that had been established inland. The area between was laced with swollen streams and treacherous swamps. The party struggled through thigh-deep mud that sucked the shoes off their feet. There were no native carriers, and each refugee had to carry his own small bundle of belongings. There were sick and wounded, also, to be carried through that dreadful night on stretchers. By 4 A.M. the pitiful procession had reached the flooded area of the evacuation camp at Butu. While they waited for dawn the assistant district officer went back to Salamaua to see if everybody had got away. When he returned he reported that from the abandoned town he could see a great column of flame and smoke towering above Lae, the capital, 25 miles to the northward. Japan's New Order had reached New Guinea.

None of the Salamaua party, which has reached Moresby, seemed to know what had happened at Lae, and it wasn't until this evening that I saw a report that had come in from one of the officers of the New Guinea Volunteer Rifles, a sort of tropical "Home Guard" which is remaining on duty on the other side of the range.

The report said that all buildings in the aerodrome area had been burnt to the ground after forty-five minutes of the most furious bombing and machine-gunning by 60 enemy planes. A N.G.V.R. detachment went into the capital to see if the scorched earth policy which had been ordered had been carried out. In the Lands Office they found everything left in perfect order—including a stock of printed maps of various New Guinea districts which would have been of the utmost value to the enemy. The office and its contents were destroyed, together with fuel dumps and abandoned motor cars.

The natives were looting the liquor stores (always extensive in the tropics!) and these had to be blown up also, to quell the rioting. As they left Lae blinding rain was falling. Every track was a slowly moving stream of treacly black mud. The rain hissed in the water-filled bomb craters and wrecked and charred buildings. The troops moved into the jungle and left the capital of British New Guinea abandoned and silent.

Moresby's anti-aircraft guns opened fire for the first time this afternoon, which makes it the first time on Australian soil that a gun has gone into action against hostile raiders. The plane was a twin-engined Mitsubishi bomber, apparently on reconnaissance and right up at 23,000 feet. The A.A. battery is all Militia, and most of its personnel are the merest kids. The average age is eighteen and one-half years.

They might have scored a hit with their second shot. The burst seemed to be right under the port wing of the Jap, which dropped thousands of feet before steadying and then pulling up again slowly. Without having dropped any bombs it circled away and headed for the Owen Stanley Range. But those ranges have to be crossed, and peaks rising up to 13,600 feet, with bad weather more common than good, are tough obstacles for any damaged aircraft.

Everyone is convinced that the reconnaissance plane was checking up on targets for a big raid. At 6 P.M. the report came in that a heavy enemy bombing force was heading this way and would arrive within half an hour. But it didn't come.

Our only defense against air attack is the battery of A.A. guns on the hill. No fighters. If the Japs care to come with the force they used on Rabaul three weeks ago they can smash our defenses in a few minutes. Nobody is very confident. Senior officers keep asking us to write articles appealing for more recognition for Moresby and its "forgotten men."

"For God's sake tell 'em how much we need a fighter squadron," one major was saying today. "Surely they aren't going to make another Singapore out of this place! It's a bit too close to home for that."

But what can we do? Anything we write is censored into innocuous nonsense. We haven't had time yet to recover from the "cover-up" censorship that was so lamentable in Malaya and almost everywhere else. The outcry over Singapore is already bringing a bit of logic and reason into it; but, even so, if we write stories telling the truth about the defenses of Port Moresby, appealing for more men, more guns, fighter planes, the most interested people will be the Japanese. They'll come in like a shot and take the place by sneezing. As it is we have a chance of bluffing them into thinking this place is stronger than is actually the case. So our stories tonight carry the sentence: "Send *more* fighter planes to Moresby."

All the people who read this dispatch will believe that we have at least some fighters in Moresby. I wish we had. I also wish we were able to tell Australia what a weak reed they are depending upon for the defense of Australia from the northeast. But what can we do?

### *"Jeez! 'Slike Fire!"*

Port Moresby looks entirely unsuited to war. The bomb craters and the shattered houses and the coconut palms shredded by blast, the sun-bronzed men in khaki hats and khaki shorts, naked to the waist, hewing gunpits and filling sandbags—all these sights don't fit into the Moresby scene. It's still a quiet, sleepy tropical port. All round the splendid harbor are the brown, stunted hills and islands. Beyond, linked with the main harbor by a wide channel, lies the magnificent anchorage of Fairfax Harbor, where the Australian Navy was hidden in the last war, and where you could hide a whole battle-fleet today. The vivid emerald green of the reef lies across the main entrance, with the wreck of an old Norwegian steamer piled up on the coral. Tucked away just beyond the port is the native village of Hanuabada, with its hundreds of cane and grass huts built up on wobbly stilts over the shallows.

Dust eddies from the earthen tracks leading to the one spindly wharf and the few small jetties for trading schooners and luggers and native canoes. Dust eddies from the shimmering, iron-roofed buildings, the Burns Philp store, the ramshackle copra sheds, the battered workshops of a marine engineer beside a crazy slipway. Sprawled round the hills are the civilian bungalows, all built to the same ugly pattern, nearly all decrepit and sadly in need of a good coat of paint.

Strewn all over the main street are pieces of twisted corrugated iron, splintered plaster and smashed timber—souvenirs of the two night raids. A few houses and shops have been blown to pieces and scores of others damaged by blast. Practically none of the lath and plaster buildings in Port Moresby would be able to stand up to the blast of a fair-sized bomb and it is evidence of the inaccuracy of the Japanese bomb-aimers that half the town isn't in ruins. Actually the damage is quite slight. Casualties have been one man killed and a couple slightly injured.

The consensus of opinion is, of course, that the town will be wiped out when the Japs really get started. For that reason it has been completely abandoned. Today there isn't a soul living in the town area proper, which is generally referred to as "Bomb Decoy No. 1." There is plenty of activity by day, but at night Papua's capital is abandoned and in the hotels and houses, where there were the sounds of tinkling ice and swing music and laughter only a few weeks ago, now there is no sound but the buzzing of the insects and the *kek-kek-kek-kek* of little gecko lizards.

The troops are not waiting for the town to be wiped out. Looting has been going on for days, and in some cases it's looting on a grand scale. I agree with what might be termed "organized impressment" under these conditions, but this has been carried into the realms of sheer vandalism.

I went into some of the stores today and the picture was staggering. Shelves had been torn down from walls and their contents were thigh-deep on the floor. I had to wade through one sea of ripped women's frocks, over which had been spilt bags of flour and scores of tins of paint. On top of this chaotic mess were dozens of shattered hurricane lanterns. I don't think the troops will need women's frocks, nor will they find much use for bright red and yellow enamel. But I'll swear there'll be a lot of people wanting hurricane lanterns before long!

Never having worked in merchandise I have no idea of the value of the ruined goods that I saw in this one store alone. A local retailer, now drafted into the army, estimates that $300,000 worth had been spilt, torn to pieces or trampled underfoot.

Number one priority for the looter was, naturally, liquor. And war came to Port Moresby at a time when there were very good stocks in the town, in the bond shed on the wharf, and in most of the homes. By a process of transportation that would have been admirable in any army, this considerable stock of spirits and ales was transferred to army camps and establishments for miles around within a few hours. Papua imported most of its liquors direct from Europe, tariff free, and as a result the stocks in the town were good stocks—the best brands of liqueur, genuine Scotch whisky, English gin, French vermouths and spirits, Spanish wines.

Tonight I was walking along the track back to our camp in the Laloki Valley. The flap of a tent parted and a voice cried thickly: "Eh, you! C'm'n 'ave a jrink! Go' plen'y 'ere. C'm on! C'm on!"

I went over and in the tent was the drunkest man I have ever seen. In his hand was a huge water tumbler, empty at the moment. "What are you drinking?" I asked, with some respect and, seeing that he wanted me to start in with him, a good deal of anxiety!

He jerked his thumb over his shoulder toward a looted cane table that stood in a dark corner of his tent.

"Some stuff," he slurred at me. "Dunno warrit is. Green stuff." He paused and licked his lips appreciatively. He grinned. "Dunno warrit is, but, jeez, 'ts blurry powerful stuff. 'Slike fire. Try some. Bottlesh over there."

I went over. Four bottles of imported Crème-de-menthe! Three empty. One half full. I looked from the bottles to the huge water tumbler in his fist.

"Do you drink this stuff by the glassful?" I asked.

He looked at me owlishly, as if I were a fool.

"Course I do! Jrink 't by the bucketful if I could. Never seen shtuff before. But—jeez it's gotter kick like a mule!"

*Premium on Glamour*

It's little more than a week since I left the cold winds of Melbourne. It seems months. So now I know just how the soldiers up here feel when you tell them you come from Melbourne. They swarm around you, asking what appear to be the most infantile questions—until you've been here a little while yourself. Then you realize their questions aren't infantile. They ask you, with a joking wistfulness, if the town hall is still in the same place, what the girls look like in their summer frocks, how Melbourne is taking the war, when they are going to send up some air support.

This place is an outpost of Empire—and, believe me, there is no cliché about that. It's a new world of swamp and jungle (although the jungle doesn't come very close to Moresby itself) and flies and mosquitoes, and fuzzy-headed natives with bright red skirts and frangipanni in their hair. It is a world of war, of steel helmets and tommy guns, and great military convoys lurching and roaring up the steep mountain sides. It is a world of suspense and sky-searching anxiety, a world far removed from the complacency of southern Australia where I left people grousing only about petrol rationing and the shortage of cigarettes.

For sheer unadulterated loneliness, discomfort and monotony let me nominate Port Moresby as the toughest military station in the Empire. News of home is more important than anything else. The few men who own radio sets are besieged each night by men who sit in dozens outside in the darkness silently listening to the news. After it is over they disappear into the darkness as quietly as they came. Every new arrival is inundated with requests for mainland newspapers, because the only newspapers you see up here are two months' old—and there are very few of them. They certainly won't go round the thousands of men in the hills and jungles of the territory. Every man reads every word—even the advertisements—and there are few newspapers that will survive that sort of handling by many men.

Mails are quite irregular, but every day there are queues at the postal depots, and every man asks the same lonely question: "Any mail today? Any letters from the south?" News from home can be very important when there is nothing for a man to do but think of home. Most of the troops I've spoken to would willingly sacrifice a couple of meals to get one letter.

Reading that last sentence over again it occurs to me that the loss of a meal or two wouldn't be much of a sacrifice anyway. Most of the food comes out of cans. That can't be avoided. Fresh meat and fresh vegetables are rarely seen. Papua is experiencing a tough drought in the middle of the "wet" and the natives can't grow enough food even for themselves. And so we all have interminable meals of tinned meat, tinned fish, tinned vegetables, tinned fruit, tinned butter and tinned milk.

Even the food is not as bad as the monotony. After the day's work is over there is absolutely nothing to do. There are no picture shows, no cafés, no billiard saloons. The nearest town that has a picture theatre which shows Clark Gable and Mickey Rooney and the rest of the Hollywood heroes is 480 miles away—480 sea miles. That may be a good thing—when I think of Mickey Rooney! But the width of the Coral Sea lies between these soldiers—most of them are kids—and the civilization that is represented for them by bright lights and honking motor horns and pretty girls and a nightly change of programme at the theatres. There are no girls here at all. The last white woman has left the territory. Today I spoke to a young Melbourne signalman who is camped in a real tropical jungle miles away up the coast. He told me he hadn't heard a female voice for five months. There must be hundreds like him.

The swing of the pendulum from peace to war has brought the complete antithesis of the tawdry luxury of civilian days. Personally I think the thing has been carried to the opposite extreme, and there is really no reason why the troops should have to live in conditions as primitive as these. They wash in a hand basin, race the flies to their meals, slap mosquitoes for hours each day, and, if they're lucky, occasionally have a swim in a pool in the Laloki River, which is reputed to be "stiff with crocodiles." They look as fit as any young man I have ever seen. But that fitness is deceptive. Many go down with malaria, dengue fever, tropical ulcers, dysentery, tinea. But they have the right spirit. I have spoken to a good many who were obviously sick men. They told me they wouldn't report to the M.O. for fear they would be boarded back to the mainland.

It is surprising how seldom you hear them complain. At the

moment there is more than a shortage of cigarettes. I doubt if you could buy a packet of "tailor-mades" anywhere in New Guinea or Papua. They just grin ruefully when the canteen sergeant shakes his head and buy "the makings." Often there is no beer in the canteens. They drink water. They have to. The nearest pub is also 480 miles away.

At night there is nothing to do but creep in under a stuffy mosquito net. With the strict blackout not a glimmer of light can be shown anywhere. That means you can't even write a letter at night. So if you don't want to be bitten to pieces by the mosquitoes you have to get into bed and under the net. Not very pleasant when the nights are only one degree cooler and infinitely more humid than the days—and, God knows, the days are hot enough! If you lean your elbow on the table for a minute a pool of sweat forms on the surface.

Today a Japanese bomber—so high it was merely a shining speck against the cirrus-streaked cobalt of the tropic sky—turned and circled over Moresby for half an hour. It dropped no bombs and the muzzles of the A.A. guns followed in silence, holding fire so that gun positions would not be given away to one lonely reconnaissance plane.

There was some significance in that bright speck circling thousands of feet above us. It was another land-based bomber. The Japs are taking an interest in Moresby and the days of hide-and-seek may soon give way to the sudden hammerblow of outright attack.

The Japanese have been surprisingly cautious. Their visits to Port Moresby have proved already that they want to size up the opposition before they start hitting. They did the same thing at Rabaul. Reconnaissance, reconnaissance, a few feeler raids, then the smashing assault. It looks as if they are trying the same stunt with Moresby. If they can grab this garrison the next step is obvious. The distance from Moresby to Cairns is shorter than the distance from Rabaul to Moresby. With heavy bomber bases established by the enemy on the south coast of Papua they could hammer the Queensland towns after only a three-hour flight; they could close Torres Strait; they could even gain a foothold on the mainland, on the York Peninsula, and hold it by air support based on Moresby. Most people here seem to think the Japs are almost ready to have a shot at it.

Today a young infantry subaltern said to me: "Don't the people of Australia realize what this means to them? Does everything have to be decided on a basis of vote-catching? Any day now we'll be fighting to save New Guinea. I suppose we'll do that willingly enough because we'll be fighting to save Australia. With Singapore gone, it won't be long now. I hope to God it isn't another story of 'Too little, too late!'"

He is right, of course. If it were lost, the Battle for New Guinea would be the curtain-raiser for the Battle for Australia.

I find a lot of anxiety here. But I don't find any of the "glamour" of the tropics. There is more glamour in one block of Sydney or Melbourne than in all of Port Moresby. And I'm sure the boys would die laughing now at a Dorothy Lamour film!

### Diversion

Opinion in this town varies like the pointer on a weather vane. Yesterday everybody was confident that attack on Moresby was imminent. Today everybody seems just as certain that Moresby will be bypassed and that the Japs will strike at Australia from the northwest, through Darwin.

The reason is that the Japs have raided Darwin heavily, with about 100 bombers, fighters and dive-bombers, coming over in about eight waves, the first of them only two minutes after the air raid sirens had sounded.*

On the other side of the picture there's a more encouraging story today. An enormously big American convoy has arrived at Australian ports. If Australia is to be built up as a supply and striking base for the United States in the southwest Pacific, then Port Moresby must eventually be recognized as a garrison of primary importance.

The convoy came on a course that took it south of New Britain and the Japanese decided to try out their new striking bases at Rabaul and Gasmata. They sent over 18 bombers to attack the ships, but U.S. naval fighters took off from one of the aircraft car-

---

* Later reports indicate that about 250 people were killed, about 500 were wounded, and nine ships were destroyed.

riers protecting the convoy—the *Yorktown,* I think—and 16 Japanese planes were shot down into the sea. Only two got home.

## They Were So Few

There's a good deal of excitement tonight in the R.A.A.F. mess, particularly among the men flying Lockheed Hudsons. Johnnie Lerew, given up as dead nine days ago, has turned up safely. Lerew was—or, rather *is*—C.O. of the squadron.

On 11 February he led a formation of three Hudsons in a bombing attack on Gasmata, a tiny village on the south coast of New Britain, only 180 miles from the New Guinea coast, which had been occupied the previous day by Japanese troops who came in two transports escorted by cruisers and destroyers.

With only three slow Hudsons with which to carry out an attack on the enemy ships Lerew decided to hit in daylight and to hit hard. He led the planes in to Gasmata at an altitude of less than a thousand feet, dived down to make his bombing run at masthead height. Anti-aircraft guns already established ashore, as well as guns from the warships, poured out a heavy barrage as the three Lockheeds came in with six Zero fighters diving down on their tails.

The Australian planes kept formation, went in with their bellies almost scraping the masts of the Japanese transports. Bombs fell squarely on the decks of the two big transports, both of which burst into flames. Then the bombers climbed to give combat to the Zeros. One Japanese fighter pilot gave up the struggle after bullets had ripped into his cockpit. Another Zero went in flames. But the Lockheeds were hopelessly outnumbered. One blew to pieces in mid-air when a burst from a Japanese cannon hit the fuel tanks. Three Zeros then turned in to attack Lerew's plane, pouring cannon shells and bullets into its tail. It went spinning down, out of control, with flames streaming from its fuselage, and crashed on the beach. Bill Pedrina, pilot of the only surviving plane, made a final circle to check up on results of their attack and to get a visual picture of Japanese positions, fought off the remaining Zeros and returned to Moresby to report: "Operation accomplished; two planes destroyed; all personnel missing, believed killed."

That's what everyone thought until yesterday, when news came in that a very unkempt and very hungry Johnnie Lerew had turned up on the north coast of New Guinea and was being flown down to Moresby.

When his plane started to go down in flames he yelled for the rest of the crew to bale out. There was no response. He looked round. The whole of the rear of the plane was a mass of flames and the members of his crew had been incinerated. Lerew's escape hatch was jammed. He kicked his foot through a window and clambered out. He was about to leap when he realized that he had no parachute on. He climbed back and snapped the clip of his 'chute, dived head first through the window, and pulled the ripcord. He had donned the parachute upside down and the sudden pull of the released cords almost strangled him. But he didn't have far to fall. He landed in the highest branches of a tall tree. As he hastily lowered himself from branch to branch by the parachute gear he could see a party of Japs running toward him, firing rifles wildly. He fled into the jungle as a few bullets zipped harmlessly over his head.

For three days he wandered, without food and with little water, through a maze of jungle and treacherous swamps, until he met a friendly native who agreed to guide him to the southeast coast of the island. That night he met another white man, who had been hiding in a cave for weeks, living on yams and contaminated water, frightened that the Japanese would capture and kill him if he left his refuge. Lerew convinced him that the best hope of reaching safety was to start moving. At dawn they found a damaged native canoe, and paddled it down the coast. Other white men hiding in the sea caves were picked up until eventually the party numbered eight whites and several natives. Numbers had grown too big for the canoe so they walked until they found an abandoned ketch anchored offshore. The battered craft leaked like a sieve, and had only nine inches of freeboard, but they sailed her through three heavy gales across nearly two hundred miles of open sea to the north coast of New Guinea. All the refugees, including Lerew, were brought down here by flying boat.

Lerew, who wears a huge and bristling red moustache and a permanent grin, is the best known and the best liked flyer in New Guinea today. He commanded what tiny air forces we had at Rabaul before the Japs came, lost all his Wirraways but managed to save all his Hudsons, and became quite famous for the signals he sent to the Air Board—sarcastically jesting signals, the pick of which was one sent in Greek: the classical "We who are about to die salute you!"

Pedrina—"Pedro" to every man in the air force—is a permanent officer of the R.A.A.F., and one of the coolest pilots I have ever seen. For weeks he has been doing some extraordinary jobs of long-range reconnaissance. Yesterday he was ordered over to Rabaul to get some pictures of the Japanese shipping concentrations which are building up in Blanche Bay. Despite the persistent attentions of two Zeros he carried out a complete "recco" of the area, and didn't leave for home until he was quite satisfied that he'd obtained every picture needed.

By that time one of the Zeros had been shot down from 14,000 feet and the Lockheed was badly damaged. There was a 500-mile flight over tough country, but Pedro brought the crippled plane back to Moresby with a dead gunner in the turret, the fuselage chewed by cannon shells and machine-gun bullets, the metal peeled in strips away from the wings, flap cables snapped off, and one landing wheel shot away.

The photographs were perfect, and that's all that Pedro ever worried about—doing the job properly.*

David Campbell is another fine flyer in this little bomber reconnaissance squadron. Two weeks ago he carried out a lone reconnaissance of Japanese positions and was tackled by enemy fighters over Rabaul airfield. Campbell continued his photographic run and got a fine set of pictures. O'Hea, the turret gunner, pumped a burst of 100 rounds into one of the Zeros at a range of only 300 feet before Japanese bullets ploughed through the glass cupola and wounded him in the legs. Bullets and cannon shells carved great slices out of the Hudson's fuselage. Almost all the control board was shot away, landing wheels were punctured and petrol tanks holed. A bullet smashed Campbell's left hand. Seated beside him, Lauder, the co-pilot, had two fingers of his right hand shot off, his leg broken and torn open by a cannon shell, his arm shattered. The last burst from the Zeros, before the action was broken off because of shortage of ammunition, ripped through the fuselage and exploded one of the sea markers filled with aluminum powder.

---

* Pedrina was killed just south of Buna in December 1942, when a Lockheed he was piloting, to drop biscuits and bully beef to troops in the front line, crashed into the jungle.

Crowds of fine silver dust spread through the lurching aircraft while Thompson, the wireless operator, the only man unwounded, went from one man to another, attending to wounds and finally tearing his own clothing to shreds to make bandages for his comrades. Almost blinded, coughing and choking in the dust-filled bomber, and with his shattered left hand strapped to his right shoulder, Campbell piloted the crippled Hudson nearly 600 miles back to Moresby, across sea, through a terrific thunderstorm and over some of the world's most terrible alpine jungle country. He landed the plane on one wheel with the last drop of petrol in the tanks.

Every time these Hudsons go out on a job they seem to come back with a story—and there never seems to be a day without at least one of them out on some job or other. The squadron has an unwritten rule that it never fails to carry out an order, however tough.

However long the war lasts, the record of this squadron will be hard to beat. Worn out by overwork, the men take these old planes up day after day on missions that could reasonably be called suicidal. They have never turned for home, while there has been petrol in the tanks, until they have reached their targets. And although they have been fighting faster, better armed, and more manoeuvrable planes, their losses have been surprisingly slight. Their training has been as good as their morals.

The squadron, then based on Rabaul, began its operations in the Pacific when the Japs declared war last December. The Hudsons went out and raided the Japanese base at Kapingamarangi (Greenwich) Island, south of the Carolines, smashing up a concentration of invasion barges and aircraft equipment. Truk, in the Carolines, remained the big Japanese feeder base threatening New Guinea, but a raid on Truk involved a hazardous 800-mile hop across the Pacific, and 800 miles back, probably pursued by a swarm of Zeros. Last month Bob Yowart, a mere youngster, made the attempt as an experiment. It worked. The great Japanese arsenal of Truk became a regular "target for today."

When the Japs came to Rabaul with their air armada of 100 planes, two Hudsons were left behind when the order came to evacuate all aircraft surviving. One was hidden on the bomb-pitted runway and at midnight it took off laden with wounded airmen. Another, with its wings blown open by bomb blast, was bolted together with sheets of galvanized iron and flown off to Moresby in triumph.

We might not have very good planes, nor very many of them. But at least we have superlative pilots, and it's surprising how skill and courage can whittle away an enemy's air superiority.*

*Bombfall at Noon*

Moresby's third air raid—the first made in daylight—has just ended, and the garrison is still a little aghast at the accuracy of the Japanese bombing. Nine twin-engined naval bombers came over in as neat a bit of formation flying as I have ever seen, and dropped about 70 bombs in a carefully planned pattern. They scarcely wasted a bomb. One fell smack on one of our Hudson bombers and completely wrecked it. Another blew to pieces the little Gannet monoplane which has rescued so many people from the mining towns. The others pitted the runway and flattened every one of the new buildings of "Yankeeville"—the elaborate camp which had just been completed for the American pilots who are coming up here soon. The Japanese planes were above 20,000 feet, which makes it pretty good bombing! Some Zeros were above them as a screen, too, but few of us saw them. Casualties were only one man killed and four wounded. The troops are now convinced that the open slit trench is the best type of air-raid shelter. One 250-pound bomb fell within six feet of a slit trench packed with Australian infantrymen and not a man was hurt.

This was my first air raid. The bombs fell far enough away to be safe but near enough for me to experience that awful feeling as I listened to the hissing whistle of the falling bombs and pressed my belly flat against the earth, and felt my innards turn around and then freeze, and wondered as I heard the *whoom-whooom-whoooom* of the explosions whether they were coming my way and, if so, how far they would travel in my direction.

Sunday last was an important day in our calendar. American bombers joined with R.A.A.F. Catalinas and carried out their first raid on Rabaul. They were Flying Fortresses that had served in

---

* For the exploits mentioned in this chapter, Lerew, Pedrina and Campbell each received the Distinguished Flying Cross in April. They were thus the first recipients of decorations for gallantry in action in Australian territory.

Java. It was a grand sight seeing them come in to Moresby airfield at sunset. Bad weather prevented their doing much on their first mission. Weather in this part of the world will always be against the high level bomber, and the sub-stratosphere performance of the Flying Fortress will be of little value in an operational area where you rarely have 100 per cent visibility. In this raid the Fortresses couldn't find a ceiling at 20,000 feet and had to bomb haphazardly through the clouds. The Catalinas, with less value and more experience of the area, went down and found a ceiling at 6000 feet.

Still, the thing that counts most is that the arrival of the Fortresses is a very tangible expression of aid from the United States, and very real evidence that people are beginning to realize the importance of Port Moresby. But we still need fighters. Today's raid has proved that. For some time now there has been a story in general circulation that a Curtiss Tomahawk squadron is to arrive here. If you ask when they are expected the answer is always: "Tomorrow!"

So now everyone calls them "Tomorrowhawks."

## Ten Came Through

Survivors of the 2/22nd Battalion A.I.F. who have escaped from the Rabaul garrison have reached Port Moresby and have at last broken the five weeks of grim, anxious silence that followed the conquest of our main base in New Britain.

Ten men came in today, unshaven and bedraggled, with sunken cheeks and lined faces, many of them wearing only the shreds of their uniforms, others clad in rags and native cloth.

It's perfectly true that the Australians were defeated in this first important battle of the islands, but they fought against odds of ten to one and they did not give in until the Japanese landing force, estimated to number about 17,000 men, had suffered at least 2000 casualties.

The total Australian garrison consisted of only 1399 men. In the final decisive action they fought, without any assistance from air or sea, against a Japanese land force, an air armada of at least 150 bombers, fighters, and dive-bombers, and against the guns of a formidable naval force.

R.A.A.F. reconnaissance planes sighted heavy concentrations of

Japanese shipping north of Rabaul on 19 January, but the convoy went to shelter in the lee of Watom Island, north of the town.

On the following day the attack began with a fierce aerial onslaught against Rabaul, in which the enemy used 60 bombers, escorted by at least 20 fighters. Against this force the defenders were able to put only five Wirraways into the air; but for what it lacked in numbers the R.A.A.F. made up in courage.

The five little planes immediately tackled sixteen times their number of faster and bigger planes, and, although they themselves were shot down, they hurled at least two Japanese planes to the ground before they went. But within a few seconds the Japanese had converted an overwhelming air superiority into a complete air monopoly. Although five other enemy planes were brought down by accurate A.A. fire from our two mobile guns, from that point the Australian defenders had no air support.

On 21 January reconnaissance planes were over Rabaul, and the same night the enemy struck against Kavieng, in New Ireland. In the face of heroic resistance by a tiny A.I.F. commando force, Japanese marines succeeded in landing from destroyers and capturing the town. Another enemy force landed on the Duke of York Islands. The Japanese net was closing in.

On the following day the centre of operations again switched to Rabaul, when 110 Japanese aircraft—heavy bombers, light bombers, dive-bombers, and fighters—who had undisputed possession of the air, launched a ferocious attack against shipping, the Praed Point six-inch gun fort, and other defense positions.

At Praed Point the Australians fought back against wave after wave of dive-bombers with unparalleled courage and determination. For fifty-five minutes they held out in a hell of bursting bombs, dust, smoke, and flames, swept by a pitiless hail of machine-gun bullets and cannon fire. Hundreds of tons of bombs were hurled on the battery, but not until the guns and searchlights had been blown out of the ground were the positions abandoned by our men.

The Japanese made one attempt to land their planes on the aerodrome, but, as they roared over the runway, demolition charges were exploded, and enemy planes were destroyed or hurled upward by the blast. Two crashed and a third was brought down by machine-gun fire. Almost simultaneously a huge bomb dump was destroyed by our engineers with a terrific explosion that shook the town.

After sunset the Australians took up defensive positions on the slopes of Mount Vulcan to await the attack that they knew must come. At midnight enemy planes dropped big parachute flares. The suspense of waiting was almost unbearable. Men told each other that it was past midnight. They consulted watches every few seconds, talking to each other in undertones.

At 2:30 A.M. on Friday, 23 January, the invasion of Rabaul began. Over the black waters before Vulcan could be heard the ripple of voices. Occasionally the flash of a torch was reflected in the ebony swell. There was the sound of boat keels grating on the shingle, and the sudden glaring light of green flares—a signal to anchored ships announcing that the landing had been effected.

The Japanese were wearing black singlets and shorts, and had blackened their faces and limbs. Apparently they thought that there would be no opposition, that the aerial onslaught had crushed the Australian resistance. There was little attempt at stealth or silence.

A Japanese bugler stood on a darkened beach and raised his bugle to his mouth. He got out only three or four notes when the Australians opened fire. The bugle call ceased. Shrill screams and shouts from the Japanese revealed their panic and astonishment. There was a sudden splashing as the landing craft retreated—to make another attempt where resistance was less. There was no attempt by the enemy to return the Australian fire. In the darkness they landed at other points, and by dawn had scrambled up precipitous goat tracks to positions near the lip of Vulcan crater.

In the first light of dawn a Japanese soldier was sighted on the peak. The enemy immediately began to attack in force, using thousands of troops, under cover of warships, guns, and a force of about 100 dive-bombers and fighters. Landing barges, each carrying 50 to 100 men, were caught by fierce mortar fire from the Australian positions, and scores of Japs were soon struggling and screaming in the water. The Japanese came on, however, and at several positions the Australians were forced to retire.

At Raluana Beach, which was held doggedly by one A.I.F. unit, numbering about 150 men, the Japs attempted to land several thousand troops, but barbed wire near the water's edge trapped them, and their casualties were enormous. Direct fire and cross fire from the concealed Australian positions swept the wire with a terrible hail of lead. The water was red with blood and thick with the bodies of fallen Japanese. For an hour the bloodiest battle of the New Guinea campaign continued. As fast as one Jap fell another took his place. Barge after barge moved in, bumping over the bodies of fallen soldiers.

"Sometimes the noise of the Jap soldiers almost drowned the roar of our own fire," said one private. "They were squealing like pigs. Hundreds of them had been killed as they tried to get across the wire, and their bodies were slumped there in all sorts of grotesque positions. It was not long before the Japs realized the value of their dead. They gathered scores of other bodies and threw them across the wire. They then clambered over their own dead and came at us. Several were waving Japanese flags. They were shot down. Others picked up the flags and carried them until they, too, were killed."

Along the beach, on a front of about 200 yards, the Japanese dead were stacked six feet high. In the beach fighting and the hand-to-hand struggles that followed in the coastal gullies it is estimated that at least 1500 Japanese lost their lives, at a cost of fewer than 20 Australians slightly wounded.

From dawn onward the Japanese aircraft had been in action all the time—100 fighters and dive-bombers acting in perfect cooperation with the forward infantry units, and bombing or machine-gunning all roads of withdrawal, and every position where Australians were resisting. One A.I.F. company, which had dug in at prepared positions, was driven out by wave after wave of dive-bombers. The Japanese were advancing in parties of 12 men—each man armed only with hand grenades. One party dashed forward, hurled their grenades, then fell back as another party moved up. The most effective weapon the Australians had was the mortar, which took terrific toll of the enemy forces.

By noon the Japanese were swarming everywhere and further Australian resistance was useless. Some of the Australian units had already gone through Kokopo toward the bush.

In addition to the force which had withdrawn through Kokopo, other weary, dust-covered, bloodstained Australians moved down the Malabonga road toward the village of Rabata, 30 miles away. Almost every yard of the retreat was contested by the enemy.

Swarms of fighters and dive-bombers roared up and down the track, hammering the overladen trucks with bombs and machine-gun fire. One sapper of engineers told me that they had to stop the trucks and take cover about every 50 yards. Yet the inaccuracy of the Japanese pilots was extraordinary, for there was one casualty only—a man who broke his leg leaping into a ditch!

At Rabata food was picked up from the A.S.C. dump, and the weary troops moved into the jungle to cross the tangled, rain-soaked wilderness of the Bainings. The adventures that followed sound more like a chapter of *Tarzan of the Apes* than an incident from the Second World War.

For more than three weeks the men struggled through an almost ceaseless tropical downpour, and in all that time no man ever had dry clothing or dry feet. Rivers swarming with crocodiles had to be swum or forded. Men staggering almost at the point of exhaustion were forced to wade through slimy morasses of clinging black mud. No man possessed a mosquito net in jungles infested by countless millions of malaria-carrying insects. And these men, weary from war and hardships, were also at the point of starvation. For many days the ration to all men was one army biscuit and one-twelfth of a tin of bully beef to each man. That was the meal—the only one each day—on which these young Australians had to build up sufficient energy to keep going when every aching muscle told them they could keep going no longer.

It was many days before they met friendly natives, who helped them to find native food—taro, yams, coconuts, *kowkow* (sweet potatoes), curious edible roots. That first meal of crude native fruits was like a banquet to most of the men. But in that appalling retreat such days were rare. It was more usual for the men, night after night, to crouch together in the jungles, squatting and sitting through the hours of darkness in the drenching rain. Many were going down with dengue, malaria, dysentery, ulcerated limbs.

Few men in all history could have plumbed such depths of misery as these little parties of soldiers who fought blindly for safety in unknown equatorial jungles. Precipices had to be scaled by ropes fashioned from lawyer canes and swinging lantana vines. Great mountains had to be crossed. Weary men had to bridge chasms by swinging across from vines which hung from the great jungle trees. Men began to lag behind. Some gave up the struggle and lay down beside the muddy track to die. Some were carried on the shoulders of men almost dropping themselves, or were carted along on crude stretchers made from tree branches and plaited grass. If the sick could not go on they were left at the nearest native village. A native village, no matter how squalid or dirty, gave each man a night's rest under a roof, at least partly protected from the incessant dripping of the rain. Rude beds of cane were vacated by the natives —many of them suffering from a variety of tropical diseases, including the terrible elephantiasis—and the moment the beds were empty, exhausted Australians tumbled into them.

The meagre diet of the men scarcely ever varied—a tiny scrap of bully beef, a biscuit, a few ounces of native food, all mashed up together, and cooked in tin hats! Yet on this food the troops covered hundreds of miles through some of the most terrible jungle country in the world—country where, previously, few, if any, white men had ever set foot.

### Problem in Indigo

The transfer of Australia's own Papua and the mandated territory of New Guinea from civil to military administration has at last become general knowledge throughout the tribes and villages of both territories. Village headmen are now discussing how it will affect their present living conditions and their future status.

The news went among them by the mysterious "bush telegraph." It travelled from tribe to tribe, from village to village, it travelled across hundreds of miles of sea, across impenetrable jungle and terrible swamp. It went over mountains and ravines. And by next day natives in villages that had seldom seen a white man were discussing in the council houses the pros and cons of the new order.

You can't try to explain this bush telegraph. District officers and magistrates who have spent fifteen years among the New Guinea natives will not hazard a guess. The news just travels mysteriously through the jungles, almost with the speed of an electric telegraph. Patrol officers have told me of seeing something happen at noon and of hearing full details at a village 100 miles away at nightfall. In other places the death of a man on an island has been reported on the mainland—200 miles across open sea—within a few hours. You can't explain that sort of thing. In New Guinea they use signal drums, but the bush telegraph works even when the drums are silent. And in Papua, where the bush telegraph is most effective, there aren't any drums.

Sometimes the bush telegraph is inaccurate. The natives love to romance, love to color and embellish the most trivial story. In recent weeks the natives have given erroneous reports of parachute landings by Japanese troops, of mysterious ships off the coast. But when dealing with matters of deep concern to the natives themselves the accuracy of these strange reports is unquestioned.

The fierce Japanese air attacks on Rabaul turned the native "walkabout" into a magnificent example of mob hysteria—an hysteria carried by the bush telegraph from village to village until within a few days native affairs throughout the area of hundreds of thousands of square miles were in a state of complete chaos. The civil administration, which for decades had had the welfare of the natives at heart, had built up a machinery which could not hope to deal with such an extraordinary set of circumstances. Control was lost, and in the inevitable friction that followed between the administration and the military (which needed native labor for much of its activity) the position steadily deteriorated, Civil authorities decided to close down the prisons and disband the police. Prisoners were released, and criminals, warders, and policemen went bush together. Not long afterwards banks closed down, and business virtually came to an end. Semi-civilized natives were the biggest sufferers. They had come to rely on the trading stores for their rice and tinned meats. With the stores closed they began to pull in their belts . . . and they began to lose confidence in the white men who had protected them for so long.

Some form of control was imperative, and in an operational war station military control seemed the soundest choice. The army took over the administration, ordered selected men from the civil administration (taken into the army and given rank) to get to work. Their job was to bring order out of chaos, to restore confidence among the natives at all costs.

The phrase "Papua for the Papuans" had been a slogan for decades. There were some among the whites who actually took the view that Japanese control of Papua would be quite as acceptable as Australian control—provided the natives were treated correctly! The theory might have been good enough for some future World

State as visualized by Olaf Stapledon, but it wasn't a theory that would help to win the Second World War.

To regain control over the natives was a big job. The disbanding of the native police force caused anxious bewilderment among the policemen themselves and among the men of every tribe and village. Many of the policemen had given loyal service for fifteen to twenty years—one man had given 30 years. They couldn't understand why they had been "dumped." In Port Moresby alone 130 police boys were thrown out. Within a few days the military authorities had rounded up 120 of them and had formed them into a handy native force with which to bring back most of the other natives. Slowly the exiles returned. I have seen them marching back into the towns, wild-looking fellows with bows and arrows and spears, and flowers and egret plumes in their frizzy mops of hair. They were glad to get back. The spectre of drought was over the jungles and villages, and there was little food to be had. They were glad to get back to the regularity of army rations and sticks of pitch-black trade tobacco.

For a couple of weeks they retained their uneasiness. When bombs fell or when the anti-aircraft guns opened up they lost no time in beating it for the back country. The army men went to work painstakingly every time, and they dribbled back again. They are getting confidence now. They have seen bombs fall in tons— and they haven't been hurt. They are beginning to pay just as much attention now to air raids as they previously paid to the sight of a motor car.

As war comes to New Guinea the future of the natives is undoubtedly one of Australia's biggest responsibilities. Hand-to-hand fighting in these jungles means killings, murder, swift death. And the natives are always anxious to emulate the white man in everything he does. This factor would be less important but for the stark fact that only a couple of generations ago these happy, friendly natives were vicious head-hunters. Many of them were cannibals. In those days human life was cheap among the natives.

What will be their reaction when they find—if they do—that human life is even cheaper among the so-called civilized, superior whites? A reversion to type is not impossible . . . and if that happens fifty-four years of hard work will be swept away by a few bayonets, a few dive-bombers, a few machine guns.

Now that the military authorities have taken over control of the natives they have a double responsibility—they must care for the natives now and they must be responsible for their future.

Military administration will be carried out, as before, by patrol officers, and the natives will be bound by the simple laws and ordinances now existing. The army's problem of native affairs is a big one. Already they have taken their first steps. Already the natives are declaring their confidence in and satisfaction with the new order. They are setting up native canteens in place of the abandoned stores. Soon the spectre of hunger will be banished from the villages. At the moment that is the immediate problem. Once the native stomachs are full the job will become easier.

### War Comes to the Papuan

The Japanese bombing formations are getting larger. The force that came over today to carry out the fifth raid consisted of 18 heavy bombers with fighter escort. Again the casualties were negligible and there was practically no damage. Morale is improving enormously with these raids. In the last few daylight raids the enemy has been using a lot of fragmentation bombs—daisycutters—aimed apparently to kill troops. Today I was driving past the target area just after the bombs had fallen. One daisycutter had fallen squarely in the middle of the road, making only a small depression in the bitumen—no larger than a meat dish. Fragments, however, carved all the grass and scrub down for quite a distance and ripped a roadside tent to ribbons. A steel-helmeted head poked through the flap of the shattered tent and looked up to the sky where the bombers were streaking for home with the cotton-wool puffs of anti-aircraft bursts following them.

"Cripes! What was that?" came a voice from inside the tent.

The soldier peering at the sky grinned and looked back over his shoulder. "Oh, it wasn't anythin'," he said. "Just one of the little yeller bastards dropped his crash helmet on the track."

The other day a stick of Japanese bombs—big ones, too—fell with a running roar of thunderous explosions almost alongside the native village of Hauabada, a village standing on crazy stilts over the sapphire waters of Port Moresby. I could see the glistening backs of natives as they crouched in the slit trenches.

Five minutes later I walked past the village. Some of the natives were lolling back on the sand. A couple were caulking holes in their "lakatois," the outrigger canoes used by the natives for fishing. The raid had left them quite unperturbed. This was an extraordinary thing. It showed with amazing clarity the reactions of a primitive people to one of the latest and most widely used of our modern "civilizing influences." Even before the first raid on Moresby the natives were thoroughly scared about the unknown possibilities of bombing. They fled into the bush in panic as soon as a plane was heard overhead. It didn't matter if it was an Australian aircraft. They never waited to check on identity. When the raids really started the panic became worse. As soon as the first bomb fell the tracks were choked by scurrying natives heading for the hills with a few belongings wrapped in trade cloth and a bunch of green bananas slung on poles over their shoulders. Their women staggered behind them, each almost bent double by a great sack of rice and tinned food. Along the coastal track between Port Moresby and the big village of Porebada you could see a long, black, serpentine column of people—looking for all the world like a line of Italian prisoners after the first Libyan campaign—and the screen of dust kicked up by countless scurrying feet scarcely had time to settle.

One native boy heard the first bomb fall about a mile away. He excused himself and left his master. Exactly an hour later his master was driving along the road and he discovered his boy nine miles from home and still making exceptionally good time!

The white man sternly asked him why he had deserted.

"Everybody else ran quick time, taubada," replied the native. "Me don't know why they run, but if they run, me run too!" Which seemed primitive logic, but understandable.

During the same raid one native jumped into a crazy old motor truck, filled it up with his colored friends, and jammed his foot down on the accelerator. The car gave a terrific lurch forward, which hurled the native who had been seated on the tailboard of the truck clean out of the vehicle. He described a graceful parabola before hitting the roadway. The victim literally bounced. He hit the road on the flat of his back, bounced three feet into the air, and came down on his feet with his legs set for running. The movement was instantaneous. He was running as soon as he touched the ground the second time! I would have loved to have trained him for an Olympiad. He disappeared round the corner in the wake of the truck with his feet seeming to hit the ground only every twelve yards or so!

After the first raid the natives weren't so eager to go bush. The first retreat had ended in numberless villages in the back country. But there was drought in the land and no food for refugees in the starving villages. After a while they began to straggle back. After all if a bomb did kill you, at least you'd be able to die with a full belly!

It was at about this stage that the natives learned the value of the slit trench, and an air-raid alarm was a signal for every Papuan native within hearing to join in a blind rush for every trench or ditch. They were quite oblivious to the fact that a slit trench—or ditch—has a maximum capacity.

I saw a large party of natives make a concerted rush at one ditch. They piled in (piled is an orderly word to describe the cataract of black humanity that descended on the ditch!) all from one end. First arrivals were crushed and sandwiched, and eventually pushed out the other end by the endless stream of natives pouring in. Those ejected dashed round to the other end and joined the arrivals still pushing in. If the air raid hadn't ended eventually the world would have discovered some form of perpetual motion in Papua. Each native pushed into the ditch had a few moments of safety (apart from the risk of suffocation) before he was pushed out the other end and had to start all over again. This continued for the duration of the raid—the bombs fell five miles away—and for five minutes after the all clear had been sounded.

Now the natives are seeing and hearing a lot of bombs fall—for very little result. They don't worry so much now. Today, when I was watching the Japanese bombers through binoculars, I felt a respectful tap on my shoulder. I turned round. A native was standing behind me, grinning hugely. He pointed upward in another direction.

"More Japanese come that way, taubada," he said with a chuckle. These natives, incidentally, can spot planes with the naked eye before most white men can pick them up with field glasses. I followed his finger. Another wave of Mitsubishis was coming in from seaward, almost overhead. The native grinned again. "Japanese no good," he said. "They never hit anything!" And he laughed again with the sheer joy of living.

### The Years that the Locust Has Eaten

Some of the officers are round tonight, yarning and helping us to drink Scotch and liqueurs and gin. The scene is rather like a setting for *White Cargo,* without the Tondelayo. A turned-down hurricane lantern casts black shadows on the cane walls of the native hut which is our home. Outside the rain is coming down in an unbroken gray wall. A good deal of it is dripping through the grass thatch and forming big pools of water in the middle of the floor, and in my blanket. Up in the blackness that hides the dust-covered rafters a gecko lizard is clucking. Everybody is stripped to the waist and the lamplight is shining on skin dripping with perspiration. There are pools of spilt liquor on the ramshackle table, on which stands old crusted, cobwebby bottles of sherry, dug up from some abandoned cellar, and a couple of squat bottles on which I can read the words, "DOM Veritable Benedictine."

Every few moments the whole scene is lighted weirdly by the blue-green flash of lightning. The thunder is rolling and crashing from the nearby bluff of Hombrom. The little room is crowded. There is a temporary shortage of plebeian beer, but a plethora of high class wines and spirits. Everybody is sick of them and is pining for some good, cold ale.

Pretty soon the conversation turns, as it often does up here—where most of us think the "too little, too late" policy is being continued—to the shortsightedness of the democracies in not waking up to the "Japanese menace."

Australians are paying dearly now for their errors of the past. They say there's no sense in crying over spilt milk. But perhaps we can be permitted to shed a silent tear or two for the things we didn't do in the years that the locust has eaten, things that could have been done but weren't, and things that shouldn't have been done but were. "Our little friends, the Japanese"—the phrase was used more than once in the years before the Second World War began—are raining bombs on Australian territory in New Guinea and on the mainland itself.

That the Japanese are now using bombs which contain scrap metal exported from Australia is undeniably a probability. And most of us will remember the constant spate of protests against the export of Australian scrap to Japan. Protests were made because we thought the scrap was for bombs which would be used against the Chinese. Well, we're getting a few of them ourselves now.

The waters of North Australia and the surrounding island groups are now waters of war. We knew for years what was happening, but we never bothered to do anything about it. For the last ten years almost every Japanese lugger which ostensibly sought pearl shell and trochus carried an officer of the Japanese Imperial Navy, who worked as an ordinary seaman when any strangers were about, but who spent the rest of the time taking observations and soundings for charts.

It is doubtful if there is any anchorage or any reef in the northern seas unknown to the Japanese, and that information is very valuable to them now. For years a dirty little 200-ton Japanese steamer ran regularly between Truk, in the Caroline group, Rabaul, in British New Guinea, and even occasionally to Port Moresby, in Papua. She never seemed to carry any cargo, but nobody worried very much about her. Then when Japan struck in the South Seas, the Truk-Rabaul supply line became enormously valuable to the aggressors. The invasion fleet that crushed resistance at Rabaul and conquered the former capital came from Truk. And now that Rabaul has become the centre of enemy operations against New Guinea the Japanese holding force is being supplied from Truk. Perhaps now we can understand why that little steamer painstakingly covered that route for year after year in all sorts of weather conditions. The crew always mixed freely with longshoremen when in port at Rabaul. When the attack was made, months after the steamer had made her last visit, there was every evidence that the defense set-up was an open book to the attackers. Other greasy little Japanese freighters made similar passages—usually without cargo—to the Gilberts and Solomons, where attacks have since been made.

The Japanese didn't make the same errors that we did. Truk was built up as an immense defense arsenal for future aggression—an arsenal and air base and naval base only seven degrees north of the equator. We pottered around with our strategic defense bases, doing a little bit here and putting the rest off until the weather got cooler. It was a nice attitude of mind provided you knew for certain that the Japanese would never come south. Nobody knew for certain. But it was generally agreed that there would be plenty of warning when the time came. Rabaul had about a week's warning. And you can't manufacture anti-aircraft guns in a week from coconut palms. The one outstanding fact of the Second World War is that you don't get warning of what is coming. So far we have taken all the kicks for our stupidity—and we have cheerfully made our innumerable strategic withdrawals, straightened our lines, warned the enemy that they are stretching their supply lines too far, and then discovered that their supply lines are going even farther, and that our defense lines are falling back more and more in the direction of Antarctica. We've cheered ourselves up with the thought that the British lose every battle except the last, until we Australians suddenly discover that *this* is the last battle, so far as we are concerned. Perhaps it isn't too late, even now, to wake up to ourselves. We have a lot of time to make up.

Japanese activity in the South Seas has continued for a long time, and although she was forbidden under the Washington Agreement to fortify any of her mandated islands (she has well over one thousand of them in the Pacific), there is no evidence that she kept faith. Ships steaming near desolate little islands off the beaten steamer tracks of the South Pacific have been swept by 11,000,000 candlepower searchlights. Captains of the ships felt justified in thinking that grim gun barrels were trained along those blue-white shafts of light. They didn't know for certain. Only Japanese ships were allowed to visit those islands, and the number of Nipponese ships that called there was out of all proportion to the trade and resources of the islands themselves.

Jaluit, in the Marshalls, and Pulap, Ponape, Truk, and Yap, in the Carolines, were admitted by Japan to be coaling and oil stations. But the harbors were deepened for ships that never went there, and the Japanese indignantly denied at Geneva that the dredging might have had something to do with submarines. Two years after war broke out between Britain and Germany the Japanese South Seas Bureau was enormously enlarged (Japan was then a member of the Tokyo-Rome-Berlin Axis), and a tremendous amount of research work was undertaken by huge staffs among the islands under Japanese mandate in the south Pacific, while shiploads of sea scouts were sent out to the islands on educational excursions, which were financed and patronized by Prince Chichibu.

It was a curious fact that ships which left Kobe or Yokohama with hundreds of scouts returned practically empty!

When war came to the Pacific the full extent of our blindness and folly could be realized. Reconnaissance aircraft found Truk a miniature Gibraltar. Huge store and ammunition dumps had been built, and aircraft carriers and warships were anchored offshore. Midway between Truk and the Bismarck Archipelago was the island of Kapingamarangi, with warships and aircraft and a whole flotilla of invasion barges. Japan had observed the terms of the League of Nations mandate—in her own particular way. War had come to the Pacific. Her bases were ready for her first drive south of the equator. Not long afterward Rabaul, an Australian garrison, was overwhelmed.

And in Australia members of Parliament hurried to their publicity officers to get drafts of speeches deploring Japan's criminal aggression—the same members of Parliament who had condoned and excused everything the Japanese had done in the years that the locust had eaten.

### Curtain Rising

The little tropic sideshow is ending. The Japanese have invaded New Guinea. It is Sunday, March 8. We had expected the blow to fall on Port Moresby, but instead they have struck on the north coast, and tonight Lae and Salamaua are in Japanese hands. It has all happened almost as baldly as that. Our defense of the north coast didn't exist as such. A handful of guerrillas went in to blow up the Salamaua airfield. The N.G.V.R. is still in the jungle, somewhere. The thing that really counts, of course, is that the Japs, who until today were 550 miles away, are now only 170 miles to the northward—380 miles nearer Moresby, 380 miles nearer Australia.

For two days we've known that something was going to happen. The only question was—where? On Thursday night the Kawanisis were over twice, at midnight and at 3 A.M. After daybreak another enemy bombing force began to concentrate on Lae. We can see now that it was a softening-up process. The real anxiety began on Friday when a report came in that four Japanese destroyers had steamed out of Rabaul harbor followed by a number of transports. Rumors were spreading everywhere and gathering flavor as they spread. A dozen times I was asked if it were true that a Japanese invasion fleet of forty ships was in the Coral Sea, south of Moresby. There were ships south of Moresby, but one was an American aircraft carrier and the others were allied cruisers and destroyers. That was some encouragement.

In the garrison itself the excitement occasionally almost bordered on panic. Military trucks were streaming up the road packed with food and ammunition for the rear lines—"just in case," I was told, "we have to fall back and fight a stand in the hills!" Panic of this sort is contagious, and yesterday I passed hundreds of natives hurrying up to the hills with their pathetic little bundles on sticks over their shoulders. A Jap bomber that came over convinced everybody that it was reconnoitering the positions in preparation for the landing.

Yesterday there was a little more information about the Japanese intentions. Our Catalinas and Lockheeds had been shadowing the convoy all the way from Rabaul. By yesterday morning they were off Gasmata and by the afternoon twelve ships, including four warships, were heading westward in the direction of Salamaua. At the same time ten heavy Japanese bombers raided Moresby airfield to make sure that our aircraft did not attempt to interfere with the movements of the convoy.

The Japanese ships came into Salamaua about midnight. The first Australian to see the approach of the invaders was Captain A. G. Cameron, an officer of the 2/22nd, who had reached Salamaua a few days before with a party of refugees from Rabaul. With three men, he decided to stay for a while to see if he could hinder the Japanese a little. In total darkness the four men crouched on the outskirts of the airfield, watching the Japs coming ashore from barges and ships' boats. Cruisers were waiting offshore for dawn to break so that they could move north to Lae to begin the bombardment that would pave the way to the Japanese occupation of the capital of New Guinea. In the warm quietness of that tropic night the enemy was making his first major move since the conquest of Rabaul forty-four days before.

By 2 A.M. the Salamaua landing had been completed. Rather to their astonishment, no doubt, the Japanese found the pretty little town on the isthmus completely abandoned, all vital installations destroyed except the airfield. That would have pleased them. Main purpose of the landing would be to obtain the airfield so that air attacks against Moresby could be intensified. The invaders moved like black shadows through the silent night. They wore rubber-soled shoes and dark-colored uniforms. But among the palms were other shadows—the figures of Cameron and his three Australians moving like phantoms from tree to tree.

The Japanese knew nothing of their presence until a burst of revolver shots echoed through the trees. The commander of a Japanese platoon fell dead as the night suddenly filled with the yammering clamor of startled Japs. Soft footsteps pattered. There was scattered and bewildered rifle fire from a dozen separate enemy parties, and the sharp, light crackling of the Japanese .256 automatic rifles was answered by the heavier reports from the Australian .303's.

Within twenty seconds the Japanese invasion force was in an uproar. Men fired wildly in search of the Australian snipers, whom they could neither see nor hear. The Australians were crouching in the undergrowth only two yards from the track along which the search parties were pattering. The noise of the Japanese thrashing through the tangled vines and undergrowth died away, and the Australians slipped silently toward an abandoned house, where a detonating set was hidden, its wires leading to the heavy demolition charges already set in the airfield. Cameron seized the plunger while the other men stood guard outside. Two seconds later the houses of Salamaua shook to the strangely muffled explosion of hundreds of pounds of carefully packed high explosive.

The diminishing echoes of the explosion, designed to destroy Salamaua aerodrome, were sullen undertones to the sharp crackle of rifle fire as the tiny band of Australians shot their way through the Japanese lines to the safety of the jungle.

That little skirmish has begun the war of the shadows in New Guinea.

Soon after dawn today the Japanese planes came roaring in to make their landings on Salamaua drome. The first pilot put his plane down on the runway, taxied a few feet. Then the ground caved in and the plane fell in an enormous crater and burst into flames. The demolition charge fired by the Australians a few hours before had spread the explosion horizontally, undermining the airfield and leaving only a thin crust of apparently solid earth which the weight of a plane was sufficient to collapse!

At 9 A.M. the Japanese invasion force had reached Lae, 25 miles to the north of Salamaua. Cameron's exploit had shaken them. Before a landing was attempted at the capital a force of 12 bombers rained high explosive on the town, and salvo after salvo of naval shells poured over into the abandoned and completely undefended town.

All our bombers are out today hammering the Japs at their new beachheads. American bombers are streaming in from the mainland to help in the attack, and Douglas Dauntless dive-bombers from the American carrier in the Coral Sea have been going backward and forward all day long.

At least this crisis has produced some of the air support we've been looking for during the past weeks! Six of the Japanese ships had been sunk or damaged by this afternoon, the pilots say. One took a 500-pound bomb down the funnel and blew to pieces. Despite furious anti-aircraft fire from the Japanese ships our planes attacked consistently, hour after hour, from an altitude of only 400 feet.

Well, this business should lay the cards on the table. The game of hide-and-seek may be over. . . .

### Battle for Bases

At least one of the reasons for the Japanese occupation of Lae and Salamaua is now clear to everybody. They have two good bases from which to attack Moresby by air. And they are proving that it can be done. Since the landings, in the six days that have passed, we have had only one day without an air raid.

In those six days there have been a few things happening. Day after day American and Australian bombers have been hammering the Japanese ships and shore installations in their new bases and at Rabaul and Gasmata, from which the landing forces are being supplied and fed. One Japanese cruiser foundered after bombs had dropped squarely on her superstructure. Three other ships, including a very large transport, were sunk, four left in flames and another beached with its stern under water.

The Japanese, however, made another occupation that day, when they landed at Finschhafen, a mission village 60 miles northwest of Lae.

Enemy planes went south of Port Moresby for the first time when Zeros and bombers attacked Horn Island, in Torres Strait.

Here they met a squadron of American Kittyhawks (one of which deliberately rammed a Zero when its guns jammed and cut the Japanese plane in two), and strafed the merchantman *Canberra* in the Coral Sea on the way back to Lae. The tempo of the air war is certainly being pepped up now!

At the moment, in assessing these new enemy landings, we have to look at the air warfare questions involved. Before the Huon Gulf towns were occupied the Japanese were making leisurely 1300-mile bombing raids from Rabaul to Port Moresby and back again, and doing it whenever they felt inclined, without much trouble except for the fact that they were operating near the limit of their effective range, with the troublesome barrier of the Owen Stanleys to be crossed both coming and going. A trip of similar length today, operating from new bases at Lae and Salamaua, would almost enable them to carry their bomb loads to Cairns or Townsville without even bothering about Port Moresby. And if they wanted to raid Moresby they could make two, three, or four trips a day.

That is why, I think, these new occupations are significant. In a country where a piece of flat ground is something to marvel at— and where aerodromes which would be condemned as highly dangerous on the mainland have often had to be carved from the sides of mountains—the Japanese have taken care to make their landings *only* where airfield facilities already exist. They know that air power is the decisive factor in this sort of country. If they didn't already know the R.A.A.F. and the U. S. Air Corps have taken a great deal of trouble to explain it to them!

The Japanese have made their new advances southward in complete accordance with their particular book of rules. Japanese tactics don't alter very much. Despite reports of *hara-kiri* merchants and "suicide squads," the fundamental of Japanese tactics is extreme caution. They don't like to attack some objective until they feel pretty certain that the job is going to be reasonably easy. Even the conquest of Malaya was not nearly as tough a job as we, to our cost, thought it would be.

In this New Guinea war, as far as it has progressed, there has been ten times more courage displayed by our men than by the Japs. If the Japanese had equalled our courage and determination we might be excused for feeling thoroughly scared now that they are sharing this island with us. But where our bombers go down 400 feet to raid their targets, the Mitsubishis never come below 20,000 feet—unless they are absolutely sure that their targets are without any defense at all. A torrent of high explosive bombs and naval shells was poured into undefended Lae before any landing was made—a very clear indication of the Japanese belief that it's better to be sure than sorry.

Their move from Rabaul to Huon Gulf was in accordance with most of their previous moves in the Pacific. They progressed just the distance of effective range of fighter aircraft—and scarcely a single mile more. It was the same old cautious leapfrog policy that looks only spectacular because of our own weaknesses, and because we do not realize yet that aggressive action is better than blind acceptance of a "withdrawal complex." The Japanese don't make their leapfrog jumps with seven-league boots. They make their moves only to places where they know they can still depend on their fighter planes for protection.

For Japan, the New Guinea campaign is easily the most distant it has been obliged to undertake. The supply line—Yokohama, Saipan, Truk, Rabaul, Lae—is 3140 miles long, and would be highly vulnerable if we had warships and long range bombers with which to attack it. At the moment we don't seem to have the necessary striking power, but one of these days I feel that these elongated supply lines will prove the Achilles heel of Nippon.

# II. NEGANA TUARI

*March 19, 1942—May 8, 1942*

---

*Negana Tuari*

THE natives have a phrase that they are beginning to use a good deal lately. It is *negana tuari*. A literal translation would be "fighting time," which expresses pretty well the new atmosphere in New Guinea. Most of the fighting is in the air, but there are signs that the Japs intend to use ground forces in combat, somewhere.

Today, for instance, the riddle of future enemy troop movements, which has been keeping us guessing for days, was partly solved. A fairly strong force of Japanese soldiers, with a light tank or two, are moving up the Markham Valley from Lae. I can't even guess at what this portends, for the Markham Valley leads to the westward from the sea—away from Port Moresby—and ends in a cul-de-sac formed by steep limestone spurs and jungled mountains whose peaks are lost in the clouds.

One or two of the correspondents are writing stories which suggest that it might be the beginning of an overland advance on to the south coast of Papua, but none of the Intelligence officers—who are completely unperturbed about the whole show—will give the slightest credence to the theory.

The most interesting feature of this advance is that certain Lutheran missionaries—of Australian, British or American nationality—have been acting as guides for the Japs, and our guerrillas over the other side are very anxious to meet some of the white traitors.

Now that the lid has been blown off this Lutheran business, it turns out that quite a little network of Nazi espionage and fifth-column activity existed on the north coast. Leaders were Lutherans (which is not to say, of course, that *all* Lutherans up there were involved), who had a plant for the printing of swastika flags and arm bands (hundreds of which were seized and brought into Moresby), kept air strips in good repair for the Axis landing which they were confident would one day come, and maintained a secret radio transmitter at Malahang which, apparently, was used to convey information to the Japanese in the Carolines.

For months the military authorities have been appealing to the government to take action, but nothing very much has been done up to the time of the Jap landings. One raid was made by Australian soldiers, who seized the swastika emblems, a great bundle of photographs of Nazi leaders, and the remains of the secret radio, which had been destroyed. But because questions of citizenship were involved no action could be taken. At the outbreak of war one missionary, who had been a German air ace in the Great War, donned a *Luftwaffe* uniform (the Lord only knows where he had obtained it!), boarded a private plane and left Alexishaven. He flew northward, out to sea. Where he was making for, and if he ever arrived, are questions nobody can answer.

There are stories of native children in the area round Finschhafen being taught the Nazi salute and the *Horst Wessel* song. Some of these natives, no doubt, are now acting as guides for the Japs.

All this just goes to prove that you never can tell where treachery is hidden. I would have said that Papua and New Guinea would be the one place in all the world where the fifth column would not exist. But since the Lutheran business there has been a minor purge among the troops in the garrison here and a few men in Australian khaki—found in possession of Nazi documents (mostly concerned with some German Youth Movement or other), photographs of Hitler, Goering, Goebbels and Himmler, as well as beautifully pinpointed aerial photographs of the garrison—have been sent south in custody.

In quite a few of the recent daylight raids over Moresby we had all noticed meteorological balloons floating about in the sky. The other day an air force cordon surprised a man—wearing Australian military uniform—releasing a large green balloon from the scrub alongside the airfield. He was attacked, but escaped after having fired on the air force men, hitting one on the steel helmet. Latest reports indicate that the man made his getaway down the coast.

Don't ask me the purpose of the balloons. I don't know. And neither does anyone else to whom I've spoken.

Meanwhile our force of volunteer guerrillas remaining on duty near Lae and Salamaua have set up their jungle camps and are ready to tackle the job of keeping a close eye on all enemy moves. One patrol has already made a sortie right inside Japanese-held Salamaua to gather information of Japanese strength in that town. The Japs retaliated by forcing natives to build a trestle bridge across the flooded Franciso River. When it was completed an enemy punitive force made a raid across the river, blew up the store dump which our guerrillas were using, and went back home. This little force we have over the range has great value, both present and potential, and everything is being done to keep it supplied, fed and reinforced. Specially trained commandos are to be flown into Wau to reinforce them. If you haven't seen the New Guinea jungle it is quite impossible to visualize what these soldiers have to do to live and fight. They live almost perpetually in a dripping green twilight, hiding by day amid the dank palms and underbrush and twisting vines and creepers; moving by night through an eerie, moist blackness into which the light of tropic stars seldom penetrates. They are kept supplied with food, with ammunition, with weapons equal to the world's best, with medical supplies. But often they must live for days on the primitive food of the natives, filled with an almost intolerable longing for civilized food, for just one puff at a cigarette, for one cool draught of real beer.

Their country of operation must rank among the toughest fighting terrain in the world. Distances may not be great, but there are no standards of distance by which travel in New Guinea may be measured. The so-called "valleys" are ravines, the "mountain streams" are torrents racing through awesome channels cut thousands of feet deep between beetling alpine spurs. The jungle is like an impenetrable green wall. The rivers are dangerous with crocodiles and the swamps teem with huge bloodthirsty leeches. And through every inch of this green hell can be heard the endless hum of malaria-carrying insects. Even in peace time, this mandated territory of New Guinea was regarded as one of the most difficult regions in any country of the globe. It's a thousand times tougher in war. Here are strange equatorial extremes of heat and cold:

times of breathless, soggy heat; times when there is frost on the grass and ice on the high mountain tarns.

One of these days the people of Australia will hear more, much more, about this hidden force in the jungles. At the moment we are allowed to write nothing about them. When it comes it will make a fine story—this tale of a little band of young Australians who slip like spectres through the green twilight, who swing the huge, broad-bladed jungle knives like experts, who wear razor-sharp sheath knives for silent killing, who carry their tommy guns right inside the precariously held Japanese lines.

### Hero's Arrival

General Douglas MacArthur, "The Hero of Bataan," has arrived in Australia to take supreme command of allied forces in the south-west Pacific. This is mighty interesting news to all of us. It shows, at least, that this zone of defense is to be given its proper importance. The arrival of MacArthur—as much by his own colorful personality and career as by the spectacular story of his escape from the Philippines—has done more to lift morale on the mainland than anything else that has happened in this war.

Most of us know nothing of his record apart from what we have read in the newspapers since the Philippine show began. Opinion among the officers ranges from one major's "He is the greatest fighting soldier in the world today" to a captain's "I can't get out of my mind the fact that he's just another of the united nations' fifty defeated generals!"

Well, time will give the final judgment. And, in the meantime, his arrival here has done Australia a lot of good.

Other things are happening this month. Some of them will have far-reaching consequences. One is the return to Australia of a large part of the Australian Imperial Force, which has been fighting so splendidly in the Middle East. The other is the visit to Washington of Dr. Herbert Evatt, the Australian Foreign Minister. He has a tough job on his hands: the task of "selling" Australia and the Southwest Pacific to the big shots in Washington, of getting more and more materials (particularly combat aircraft) for this theatre, of having the seat of the Pacific War Council transferred from

London to Washington. He is one of our brainiest Ministers and a fighter, and if anything can be done he'll do it.

### The "Tomorrowhawks"

All the looted liquor for miles around is flowing tonight. In our camp every single officer and man seems to be packed round a battered, half-tuned piano which somebody "found," and the night is ugly with their roaring choruses. Morale and cheerfulness have hit new highs. All because our fighters have arrived. The "Tomorrowhawks" turned out to be P-40s—Curtiss Kittyhawks—a whole squadron of them, which swept in to make their landings late this afternoon. Port Moresby has fighter support at last!

The first four fighters came in just after somebody had given an air-raid alarm. Our machine gunners had never seen Kittyhawks before and the planes bore no emblems (the stars of the U. S. Air Corps had been painted out, and the circles of the R.A.A.F. had not yet been painted on), so the gunners opened up with a hail of fire and holed every one of the four planes! None of them was seriously damaged, fortunately!

The machine-gunners are in disgrace tonight, but I doubt if anyone could fairly blame them for the mistake. Last Friday the Japs raided with six Zero fighters and no bombers. All the troops, seeing the fighters coming in low over the hilltops, dashed into the centre of the airfield, threw their hats in the air, cheered with delight at the arrival of the "Tomorrowhawks." Within a couple of seconds they were flat on their bellies, dodging flying bullets and cannon shells! Apparently they didn't want to make the same mistake today.

Twenty minutes after the fighters came in, over came a big twin-engined Japanese bomber, making the usual leisurely reconnaissance of the garrison that has been a daily feature for weeks. Young Wackett—son of the man who makes our Wirraway aircraft—took up a Kittyhawk for his first combat. The Jap tried to escape toward the mountains. The fighter streaked out and headed him off, while an excited naval radioman cleverly jammed the Jap aircraft radio to prevent any signal going out that we had fighters in Moresby at last. Thousands of men had their necks craned skyward as the bomber doubled back toward the harbor with the little fighter diving down on his tail with guns chattering. A great column of greasy smoke poured from the bomber as it crashed in flames on to the reef.

The troops were still cheering an hour afterward, and every truck that rumbled past the airfield was crowded with soldiers looking toward the line of sleek little fighters and shouting: "You bloody beauts!"

And celebrations haven't stopped since.

Even the Japs have helped to make the night livelier. The broadcasting station most easily received up here on the few radio sets in the garrison happens to be Tokyo Radio. For the last few nights they've been broadcasting, in English, vivid descriptions of the fierce "Battle of New Guinea," raging between Japanese troops and "strong Australian forces" in the mountains. Each night they have carefully pinpointed the extent of the Japanese progress. Tonight they triumphantly announced that Nippon had achieved a major victory after a series of fierce and bloody battles, and finished up with a complete description of the triumphal entry of the Japanese troops into the battered streets of Port Moresby, "devastated and laid waste by our smashing air blows."

Well, there hasn't been any fighting, and the only signs of activity in the dusty, sleepy streets of Port Moresby when I was in town this afternoon were a group of naked soldiers bathing beneath a street hydrant, and a sentry sitting outside the Burns Philp store trying to open a can of apricots with his bayonet!

### Men of Moresby

Over the rounded top of a squat hill came the Japanese Zero fighters—five of them—diving down from 1500 feet at a speed of close on 400 miles an hour, their snub-nosed engines and low, tapered wings giving them an appearance of terrifying invulnerability. Little yellow stabs of flame preceded by only a second or two the sharp clatter of cannon and heavy machine guns.

Ahead of the concealed machine-gun positions the earth spurted up in tiny spouts of red dust. Over our heads the broad leaves, cut through by whizzing lead, fell from the branches. The two men in front stood at the gun, immobile, like carved bronze statues. Suddenly there was a tautening of muscles, as arms moved with trained skill. The shattering roar of the gun was the signal for other posts to open up. All round us the air vibrated with the roar of rapid-fire guns, the curious swish of bullets.

In three seconds it was all over. Climbing almost perpendicularly, one of the Zero fighters was streaking away over the hills. Another had bounced from the ground and rocketed over our heads with a great spurt of flame spewing from the cockpit. We didn't see it crash, but we heard the rumbling explosion as it burst into a thousand pieces on a hill 600 yards behind. A great column of smoke rose from a stubby hill on our left, where another fighter had crashed in flames into the scrub and hurled the body of the pilot 200 yards beyond. The fourth enemy fighter was streaking away for the mountains with a great trail of white smoke pouring from the tail. We couldn't see the fifth machine. In the excitement of the brief action it had got away. Two shot down in flames and one damaged for certain out of five planes. It was good shooting.

The other day I saw something that indicated the boys were shaping up pretty well. The supply truck was pulled up at the side of the road. A young A.A.S.C. private was unloading stores for his camp. He reverently piled a case of eggs on his shoulder—the first eggs (fresh or otherwise) seen in Moresby for months. As he moved away from the truck the bombs began to fall. He walked on without looking up. Then one fell closer. It was still about 200 yards away, but even when they're that far off they sound as if they're going right for you! He looked up at the Japanese bombers and yelled out at the top of his voice:

"You break one of these eggs and I'll come up and break your bloody necks!"

And the troops are still laughing at one incident that occurred in a recent raid. A supply truck was moving along the road when bombs began to fall near by. The truck was stopped and the men leaped out. There was no shelter. They threw themselves beneath the truck. Unfortunately they had forgotten to put the handbrake on. The truck began to move slowly down the road. The men underneath began to crawl on all fours beneath it. The truck moved faster; the men crawled faster. The raid ended with the truck moving down the road at about 10 miles an hour, 50 yards ahead of three men crawling frantically on all fours at two miles an hour.

A steel-helmeted head rose from the bushes as they passed, and in the tropic air rose the unmusical strains of "Git along, little dogies, git along, git along!"

## Jungle Massacre

I don't like writing so-called "atrocity stories." Even when they happen to be true, they are always suspect. They've been suspect, I suppose, ever since the days of Raemaker and the *Kultur* propaganda of the Great War. But we've been requested to write the story of the Tol massacres, partly to convince a certain weak-kneed element that it doesn't do much good to surrender to the Japanese. All of us have taken great pains to check up on the facts of the story, and to talk to the two wounded men who survived the massacre.

There were three Australian survivors, but one is still too ill to be seen. They were members of a party of 10 officers and more than 50 other ranks of the Rabaul garrison who were trapped in the village of Tol, while attempting to make their way to safety along the southern coast of New Britain. The day before reaching Tol they had picked up leaflets dropped from Japanese float-planes announcing that Australians who surrendered would be well treated, but those who refused to surrender would be hunted out and killed.

While they were at Tol a strongly armed landing party of marines came ashore from a Japanese cruiser. The Australians, starving and practically unarmed, agreed to surrender, and in the beginning it seemed that the Japanese intended to treat them decently. They were given drinks and cigarettes. A party returned to the cruiser to report back to Rabaul on the incident. When it returned to the village there was a hurried consultation in excited Japanese and the whole attitude of the captors changed immediately. The Australians were bullied and kicked into line and counted. They were then ordered to empty their pockets of all possessions, which were scraped into a heap on the ground, on top of which each man was told to toss his identity disk. Then each man's wrists were tied behind his back with white cord and the men were strung up with rope into parties of ten tied together.

Each party was taken into the jungle in a different direction.

Amid the tangled green wilderness the Australians were cut off the line one by one, marched into the bush and bayoneted to death by a Japanese soldier. Each Australian officer was handed a revolver containing one bullet and told to commit suicide.

"My party was stopped after we had gone a few yards into the undergrowth," one of the survivors told me. "A Japanese officer then drew his sword and ordered his men to fix bayonets. One Australian was detached at a time from the party and led into the jungle by a Japanese soldier armed with a bayonet. We could hear the screams as our cobbers were killed one by one. One chap asked to be shot. This was done by the officer himself. Another got loose some way and started to dash into the bush. He, also, was shot by the officer. Several men were bayoneted to death only a few yards from me. Most of the Australians died very bravely, promising the Japanese, 'You'll pay for this when our chaps catch you!'

"I was the last man on the line in my party. Just as it came to my turn all the Japanese left, for some reason, except the officer. He stayed with me for a while, not talking, just looking at me. When the others didn't return the officer picked up a rifle, motioned me to walk away and then fired at me. The bullet went through my left shoulder and I fell to the ground and lay still. He fired two more shots. One went through my left wrist, the other through my right hand. I kept still, as the shot must have also caught me in the back, paralyzing my legs for a time. For hours I couldn't move, but when no more Japanese came I decided to take the risk and try to get away. I found that the Japs had returned to their warship and gone from the area, and found two other badly wounded Australian troops. The rest of our large party had been killed. After wandering in the jungle for three days we were picked up by another party of Australians, given medical attention, and taken to safety."

It appears also that the Japanese force which occupied Salamaua lined up more than 100 natives against the wall of a hangar at Salamaua airfield and shot them as a terrorist lesson to the rest of the native population. Other natives were branded with a red mark on the forehead and put to work unloading Japanese storeships. They were given one army biscuit as the day's ration. That night all the natives went bush.

*Welcome to a Prostitute*

A new type of American bomber—the B-26 Glenn Martin Marauder—has gone into action against the Japs in New Guinea, and those of us who have seen results are inclined to agree with the American pilots who fly them. "This aircraft can win the war," they say. "It's a honey!" It's a twin-engine job, with a bomb capacity greater than a Fortress and a speed that almost reaches that of a fighter. It has tricycle landing gear and looks "nose-heavy" with the two huge four-bladed propellers which clear the ground only by nine inches. It is, they say, "a tough baby to fly." The wings are very narrow for the size of the plane and it lands faster than a good many fighters. The Marauder is, therefore, locally known as "Martin's Prostitute" because it has "no visible means of support." But it's a damned good bomber, as the Japanese at Lae have already found out at the cost of 16 bombers and fighters destroyed or damaged out of 24 planes caught on the ground in a surprise sunset raid by American Marauders and Australian Kittyhawks.

American assistance is now really being seen in a big way—more on the mainland than in New Guinea, at the moment—and nobody will blame the people of Australian cities for the tumultuous welcome they've given to these fresh-faced youngsters who are pouring into the country in their thousands from the great democracy across the Pacific.

In the New Guinea operational area the guide and mentor of the young Americans is Tom McBride Price, one of the most experienced of the Australian Catalina pilots. He knows the New Guinea area like the palm of his own hand, and wears the ribbon of the Distinguished Flying Cross, which he won in the Mediterranean two years ago when he was flying the amphibian from H.M.A.S. *Sydney* as "spotter" for the British Navy's first bombardment of Italian-held Bardia.

"These American youngsters have got all the guts in the world," Tom said tonight. "They aren't frightened to go right down in the face of really tough opposition to do their job. In the last raid on Rabaul they dived in so low that some of the Marauders were holed by the splinters thrown up by their own bomb bursts. With these

Americans and Australians I think we can build up a team that will give the Japs an awful headache."

They are refreshingly boyish and enthusiastic to talk to, these kids from Texas and Colorado and North Carolina and California and Michigan and Alabama (but mostly, it seems, from Texas), and they still think it's a huge game and a grand adventure! War is actually neither a huge game nor a grand adventure, but they'll find that out soon enough—and they'll be all the better pilots for it.

The first mission for most of them was to hammer Rabaul—and they went in only 500 feet above the trees. "The Japs were taken completely by surprise," said one youngster. "We wondered what they were yabbering about when they saw us come in so low in formation. They must have thought we were going to land. They were so startled that they didn't think of running. We could see them standing there pointing at us. Then our bombs began to fall and they scattered in all directions. It was a grand experience. Oh, boy, when do we go again? We're all mighty anxious. I guess we paid back a bit for Pearl Harbor, but we've got a lot more accounts to render yet!"

In the turret of one plane was a kid from New York with an unpronounceable name—his father was German, his mother Italian, and he had just celebrated his twentieth birthday—who on his first mission had shot down one Zero for certain, and another listed as "probably destroyed."

"I was scared as hell as soon as I saw the Jap fighter coming at our ship," he said. "Then it got on our tail and I forgot to be scared all of a sudden. I opened up with both guns and he peeled off and rolled away underneath. I was just thinkin', 'Well, that's easy,' when I saw another Zero coming in from the side. He certainly looked darned ugly, but the guns got him all right. He seemed to stop dead as if suspended in the air. I could see my tracers streaming into his cockpit. Then he rolled away and spun underneath with orange flames squirting from both wings."

A twenty-year-old buck private from Minneapolis in the turret of another Marauder also scored his first kill in the same raid.

"My stomach was all knotted up inside me," he said, "but I let him come right up close before I let him have it. When I saw the plane going down in flames I had a sort of funny feeling. I didn't know whether I was sorry or glad."

I asked the pilot of this plane whether it was tougher going to the target or returning from it. He grinned. "It's pretty tough both ways. Going there you're all keyed up and anxious. Coming back you're all bubbly inside . . . and anxious. *We* certainly did some sweating coming back. Every now and then the observer would take out a photograph of his wife and look at it. I kept looking at a bullet hole in the engine coaming and wondering just what the bullet had done to the engine inside, or whether a gas tank had gone. And whenever I thought of that gas tank, slowly spilling gasoline, I'd look down at that terrible country below us. But we got home O.K. and we are all looking forward to the next mission. We like it!"

The pilots of Australia and America seem to get along very well together. The Australians naturally envy the Americans their (by comparison) princely rates of pay. The Americans envy the greater experience in this area of the Australians—although they don't envy the types of aircraft the Australians often have to fly!

There is a mutual admiration, one for the other, which is a very healthy basis on which to build the fighting team we must create to flog the Jap out of the south Pacific. Said one American bomber pilot: "Australian fighter pilots are the gamest I've ever seen. I saw one lone Kittyhawk, piloted by an Australian, dive down on seven Jap bombers with three Zeros escorting them. That was, to my way of thinking, plain suicide. But he pounced on 'em like a hawk on a flock of chickens, scattering them all over the sky, and shot down one Nip bomber in flames—and then he got away! That sort of thing kinda takes doing. Another time one of our American fighters—a P-39—crashed taking off, rolled over and burst into flames. Our pilot was trapped in the cockpit, but an R.A.A.F. warrant officer dashed through the flames, smashed the canopy glass, and, though badly burnt himself, saved the life of the American pilot."

Said an R.A.A.F. squadron leader: "One of the most amazing things of this war has been the way the Americans have jumped straight into the war with a skill and courage that comes to many only after years of bitter fighting. I saw youngsters from the States go into action for the first time against the Japs over Rabaul. The whole sky seemed ablaze with anti-aircraft bursts, and Zeros were coming from all directions. The Americans just waded in with the coolness of veterans and dropped their bombs unwaveringly on the targets from only a few hundred feet above the ground. Then they turned round to fight their way out through the Zeros. They won!"

It will require an American-Australian team to win this little war in the southwest Pacific and I think we're getting one. They are learning each other's slang, wearing each other's clothes, even educating themselves in each other's gambling.

Today two enlisted men, one an American, one an A.I.F. infantryman, met on Moresby airfield. They yarned for a few minutes and then I saw the American pull a pair of dice out of his pockets. Within a few minutes he was teaching the Australian how to "shoot crap." When it ended the Australian understood the game but had lost $20. He thought for a moment and then dived his fist into his pocket and brought out two pennies. A crowd gathered as the pennies were tossed in the air. Half an hour later the American and the Australian parted. The American, with a lugubrious grin on his face, scratched his head in mock perplexity. The Australian was grinning. In his pocket he had his $20 back, plus 22 of the American's dollars. But the American had learned the Australian game of "two-up!"

### Backcloth for Battle

A light rain is falling on the sodden ground and clouds are capping the mountains all round. The air is throbbing with the noise of aircraft. Apart from that endless whining hum, there is no evidence of war. The native boys are squatting on the veranda of a grass hut, giggling at the efforts of a youngster with flaming hibiscus in his hair to sing a monotonous but curiously catching native tune. Somewhere in the scrub some young Australian is playing "Waltzing Matilda" on a mouth organ that appears to have lost several notes. There is a constant buzz of insects and the call of birds, and hundreds of lemon-colored butterflies are weaving around the brilliant flowers.

If it were not for that drone of aircraft, war would seem very far away—until you started to walk. Then you would see roads with their edges scarred and pitted by bomb craters. If you went into the bush in a certain direction you would find the shattered remains of a big Japanese bomber. She came down yesterday in flames and five dead Japanese were carted away. On the top of another hill the charred remains of a fighter with the Japanese markings still visible is strewn like the skeleton of some prehistoric monster among the blackened sandbags of an observation post. Walk a little farther and you would find a group of tents with the canvas still ripped and holed by shrapnel. You would find buildings with twisted framework and sagging roofs and the fibrous plaster and corrugated iron scattered by blast. You would find plenty of evidence of war if you sought for it.

But you would find it difficult, as I, after two months, find it difficult, to reconcile the picture of two young native boys with crimson lap-laps and flowers in their hair, walking hand in hand beneath the palm trees, with the picture of men in steel helmets crouching in slit trenches and flinching instinctively at each crashing thump of high explosive.

The great billows of dust and smoke upflung by a stick of 250-pound bombs look incongruous before the jagged peaks of timeless mountains. The chatter of the natives as they sit on the crazy steps of their villages built up on crooked piles above the water is a sound that fits into the Papuan scene better than the chatter of the machine guns of seven fighter planes locked in an insanely whirling dogfight 20,000 feet above our heads. Look at the blue-green harbor waters and see the native lakatois skipping across the waters with outriggers dipping and rising in flurries of silver spray. That is the real Papua—not the harbor with great gouts of water upflung by poorly aimed bombs which have fallen from the triangle of ten silver specks flying three miles above the sea.

The early raids were frightening things, not understood. Men thought of Rotterdam and London. Their nerves tingled, their stomachs seemed to curdle when they first heard that sinister, ever-increasing whistling sound that stopped a split second before the first mighty roar of the bomb exploding. They pressed themselves against the unyielding earth, hearing the burst thunder closer, counting in an uncontrollable sweat of apprehension, wondering whether the stick would reach as far as their seemingly inadequate shelter. Then, after a few raids, they were no longer afraid. Men had fallen flat on open ground between two falling bombs and had been unhurt. Others had survived without a scratch when 250-pounders fell within six feet of the slit trench in which they cowered. The days passed into weeks. The Japanese tally reached a total of 2000 bombs dropped—for one man killed! Now they stand up and watch the raid and not until they actually hear the whistle of the falling bomb do they duck for shelter.

Today they represent the real Papua, because without them the other Papua—of hibiscus and frangipanni and laughing natives—would not exist. But it's still hard to reconcile the actors with the stage setting.

The noise of aircraft has died away. The only sound in the hot, steamy air is the drone of myriad insects and the cry of birds. And a string of native porters has just passed the door of my hut—strange wild men, who look like head-hunters. Violet, white, green, red, blue are some of the colors of their lap-laps. Some have hibiscus stuck behind their ears. Others have frangipanni wreaths twined in their frizzy black mops. And on their shoulders they are carrying cases of bully beef.

### Target for Today

This is really not my story at all. It is the story of a group of young American airmen; of their actions and reactions during a mission into enemy territory. It was told to me tonight by Lieutenant John J. O'Bert, twenty-six-year-old bombardier from Colorado, and it explains something of the background to those terse official communiqués that merely say: "Allied aircraft carried out an attack successfully on Japanese positions at Rabaul in the face of considerable anti-aircraft fire and some fighter opposition." Those communiqués make it sound like a battle between machines, but the human aspect of modern war—and the important aspect—is that the struggle is one, not between machines, but between the young men who handle those machines. So here is Johnnie O'Bert's story of a raid by Glenn Martin Marauders.

"On this occasion the airfield was dark. Cigarette ends glowed and men laughed and joked as they were being 'briefed' for the job we'd been allotted. Some of the jesting was probably artificial, some of it was plain high spiritedness. This was only our third job, and there was still that keyed-up, nervous tension that had to be glossed over with joking that, in retrospect, might seem kind of silly. Snatches of subdued conversation; sudden bursts of laughter; one chap yelling to another: 'We'll send your people a parcel of blotters and a note saying that the dark splodge in the centre is their son,' men in flying kits and helmets; and on the outskirts of the crowd young gunners and crewmen from the ships to be left behind, hanging around and hoping that somebody won't turn up so that they can go.

"Then the pulsing roar of engines; flicker of flares in the night, and the swift spinning of the stars as we turn above the airfield and head away on course for the selected target. Down below us streams the sombre, sleeping world. There is subdued talk, bursts of sudden laughter as we settle down to the job. Gunners are at their posts, pilot, navigator, bombardier, crews are methodically carrying out their work without fuss. Every control, every piece of equipment is tested and retested. On a job like this you can't afford to make mistakes.

"We are getting near Rabaul. How long the trip has taken us is something the Japanese would like to know. We've just sighted a Japanese reconnaissance plane away on our port side. That makes us a little anxious. He doesn't stop us and we don't try to stop him. But we know that he's reported by radio of our impending arrival, and the Nips probably will have something waiting for us. Underneath is a sea of green, thick jungle. It would be tough to come down in that country. We see a native village built up on sticks over the water. Maybe they'd be friendly and would help us; maybe they wouldn't.

"We're getting close to Rabaul, and you can feel that strange sensation as if your stomach is knotting up. None of us has had a drink. I don't think there's any law against taking a swig before you leave, but nobody ever does. I take out a pad and pencil and jot down all the things I've got to do just to make sure I do everything O.K. when the time comes. I'll tick them off as I do them. It's surprising how quickly I can read those notes. We're all talking to each other, checking the guns and equipment, and everybody is keeping a sharp lookout to report instantly anything that seems suspicious—which, of course, means Japanese aircraft.

"Reactions of the other fellows are different. I sing some of the songs I like in a loud voice that can't be heard above the roar of the engines—usually 'Jeannie with the Light Brown Hair,' I guess, because my girl's name is Jeannie, and because she has light brown hair. Another chap unconsciously always polishes his fingernails on his flying suit. Another takes out a photograph of his wife and looks at it for a second or two.

"Ahead of us now we can see the black bursts of the Japanese ack-ack mushrooming in the sky. They're putting up a barrage hoping we'll run into it. Through the clouds below we can now see scattered buildings and green clearings. Things begin to happen pretty fast. The nervous tension has gone. We're below 2000 feet now, diving down on the target. I have one hand on the trigger button of my machine gun, the other on the bomb release. Then the bombs go. We see them burst right underneath us, swelling clouds of smoke, dust, and bright red flashes of explosions. You can hear nothing above the noise of the planes—no sound of bombs —but as each bomb bursts the blast hits the plane, and it lifts and rolls a little. One of the gunners is spraying a motor truck on the ground. The Japanese are driving frantically, zigzagging to right and left. The truck crashes into a ditch and overturns. Scores of tiny figures are scurrying like ants across the aerodrome toward the air-raid shelters.

"The navigator is leaning over the open door of the bomb bay taking pictures of the bursts with a little box camera. The pictures won't come out, but it shows he's pretty unperturbed. The sky is black with the bursts of ack-ack. They're letting us have it properly, but they're well above the mark. We're not so low this time as we were on the last mission, when we went in so low that the Japanese thought we were going to land, and our ship was riddled with shrapnel from our own bomb bursts.

"Fires are blazing behind us and black smoke is rising. We got in some pretty good hits, and we're feeling cocky. We go straight on to machine gun other targets—buildings and the ships in the harbor that are blazing away with A.A. guns and flying boats on the water —but we nearly go too far. One tiny ship we tackle opens up with a flaming barrage that sends up a lot more than we send down. We bank away and head for home.

"Then we see the Japanese Zero fighters above us. We shouldn't be excited, but I guess most of us are. These Zeros are good. From now on we're on the defensive. Somebody says to me: 'Let 'em come up a bit. We want to see what they look like!' Maybe we let them come up a bit too close! A couple of slugs zip through the body of our ship. No damage. Nobody hurt. We give the Zeros a couple of bursts, and they falter and go back. A little later one drops out, but the other comes again. We're looking for every cloud to dodge into. Another burst from the Zero . . . another from us . . . he keeps away at a respectful distance.

"One of our planes is having a bit more bother. There are seven Zeros chasing him. One loops round and gives him a blast in the fuselage. He still flies on with guns spitting. It takes us twenty minutes to shake our chap off. He doesn't go until his ammunition has gone. He didn't damage us. Probably we didn't damage him, but there were a couple of Japanese bombers and about 16 Zeros up top, and we're wondering how our other ships fared.

"We check up through the plane to see if anyone is hurt. All safe. Then we check up for damage. We count the bullet holes and check everything to see it's O.K. We suffered a bit of damage, but not much. We'll get home. Somebody asked me would I like a bottle of beer. Oh, boy! We're all talking to each other now, trying to check with all hands the results of our attack. Our stories tally pretty well. We seem to have done all right. Everybody is still at action stations, but the strange knotted feeling inside has gone. Some of us feel a bit tired. One of our gunners says, 'After last raid I dreamed that Japanese were chasing me all night—I hope they give me some peace tonight!' Another man remarks slowly: 'I'll strike the first man who asks me was I scared 'cause he knows damn well I was!'

"As we near our base we go up high to check all controls before coming in. Everything seems O.K. We begin to think more and more of a long cool drink and plates covered with food.

"Well, that's another raid over. Maybe next time we won't let the Japanese Zeros come quite so close. The plane that was tackled by seven of them is in. He got back all O.K., but the ship is shot up some. A cannon shell burst inside the plane. Nobody is hurt. Now for that beer.

"Later on comes the nasty part of it. One of our planes crashed taking off. My best friend was in it. I have the job of packing his gear together to send home: papers, letters, photographs, a collection of phonograph records, classical stuff; a volume of Shakespeare. He was a grand guy."

*"Bombs, Boongs and Bully Beef"*

The fighter pilot waved his hand round the dusty, brown-green valley over which a flight of Kittyhawks roared into the air, their engines pulsing as they circled to gain height. We both wore tin hats, because we were expecting a raid, and the interceptors had already gone up to meet the incoming bombers. The pilot was still suffering from a slight wound, and was having a day off.

"What a country!" he exclaimed. He pointed to a mass of bomb craters in the scrub, a party of natives hurrying uphill toward the slit trenches, a dump of cases of canned beef stacked beneath the branches of trees that were wilting in the heat.

"The land of bombs, boongs,* and bully beef," he said. "If Port Moresby represents the glamorous tropics, I'll take Spitzbergen. Or even Tristan da Cunha.

"And yet, last month I went down to the mainland on leave. I saw a capital city again, trams in the streets, picture shows, pretty girls. I jostled among the crowds of people outside my pub and loved it. I went out without a greatcoat just to see what it was like to be really cold again. I drank beer that was cold, and ate fresh meat and fresh vegetables, and had fresh milk in my tea. And, will you believe it, I'd only been there two days—just two blanky days —when I began to wish I was back here. In this dirty hole, mark you! By the end of a week I was just eating my heart out to be back here."

He was looking contemptuously across the valley to where the dusty, stunted hills stood dwarfed by the great saw-toothed ridges of the main alpine spine, incredibly blue in the shimmering sunlight. Suddenly he swung round and peered into the sun. "Better move along to that trench," he said. "Here they come." The throbbing drone of Japanese engines was growing clearer . . .

The line of dots after the last sentence indicates that the curtain has been lowered to denote the passage of twenty minutes. In that time a great pattern of H.E. and A.P. bombs (demolition and daisycutters) had hurled gouts of brown dust and gray smoke into the air, and the dust still hung across the valley like a screen. A tenuous

---

* Natives.

spiral of black smoke rose from a hill on our left where a Japanese bomber had crashed in flames.

Our fighters began to come in. There were new bomb craters on the airfield, but none on the runway. The sleek little machines came down one by one.

There were bullet holes in three planes. One of them had its tail almost shot away. The pilots pulled off their helmets and stood, puffing at cigarettes, while Intelligence officers questioned them. They showed only slightly the evidence of the strain of that twenty minutes of combat. They were all a little relieved because most of them thought two of our fighters had been shot down, and they now discovered that one man (the pilot of the machine with the shattered tail) had brought his down safely. They spoke little about the man who had gone down in flames into the sea. It was not callousness. It was just that they don't do that sort of thing in the air force.

The questions asked by the interrogating officer reminded me of a very hardbitten Crown prosecutor I saw one time in a Melbourne courtroom. The only answers he wanted were "Yes" or "No." If the witness hesitatingly said "I think," the prosecutor snarled sarcastically, "The Court is not the slightest scrap interested in what you might think."

One pilot said he saw tracers from his guns smacking into the belly of a Zero, after which the Jap dropped toward the earth in a flat spin.

"See it crash?" asked the prosecuting counsel.

"No, Mac, but I don't think he could have pulled out," was the reply.

"Not interested in what you think. Did anyone else see it crash?" He looked round the group of pilots. Two others thought they'd seen a burst of smoke in the scrub.

"Sorry, not good enough," said the prosecuting counsel. He turned to the first pilot. "You can't claim, you know. Best we can do is 'hit and possibly destroyed.'"

"Good God, yes!" came the reply. "Never intended to claim it as a certainty, you know."

Some of the pilots left the airfield. Others waited in their flying kits in case the Japs came over again. Mechanics were working like maniacs on the fighters, stuffing the great belts of machine-gun am-

munition into the slender wings. A mobile petrol pump was pump-
ing high-octane fuel into the tanks. Over on the drome dust clouds
were rising as bulldozers pushed the upflung earth back into the
bomb craters which scarred the field. Beyond, American mechanics
were working on a big bomber which had suffered damage from a
Zero's cannon shells while over Rabaul the day before. A convoy of
military trucks carrying cases of the inevitable bully beef rumbled
along the rutted road. The soldiers, stripped to the waist, waved
their slouch hats at the fighter pilots, for whom they have always
had the most unbounded admiration and affection.

The dust had settled from the explosions. "The "boongs" came
splayfootedly down from the trenches, their gaudy lap-laps so brilliant in the midday sun that you needed dark glasses to look at
them in comfort.

The fighters were all parked, with their noses turned to the runway so that they could take off the instant the warning was given.
The pilots looked tired, but there was something in their expres-
sions, something in the set of their jaws, that made me glad I was
not a Zero pilot.

The job these youngsters of the Port Moresby fighter squadrons
—both Australian and American—and the allied bomber squadrons
have done will not be told fully until this war is over. It will be an
epic story of courage and endurance. So far we can tell only fragments of that epic. The story, for instance, of Johnnie Jackson, who
took a single fighter across to Lae on a daring reconnaissance, who
saw his own brother shot down into the sea, who was shot down in
flames over Lae, and made his way through terrible jungles and
swamps to reach a rendezvous with an American dive-bomber,
which took him back to Moresby through the spattering lead of a
Japanese fighter force that was raiding the base. Of how Johnnie
Jackson, still ill from his dreadful ordeal, insisted on taking his
fighter up against an overwhelming force of Zeros, and died as he
had lived—with consummate bravery.

Or the story of how John Engleman, an American sergeant-
gunner, hung by a rope in space from a speeding American bomber
to close the bomb bay doors which had jammed while in action over
Rabaul. Or of how another American bomber, its petrol tank holed
by Japanese machine-gun bullets, came into Moresby in a belly-land-
ing after the pilots had flown for thirty-five minutes "on the red

light." If you don't know what that means in nervous strain visualize flying a heavy bomber over some of the toughest mountain jungle country in the world with the red light glowing on the petrol indicator to show that the tanks were empty. Watching that glowing light for thirty-five minutes, not knowing at what instant the engines would splutter and the plane would go down, carrying its crew to certain death!

"We landed the plane, though," the pilot told me. "You could have thrown a lighted match into the petrol tank. That trip certainly made us sweat."

These men lived under tough conditions, fought under tough conditions. They knew the Japanese planes were good. But they never flinched from combat, and the toll they took of Zeros and bombers shook the Japanese back on their heels and gave them a new respect for Australian and American airmen. These pilots lived in the bush, in tents, or rough native shacks or even on the ground under the spreading wings of their planes. They ate food when and where they could get it. Often they ate nothing for a whole day. Sometimes it was impossible to get a cool drink. Their food was generally tinned baked beans and bully beef. They saw many of their comrades go down in that sickening plunge that meant quick death. But they saw many more Zeros and Mitsubishi bombers take the same final spin toward the earth.

They lived on their nerves—and we should be thankful that those nerves were of iron. And at least they had the satisfaction of seeing the Japanese beaten back, they saw the day when we were able to deal out to the enemy much more than we'd had to take.

And there was the fighter pilot talking to me in the dusty valley of the Laloki, and he was telling me of his leave in Sydney and of how he was eating his heart out to be back in Port Moresby.

### "It Won't Be Long Now!"

The most commonly heard remark today, May 8, is: "Well, it won't be long now!" The curtain will go up at any moment. The signs are too clear—and too numerous—for there to be any false alarm this time! Japanese planes have been pouring into Rabaul, Kavieng, Gasmata, Lae and Salamaua. The big Japanese naval force, including aircraft carriers, which launched the enemy's attack in the Bay of Bengal recently, has been to Truk and is now moving south. The transports and warships in Rabaul harbor—observers count them in scores now—have put to sea. Every available bomber, fighter, dive-bomber and reconnaissance plane that can be spared has been rushed to North Queensland or New Guinea and for nine days our air attacks against what the official spokesmen call "enemy invasion concentrations" have been interrupted only by darkness (sometimes not even by that) and execrable flying weather.

As usual in times of crisis, there has been a heavy clamp on all information, and an even heavier censorship on every word we write. It is difficult to get any picture of what is happening. It is even more difficult to try to convey that picture to the public.

The Japs seem to be throwing in everything they have. They are even supplementing their Zero fighters with Mitsubishi S-39 pursuit planes—a type that became obsolete more than two years ago. They have boosted Moresby's total of air raids to forty-five in an almost non-stop blitz that is only just beginning to show signs of petering out—largely because of our persistent hammering of their airfields and resolute interception by our fighters whenever they come over. In these desperate struggles in the clouds high above the jungles of New Guinea fighter strength is playing a more important part than bombing strength. Most of the raids have been made by high-speed, low-flying Zeros in a series of vicious ground-strafing attacks. The fight for air command of the Papuan skies has never been more bitter. Nor, I think, has so much hung upon its outcome.

There's not much of the old-fashioned chivalry about air fighting now. One of our fighter pilots who baled out was machine gunned by a Zero on his way to the ground. Peter Turnbull,* ace of the R.A.A.F. Kittyhawk squadron, which has now been relieved by American-piloted Airacobras, believes that there's something big cooking and that the Japs are going to desperate lengths to ensure that no information falls into our hands. Turnbull is an experienced pilot. He won the D.F.C. in Libya, where he was credited with nine Axis planes for certain, and he has added quite a few Zeros to his tally up here. In a recent dogfight over Moresby a Japanese fighter was shot down into the sea. A few minutes later Turnbull

---

* Killed in action at Milne Bay in September.

saw the Jap pilot swimming toward the shore from his wrecked plane. Another Zero immediately dived down and machine-gunned the struggling pilot until he disappeared beneath the reddened waves. "At the same time," added Turnbull, "it's plain nonsense to talk of them as hara-kiri merchants. They are no more suicide pilots than we were in Libya when we had to go up against Messerschmitt 109's in old Gloster Gladiator biplanes."

Everybody is quite unanimous in the opinion that the Japanese are about to stage a large-scale invasion attempt. But opinion is quite divided as to where the blow will fall. Moresby, New Caledonia, Northwest Australia, the South Solomons are favored in that order of among the lay prophets and armchair tacticians. The Japs have a wide circle of bases from which to strike. Since they came below the equator they have established positions at Lae, Salamaua, and Finschhafen (New Guinea), Kavieng (New Ireland), Rabaul and Gasmata (New Britain), Lorengau (Admiralty Islands), and Buka, Faisi, Kessa and Kieta (Solomon Islands).

It's difficult to break through the tangle of secrecy that surrounds everything this week, but all of us are pretty sure, also, that Tulagi, in the South Solomons, where we maintained an advanced operational base for Catalina flying boats, has been invaded and conquered by the Japs. All we know, officially, is that there has been no mention of Tulagi since the announcement that the pretty little town was subjected to a whole series of bombing raids by Japan's air force. Tulagi got two and three pastings a day at a time when the Japs were also hitting Moresby as many as three times a day, and chucking in a raid against Horn Island, in Torres Strait, just to keep us guessing. Or perhaps these raids were aimed, not so much to hoodwink us, as to smash as much as possible of our defensive aviation. In preparation for what? That's what we all want to know.

There is much excited talk tonight of a huge naval battle raging somewhere to the eastward. All the ships that were in Moresby have gone—ordered to make straight for Torres Strait and so reach the shelter of the Great Barrier Reef without delay. There's a persistent story of a huge Japanese convoy of sixty transports and warships off the Louisiades, at the southeasterly tip of New Guinea, heading in our direction. There are, in fact, so many rumors that it is perhaps just as well that the censor has clamped down and prevented us from writing almost anything except the most innocuous droolings. The censor returned to me yesterday the blue-penciled remnants of a 490-word story—factual and not, I think, sensational —which, if I had bothered to send it, would have reached my newspapers as:

> From Johnston at allied advanced base Thursday stop
> With Japanese pressure increasing hourly message ends.

At the moment much depends on the efficiency and courage of the men flying aircraft on reconnaissance missions. They have to go out night and day, in good weather or bad, and although they seldom, if ever, become heroes of the popular press, they quietly perform some of the most arduous and courageous and valuable work of this war in the islands.

For many weeks now our reconnaissance planes have been flying hundreds of thousands of nautical miles every week under the direction of Australian Air Intelligence, which knows the area better than the Americans and whose work prompted an American senior officer to say this week: "The Australian way of handling this enormous job has no superior in the world." But a great deal is being done by a single American pilot—thirty-one-year-old Captain Karl Polifka, of California—who flies an unarmed single-seater. His plane is a twin-fuselage P-38 (Lockheed Lightning). The natives call it the "flying lakatoi," because its twin fuselage bears a striking resemblance to their own outrigger canoes. The guns have been taken out and cameras installed, and Polifka relies on the extraordinary climbing ability and immense speed of his plane to get out of trouble.

Yesterday Polifka got home safely after having been tackled unsuccessfully by twenty-one Zeros—one over New Britain, ten over Rabaul, three over Lae, three over the Owen Stanley Range, and four near Port Moresby. And for a large part of the time he flew on only one engine (the supercharger of the other had gone haywire) at 20,000 feet!

These "recco" pilots say that weather is their greatest trouble in this area. Cloud masses are almost constantly present and usually very low. As Polifka says, "Sometimes a low cloud blanket will completely obscure a little island which, if it could be seen, would yield rich profits to an observer. I guess that's part of the job!"

But, from the wink Polifka gave me, I've an idea that we might hear good news soon. And if we do I think we'll owe a lot to him and the scores of other American and Australian pilots who do a grand job—seldom recognized by the public—"on recco."

# III. CHECKMATE

*May 11, 1942—July 21, 1942*

---

THE Battle of the Coral Sea has been fought and won. The Japanese invasion fleet, which *was* heading for Port Moresby, has been scattered and has fled back to Rabaul. Our bombers are still attacking the ships in Blanche Bay. Looking back on my notes of two days ago I find these words underlined: "In naval action yesterday and today Japs suffered biggest naval defeat of war. Whole situation affecting Australia changed overnight. Greatest credit to U. S. Navy for magnificent victory."

It's possible now to piece the story together. Some of the rumors of a few days ago have been proved as facts, many more have been revealed as fantastic inventions.

The Japanese had planned to attack earlier than May, but the loss of more than 20 ships and countless aircraft during our ferocious air attacks on Salamaua, Lae and Rabaul, which followed the Huon Gulf landings, forced them to postpone their plans for at least a month. They began to build up again, and when preparations were almost complete they transferred a formidable naval task force from the Indian Ocean to the Carolines, and thence down to the New Britain area. Their first job was to seize a flanking base, and they selected Tulagi. After heavy bombardment the base was captured by the Japs. We had no defenses adequate to cope with any invasion attempt, even one of moderate scale.

Soon after this the United States Navy showed its hand. Dive-bombers and torpedo planes from the *Lexington* made a surprise raid on Tulagi, where 12 Japanese ships were anchored, unloading supplies and munitions for their new garrison. The shipping was wiped out and the shore positions blasted. One small ship was

74

missed by the bombs, so dive-bombers made scores of passes at it with machine-gun fire. The sea at the waterline was boiling with the impact of thousands of bullets. The dive-bombers did not return to their carrier until the ship filled and sank.

By this time the Japanese had collected an enormous armada among the islands. Estimates varied from 65 to 92 transports and warships and an unknown number of submarines. The main transport force, with an escort of warships, moved down to the Louisiades to turn the corner and head for Moresby. The bigger Japanese ships, including the carriers, which comprised the main task force, pushed ahead into the Coral Sea and headed south. It was possibly the intention of the Japs to stage a naval bombardment of the Queensland coast, with these ships and with the aircraft aboard the carriers, as a diversion from the sea-borne attack on Moresby. There were no transports attached to this screening fleet.

Neither force was able to carry out its allotted job. The United States Navy struck first. American dive-bomber pilots, going into action five months to the day after Pearl Harbor, selected the big Japanese aircraft carrier *Ryukaku* as their principal target. The carrier was at full speed zigzagging frantically as the planes approached and then turning into the wind to launch her aircraft. A light cruiser was on each bow, four miles ahead, turning rapidly to bring anti-aircraft guns to bear. The dive-bombers peeled off, one by one, and plummeted down toward the box-shaped target slicing through the water below them at more than thirty knots. Every bomb hit squarely on the flight deck. In less than two minutes the carrier was a shambles of twisted metal from ten bomb hits and five torpedo hits. Within two more minutes she had blown up and disappeared beneath the blue-green waters of the Coral Sea.

Another carrier, the smaller *Shokaku*, was hit repeatedly and was left in flames. A Japanese cruiser blew up and went to the bottom. Lockheed Hudsons of the R.A.A.F. found two submarines and sank both of them. The Japanese crew aboard one were on deck doing their washing. The first thing they knew of the attack was when a bomb fell close alongside. The submarine went down leaving the laundry floating on the waves.

The Battle of the Coral Sea had reached its climax. To the southward the grand old *Lexington* was attacked by 108 Japanese bombers, dive-bombers and torpedo planes. Forty of the enemy's aircraft were shot down into the Coral Sea, but two torpedoes inflicted mortal hits on the great carrier, which was left in flames. She was abandoned at sunset and sank soon after nightfall.

Waves of Japanese bombers then turned their attention to the naval tanker *Neosho,* which was being escorted by the destroyer *Sims.* The destroyer was blown to pieces. There was nothing to be seen but the sudden flash of the bombs. The *Sims* seemed to split up the keel and disappear. Eighteen Japanese bombers then struck at the *Neosho.* Nine of the planes were shot down. One fell, blazing, on to the deck of the tanker, which despite ten direct hits was kept afloat by her partially empty tanks until the following day.

The American losses were trifling compared with those of the Japs. In all, we lost three ships: an aircraft carrier, a naval tanker and a destroyer. Fifteen Japanese warships were sunk for certain, including the *Ryukaku.* Twenty-two others, including the *Shokaku* and two seaplane carriers, were either sunk or severely damaged. More than a hundred Japanese aircraft were shot down into the Coral Sea.

The thing that matters most, of course, is that the Japanese forces have been completely scattered and are heading northward as fast as their Diesels and turbines will take them. This, the first naval battle of the South Pacific, has been a great victory for the United Nations.

At the moment there is little we can write about it. The bare announcement of losses is all we are permitted. We are told that it may be some weeks before we are allowed to tell the story.*

Now that the battle is over, and the men of Moresby are able to breathe more or less peacefully again for a time, it is worth discussing some of the interesting points this unique naval battle has emphasized. It *is* unique. This is the first time in history that a naval battle has been fought between ships more than a hundred miles apart; the first time that a naval battle has been fought with no naval gunfire apart from that used for anti-aircraft defense. Many

---

* Stories were released a month later, after the Battle of Midway, in which the Japanese Navy suffered an even more serious reverse on 3 and 4 June. They lost four aircraft carriers—*Akagi, Kaga, Soryu* and *Kiryu*—with an estimated number of 275 planes. Three battleships were hit and at least one was severely damaged. The heavy cruisers *Mogami* and *Mima* were sunk and one light cruiser was heavily hit. Thus Japanese shipping suffered in the Coral Sea and Midway battles to the extent of between 50 and 60 ships sunk or damaged, including six aircraft carriers.

writers are even now describing it as a naval battle in terms which compare it with Jutland (yesterday's most popular headline was "Greatest Naval Clash Since Jutland!") or Cape Matapan. It was, in fact, almost completely an air battle on an enormous scale and fought over a huge area of sea.

If comparisons are necessary, the closest parallel to the Coral Sea action would be found in the Axis dive-bombing attack on the *Illustrious* in the Straits of Pantellaria last year, or the sinking of the *Prince of Wales* and *Repulse* off Malaya.

The main fact that arises from the mass of comment and opinion over the battle is that modern aircraft are enormously superior to warships under certain conditions and those conditions exist to a very great degree in the northeastern approaches to Australia. In the Coral Sea battle there were no flaming broadsides from plunging ships, no gun duels between the ships of the Allies and the ships of Japan. It was a large-scale air battle against ships, with planes operating from fixed airfields on the mainland and in the islands, and from mobile airfields in the shape of aircraft carriers.

It has given some weight to the belief that, given sufficient numbers of aircraft of the right type and a sufficient number of good air bases places with regard to offensive and defensive strategy, Australia could defend her shores without naval assistance, with air power alone. Ships would still be necessary, of course, to safeguard trade routes and to protect convoys, and no eventual large scale counter-offensive would be possible without their assistance. But the actual defense of the mainland could be carried out with aircraft alone if we could put the necessary strength into the air whenever and *wherever* it was wanted. That strength, of course, does not exist in Australia yet. But comparing the air position in Australia today with what it was six months ago is rather like comparing our war effort of 1914-18 with our contribution to the Boer War. If all reports are true it may soon be rather like comparing the scale of the Second World War with Mafeking!

We can't have too many planes. We shall need every ounce of our present and potential strength to beat the Sons of Heaven. Five months of war have already proved that Japan ranks among the great air powers of the world. They have first-rate aircraft, excellent and courageous pilots, a shrewd directive, and an uncommonly good sense of cooperation and tactics.

They have realized for years the value of air strength in the Pacific. Their heavy fleet of aircraft carriers and seaplane tenders—the largest in any navy in the world—proves that they have long appreciated the value of a highly mobile sea force capable of striking by air over a wide area. That fleet proved of immense value to them in their astonishing campaign of swift conquest in the Pacific, because it gave them the ability to move their air strength as circumstances dictated, and to bring air superiority without delay to battle areas where air superiority was most needed.

At the same time it must be realized that the Japanese air force has suffered heavily in this Pacific war and is now numerically weaker, although technically stronger, than it was in December. In the past the Japanese have had to employ available bombers and fighters over so many widely separated fronts that, excepting where they were undertaking a major offensive or a major diversion, they could not afford to provide more aircraft than were capable of carrying out nuisance raids or defensive operations against our bombers.

Two of the biggest air attacks in the Australian zone were at Rabaul, in January, and Darwin, in February. It is permissible to assume that they were not two separate striking forces, but the same one, which cleaned up one area and was then rapidly transferred to another.

The Battle of the Coral Sea showed conclusively that Japanese carriers had returned to waters north of Australia, and it is also significant that they returned only after Tokyo had admitted that mopping-up operations had been completed on quite a number of southwest Pacific fronts. In other words, with the slackening or disappearance of Allied pressure on various fronts, the Japanese high command was able to release a substantial portion of its striking power for possible use on the Australian front, particularly as the Burma campaign was developing more and more into an outright land operation.

How many of the twenty-six Japanese divisions which Mr. Churchill said were "scattered throughout the Pacific" were also released, it is impossible to say. The fact remained that Japan, which, in the first five months of war, had been compelled to wage twelve separate campaigns, covering a total area of millions of square miles, had so whittled down resistance that she was able to concentrate on three main campaigns—Burma, China, and Australia.

The Battle of the Coral Sea was the first indication of her intentions on this third campaign. Her move was stopped by the strength of the allied combined air and sea power; but only an unreasoning optimist would consider that it had been stopped permanently. The Japanese have put far too much into their preparations for a thrust against us, or our lines of communication, to be beaten off so easily.

This campaign—the most distant Japan has undertaken in her attempt at Pacific domination—began less than a month after the Pearl Harbor attack. It is now one hundred and fifty-five days since the Pacific war began, and it is one hundred and twenty-seven days since Japan's forces in the mandated islands of the Carolines made their first thrust against Australia's island barrier by bombing Rabaul, Kavieng, and other points in the Bismarck Archipelago. The period between Pearl Harbor and Rabaul's first raid was for the Japs a period of blasting and preparation, rather than a period of conquest.

Japan's greatest successes have been obtained since the first bombs on New Guinea gave the world an open declaration of the extent to which Nippon was prepared to carry the flaming brand of aggression. Since New Guinea became a war zone, the black tide of Japan's domination has swept over the Philippines, Borneo, Sarawak, Celebes, Hong Kong, Malaya, Singapore, Timor, Burma, and the islands of Netherlands East Indies.

In addition, she gained Indo-China by Vichy's connivance, and Thailand by eleventh hour treachery. It is probable she has already obtained a foothold in Dutch New Guinea, and she has shown the length of her striking arm by dealing smashing air blows at points as far apart as Broome, Darwin, and Pearl Harbor.

Contrast this alarming picture of conquest with the plain facts of her campaign in the islands northeast of Australia. Here she has successfully completed only one large-scale combined operation.

And it is "large-scale" only by contrast with other general inactivity—conquest of Rabaul on 23 January, a conquest obtained only at heavy cost, despite the fact that she employed about 20,000 troops backed up by a terrific air and sea power to crush a virtually unsupported Australian garrison of 1400 foot soldiers.

Her other operations have constituted little more than nibbling at bait. She landed not very considerable forces in the Huon Gulf ports of Lae, Salamaua, and Finschhafen; but this was no more an attempt at invasion than the later landing on the Solomons. It was merely for the purpose of obtaining new air bases, and, incidentally, to enable her to disperse her war material more widely, and so to minimize the destruction which was being dealt out on an increasing scale by allied air forces.

On this basis it is perfectly true that she has extended a number of fingers over the maze of northeastern islands; but the fingers are still outstretched. They have made no attempt to clutch those islands into a new empire. They are still only outlying bases for attack and defense. They number at least 13—Rabaul, Lae, Salamaua, Finschhafen, Gasmata, Kavieng, Faisi, Kessa, Uka, Kieta, Tulagi, Nivani Island, and Lorengau. There might be others of which we have not heard. Apart from this, the Japanese have carried out fifty largely innocuous raids against Port Moresby, and other nuisance forays against other towns and bases. They have launched one large-scale attempt, which was forestalled and crushed in the Coral Sea. And that is all.

Where in this picture is anything to compare with the terrorizing assault on Java, the relentless pressure through Malaya, the hammer-blow assaults of Burma? The speed of Japan's war machine has proved to be capable of enormous results within the span of one hundred days. Yet Port Moresby has been subjected to Japanese assaults for one hundred and seven days, and it is infinitely stronger than ever before. And only in the last week has Moresby been subjected to raids which by World War II standards can be regarded as moderately heavy. Never in any one day have more than 50 planes attacked Moresby. Yet more than 100 planes carried out the first attack on Darwin, and almost 200 were used to batter Rabaul.

It is clear that they have never used the maximum air power available in the islands for any operation, and their intention appears to be to conserve and build up maximum air power for their major offensive.

This building-up process has been continued only under tremendous difficulty. Every gallon of fuel must come by sea from Truk, in the Carolines, either to Rabaul as a feeder base, or, more rarely, direct to subsidiary bases. In the same way the enemy must transport every bomb, every machine gun bullet, every scrap of food. On that system of supply it has taken even the fast-moving Japanese a long time to build up and equip a force capable of undertaking a military operation of great magnitude—such as an invasion of Australia, or even of a strongly held garrison like Moresby or New Caledonia. Moreover, such a force could not move off along the path of potential conquest until huge bases of reinforcement material and reserve supplies had been established as close as possible to the scene of ultimate operations.

One of the main objects of allied air attacks has been to prevent this building-up and consolidation, and our policy had paid handsome dividends. The aggregate of Japan's losses is doubtless considerably higher than claimed in official communiqués, where "doubtfuls" are dismissed and only "certainties" claimed. It is true we have suffered losses ourselves. But they are completely outweighed by the scale of the Japanese losses.

Piecing the scraps together over the one hundred and twenty-seven days of the New Guinea campaign gives the following approximate picture of enemy losses in or about the New Guinea area: Aircraft: 130 bombers and flying boats and 90 fighters destroyed, and about 200 of all types damaged. Warships: one aircraft carrier destroyed, one probably destroyed, one seaplane carrier badly damaged, 8 heavy and light cruisers sunk or damaged, in addition to 60 destoyers, 14 gunboats and fleet auxiliaries, 11 freighters, and 21 transports and supply ships sent to the bottom.

Despite this story of sustained losses and disorganized plans, the enemy has persevered with the policy of reinforcement, and it is wise for us to assume that this policy may culminate any day in the beginning of the greatest Pacific battle operation in Nippon's major attempt to nullify Australia as an allied base for a counter-offensive.

### Untouched Eden

There were two flights of Japanese bombers overhead—tiny silvered specks droning as they turned to make their runs across the target area. The driver of the bright red truck unhurriedly parked his vehicle under the overhanging branches of a broad-leafed gum tree as the first rolling thunderclaps from over the hills told of another salvo of high explosive falling on the aerodrome area.

As the bombers turned away from the cotton-wool puffs of anti-aircraft fire and made their way homeward, the driver of the red truck climbed into his cabin, put the car into gear, and moved off along the rutted road. In the back were piled neatly pressed cubes, each about eighteen inches square.

The rubber of Papua was on its way southward to the mainland. War was not interfering with production. War, in fact, could only stimulate the production of Papuan rubber, for the world's greatest production centre of rubber, Malaya, had fallen into Japanese hands, and every pound that could be produced elsewhere was now doubly valuable.

We can regret now the incompetent management of the past, the bungling lack of foresight, which has brought about a situation where a vast territory capable of immense production has remained unexploited. The rubber going out of Papua today is only a tiny fragment of what could have been going southward if we had shown any common sense in the past.

Papua will produce first class rubber. Some of the rubber plantations which have been managed with sanity and efficiency have production figures which compare with the best in the world. There are small plantations of only one hundred and fifty acres bringing in revenue of $8000 a year. Incompetent management undoubtedly did most to discourage the development of rubber production in this territory, but our Government policy of post-war years is certainly not blameless.

Papua is virtually Australia's only colony. If we accept that point of view, then we must also accept the fact that our "colonial administration" has been almost unbelievably shortsighted. Australia kept a benevolent eye on Papua, saw that the natives were well treated, occasionally encouraged a trifling amount of research into the production potentialities of rubber, quinine, cotton, tea, and other essentials that could not be produced economically on the mainland. Economically and financially, however, Australia was inextricably tied to oversea monopolies and to the great international financial and developmental organizations. Australia could not, or would not, offer worthwhile markets to Papua. In other words, we did so little to develop our only colony that we did not deserve to have a colony.

As with rubber, so with almost everything else. Now that the

Japanese have overrun the world's greatest sources of tin, rubber, and quinine, and some of the world's greatest petroleum-producing centres, Australia may begin to think about looking into the enormous, undeveloped resources of Papua and New Guinea. The tragedy is that years of work are necessary between the thought and the result, and we have blindly thrown away those years.

Here are the possibilities of Papua: Rubber grows wild, and can be cultivated freely on a large scale. Quinine, tea, nutmeg have been grown in a small way experimentally, but have never been developed. Coffee plantations in the northern areas have been developed by the administration and operated skilfully by natives under the supervision of white men; but again production has never gone past the experimental stage. Political interference has been the only barrier to enormous production of first quality sugar. Rice will grow here without the slightest trouble. Tobacco is indigenous, and could be grown without limit in the high mountains, where almost anything will grow. Tea can be produced on a large scale. In other words, Papua and New Guinea could produce for Australia almost every commodity that Japanese aggression in Asia and the southwest Pacific has taken from us.

Since the first payable goldfields were discovered in Misima Island fifty-three years ago the story of mineral possibilities has been one of enormous potentialities and negligible exploitation. The territory contains gold, copper, osmiridium, petroleum, phosphates, lead, iron, sulphur, coal, zinc, manganese, gypsum, tin, bismuth, silver, platinum, magnesite, meerschaum, barite, and wolfram. There are also such gems as topaz, sapphire, amethyst, garnet, agate, spinel, epidote, beryl and olivine.

It is very likely that some of these minerals—perhaps almost all of them—can be obtained in very great quantities. Coal, for instance, of a proved high quality has been found on the Vailala, Purari, and Kikori river areas, with very large seams and outcrops above the surface in wide reefs. But do you ever hear of exports of Papuan coal?

The agricultural possibilities of Papua are enormous. Kapok, coffee, cocoa, and sisal could be produced on an enormously rich scale. Every type of land is available for production. There are extensive and unbelievably rich coastal flats, fertile valleys and plateaux, and huge areas capable of extensive cultivation in the hills and valleys up to a height of 6000 feet above sea level. Rainfall varies from 37 inches annually in the Moresby "dry belt" to 230 inches a year in the rich alluvial delta country.

Papua is an almost untouched land of plenty. Its potential riches cannot be ignored indefinitely. At the moment its importance to Australia is strategic. But the time will come when its economic importance to the mainland will be even more vital. With every week of war and Japanese conquest that time comes closer.

### Three Minutes

Three youngsters flying Marauders—Hap Jolly, Bud Flint and George Kahle—came in tonight almost bursting with excitement, because the three American bombers they were piloting had shot down six Zeros in three hectic minutes over Rabaul.

The three young Americans—Jolly, at twenty-five, is the veteran by several years—took their planes over Rabaul to hit Jap concentrations of ships, which seem to be building up there again. They got a sight on 20 large transports anchored in the stream when 17 Zeros dived down on them from the clouds. This must have put them off their job, because none of them has claimed even a possible hit on the ships. There was very intense anti-aircraft fire and tracers from heavy machine guns even before the Zeros came.

The Zeros came in head-on attacks at the outset, but the Marauders were moving too fast for them. All the pilots seem to think the Jap pilots were rookies. "They acted like another box had been opened," said Jolly. The Zeros came swarming round and ranged alongside, immediately laying themselves wide open to the concentrated gunfire of the three bombers. One Zero tried to get out of the mess by diving down between the planes piloted by Jolly and Kahle. Tracers from both planes ripped his fuselage to ribbons and he went into the sea in two pieces. Jolly's turret gunner had caught another and he spun down in flames.

Meanwhile Flint was having a field day. In less than two minutes he sent three Zeros down in flames—one to the nose-gunner, one to the tail-gunner and one to the turret-gunner.

In Khale's plane there was a lot of excitement. Carl King, the co-pilot, has a funny habit of brushing his teeth before making the target run. "He forgot to take the goddam thing out," Kahle explained to us, "and he was trying to point Zeros out to me in the middle of the attack, and getting quite excited because he couldn't talk with his mouth full of toothbrush! Down beyond, Lou Skeadus, our Greek turret-gunner—his father was a Greek fighter pilot in the last war—was shouting instructions about Zeros in the interphone, but in his excitement clean forgot to talk English. Then Lou got one—our sixth victim—and immediately afterwards his gun caught fire. The plane was full of smoke and the interphones were full of a strange mixture of Greek, broken English, and good old Bronx cusswords!"

The bombers shook off the remaining Zeros by dodging into rain clouds, but about fifteen minutes later two more Zeros came up alongside Jolly's plane and stayed there, one on either side, "just like a couple of vultures." The American gunners let them have it, and one went down in flames, making the day's tally seven. Altogether the three bombers sighted 26 Japanese fighters and were attacked by 17 of them.

Jolly forgot to tell us that his landing brakes had been shot away and that when he landed he ran right off the end of the airfield and crashed his plane! It is a total write-off.

Just to square the ledger the Japs came over Moresby twice today —classed as two raids officially, although there were only a few minutes between attacks. They used 48 planes, which is the biggest raid yet, but the Airacobras shot down three Zeros without any loss on our side.

### Death Is the Penalty of Error

The silver oak leaf of a U. S. lieutenant-colonel was new and shining on his khaki shirt. He was the first American air ace of the Pacific war: Lieutenant-Colonel Boyd D. Wagner, twenty-five-year-old fighter pilot of Johnstown, known to everybody as "Buzz." * He yarned to me over glasses of cool lager on every subject under the sun except one—the exploits of "Buzz" Wagner.

Yet Wagner, two weeks before, was a lieutenant. And in the U.S.A.A.C. you don't jump over the ranks of captain and major in a fortnight without some very good reason. That reason was to be found in the first Japanese drive in the Philippines.

* "Buzz" Wagner went back to the States later and was posted missing on a routine flight near Florida.

The sky was thick with Nippon's aircraft—dive-bombers, medium bombers, heavy bombers, fighters. The debacle of Pearl Harbor was not allowed to occur in the Philippines. United States pursuit planes roared into the sky. Crouched behind the control board of one of the interceptors was Wagner. He made a lone-handed attack on five Zeros—a feat that is almost asking for sudden death. But two Zeros fell flaming from the sky, and the other three were driven off. Wagner dived down seeking more victims. On the captured airfield were lines of parked Japanese aircraft—12 planes all told. Through the black hell of an anti-aircraft barrage he dived at 400 miles an hour with his guns spitting tracers. Five Zeros burst into flames. Machine gun bullets from ground fire riddled Wagner's plane, shattered the glass canopy over the cockpit, and hurled needle-sharp slivers of glass into his eyes. With blood streaming from his injured eyes, he completed his attack and returned to his base safely.

After Wagner had left another senior American officer said to me: "Buzz has got tons of guts. But the main thing is he is really a miracle man with a gun. That's why he's so successful. In a pursuit plane marksmanship is everything. We had another young pilot who went up and tackled a Zero. He got on his tail, but missed with his guns. The Zero came round and didn't miss. He lost. In fighter combat the penalty for error is usually death."

There are scores of young fighter pilots in the north now, Australians and Americans, who live from day to day with the knowledge of the truth of those words: "The penalty for error is usually death."

There were bombers over the 'drome the other day and Zero fighters streaking across the sky like bats out of hell. The rumble of high explosive was near, dust and smoke were drifting across the low hills. Directly above our heads were five Zero fighters. Out of the clouds darted two Kittyhawks. In a moment machine guns were chattering and seven planes were circling and diving and turning at breath-taking speed. Hopelessly outnumbered, the two kids flying those fighters never thought of diving out of battle. For ten minutes they kept going. One was dodging a Zero in a screaming dive. You could hear the "blue note"—the strange squealing whine that indicated that the plummeting plane had almost achieved terminal velocity. We could see the Japanese tracers spitting.

"I'd blacked out twice," the pilot told me later. "I couldn't see the controls, but I managed to keep some sort of consciousness by pushing my chin down on my chest and screwing my head round against my left shoulder. The purple screen across my eyes drifted away, and I pulled out of the dive. The Zero came after me. I didn't seem to be able to get away. And then I saw our other Kitty racing in from the side. He drove right through us between the Zero and my tail, taking every Japanese bullet right down the length of the fuselage. His tail was almost shot away, and the pilot took a bullet in the arm. But he saved me. How we avoided a triple collision I don't know. The Japanese pilot must have almost pulled the joy-stick out doing that loop turn to dodge away. But he'd lost the chance of getting me. I knew I had him now. I could see my tracers streaming into the rim of his cockpit. A lick of black smoke squirted out, and he went down ablaze in a flat spin. I looked round for my cobber, but he'd gone. Later I found that he'd shot a Zero down himself and then landed his riddled plane safely. How he got her down with the rudder just hanging in ribbons will always be a mystery to me."

One of the toughest things about flying fighters in this country is the terrible terrain that the unlucky pilot who's forced to bale out has to come down into. Men have been impaled on the spiky jungle growth as they parachuted, men have landed safely in the jungle only to meet a slow death from disease and starvation. It is amazing, when one sees this terrible land, how many have been able to struggle through to safety.

When the American P-39 squadron first went into action "Buzz" Wagner—grounded because of the injury to his eyes—came to Moresby to wish them luck on their first mission, a strafing attack on Lae. It was too much for Wagner, so he went along as "guest pilot" to lead the squadron in its first operation.

The Airacobras attacked the Lae airfield in two waves. The Zeros were well dispersed in the scrub, but there were 12 to 15 brand new bombers of a new type lined up on the runway as the fighters dived in with machine guns and cannons roaring out that unpleasant *pap-pap-pap-WHOOF-pap-pap-WHOOF-pap-pap-pap-pap* that the Zeros over Moresby had made *us* accustomed to.

"It was all over in five seconds," said Wagner. "I'm sure practically every bomber was hit, but we moved too fast to see how many were destroyed. As I looked back I could see great columns of black smoke rising. We still had plenty of ammunition left so I signaled the rest of the squadron to head for Salamaua and take independent targets.

"A couple of us machine-gunned the airfield and huge flames burst above the tree-tops, so I guess we hit something. We pulled up over the hill and then all of us saw a lovely target—a neat, white-painted shack with a big radio mast alongside. We dived down almost to the ground and about a dozen Japs came streaming out. They fell as they ran into our stream of fire. Then our bullets and shells smashed the side right out of the shack, and we pulled away leaving it destroyed and burning. That took about ten seconds.

"Immediately afterward I spotted Zeros—seven in one formation, five in the other, and more specks way out on the skyline. They were roughly 4000 feet above us, so I called for the needle and gave full throttle and we headed for home. But two pilots at the rear of our formation said, 'What the hell! Let's have a go at 'em!' and peeled off. Next thing 12 Zeros were on to two of our boys, so we all turned back to join in the fun.

"Then for the next twenty-five minutes we had the best dogfight I've ever seen in my life. We chased each other from Salamaua to Lae and back again, and we never got above 1000 feet! We fought down almost to the ground, just skimming the tops of the waves, and almost scraping our bellies on the tree-tops. Three of the Zeros were shot down into the sea. I didn't see any Japs bale out. Three of our boys went, too. Boy, it was the most terrific dogfight I've ever seen in my life! We were evenly matched and nobody gave any quarter. It was a honey—and it was a marvelous experience for these youngsters on their first job. It taught them, in less than half an hour, more than they would learn in ten years of training. I wouldn't have blamed any of them for beating it back home when they saw 12 Zeros ready to dive on them, but instead they turned back to fight it out."

It wasn't until I talked to other pilots of the squadron an hour later that I discovered that Wagner himself had shot down all three of the Zeros which were destroyed!

He gave the boys a good start. Last Monday one of the Airacobras was cut off from its formation during dogfights that occurred during a big Japanese raid on the Moresby airfields. The Japs came over with 34 heavy bombers and 15 Zeros. This particular pilot climbed through a cloud bank in search of his comrades and ran straight into the packed formation of the 31 surviving Japanese bombers heading back home after the raid. He went straight at them, in a head-on attack, with all guns blazing. The Japs scattered, all except two of them, which swerved out of formation and went into flat spins with smoke streaming from their engines.

Despite the courage of our pilots, the Japs still have a very definite fighter superiority, and their weight of numbers has also given them a tactical superiority. It is important for us to realize that the Japanese in the air is a foe to be reckoned with.

Japanese bombing aircraft are generally solid, well-built planes, with good carrying capacity, reasonable speed, and a range completely satisfactory for most operations in the northern theatres. Although below the performance of our most modern planes, they appear to be peculiarly suitable for tropical operations. They bomb almost invariably to a set pattern, which is apparently worked out on the ground before the raid, probably by superimposing a drawing of their selected "pattern" over an aerial photograph of the target to be bombed. Once having gone to this trouble, it would take a tornado to shift them from their purpose.

I have seen large, tightly packed formations of Japanese bombers attacked by allied fighters before reaching the target, and hammered over the target by fierce A.A. barrages. Their formations never faltered. Once I saw four bombers shot down in flames out of a formation of 18, and the remaining 14 roared on over the target as if nothing had happened. The attack is apparently directed by the formation leader, probably because all the Japanese bombers do not carry bomb sights, taking as the signal for release of their own bombs from the leading plane. In night raids I have seen, the moment for release of bombs has invariably been indicated to the raiding force by a red Very light fired from the leading plane. In more than sixty raids on Port Moresby, mostly by daylight, methods of attack varied little, and targets were almost always limited to aerodromes, port facilities, and (only once or twice) ground defenses. All bombing has been from a high level—between 18,000 and 26,000 feet. (Remember the "authorities" who said before the war that the Japanese were no good as pilots because they couldn't stand high altitudes!) Although they have often gone very close to their targets, they have caused little military damage and negligible casualties.

Japan appears to have pinned its faith in the development of one main fighter aircraft, in the same way that Britain pinned its faith to one plane, the Spitfire, in the early days of the war. The original Zero is two or three years old, but alterations and modifications have made it now very much a 1942 model fighter. I have many times seen both the old Zero and the new Zero in action, and although when one has dodged machine-gun bullets and cannon shells from a plane he is likely to have an exaggerated respect for that type of machine—I say unhesitatingly that the Zero, properly flown, is today one of the world's best fighting aircraft. The Zero has a heavy body that looks unwieldy alongside the bullet-like fuselages of the Kittyhawk and Airacobra, wide tapering wings, a heavy cowling over the pilot's cockpit which is larger than in most fighters, and a huge radial engine which some air fighters believe is a combination of, but probably an improvement upon, the best features of the Wright Cyclone and the Pratt and Whitney. Having seen their Zero in dogfights, I have a profound respect for the Mitsubishi people, who by adaptation and improvement have turned out a first-rate aircraft which has good speed, almost unlimited manoeuvrability, good firepower (cannon firing through the propeller hub and machine guns from the wings), and a general performance which is good at low altitudes and little affected by extremely high altitudes. I have seen these Zeros—or, rather, I have seen their vapor trails, because the fighters were so high that they were not visible—at 29,000 feet acting as a screen for bombers 5000 feet below them. They are sturdy, well built, and (the newer types) of all-metal construction with an armored compartment for the pilot.

The Japanese naval fighter pilots lack neither skill nor courage. It is fortunate that they are matched in New Guinea against allied fighter pilots who also have any amount of both qualities. The result is that some of the New Guinea dogfights must rank among the most spectacular and most bitterly fought of any in this war of air power. Other Japanese fighters have occasionally been in action —Nakajimas, Mitsus, once or twice German-built Messerschmitt 109's, and occasional naval floatplane fighters—but the enemy has realized that he has a good thing in the Zero and has stuck to it.

The Japanese fight well and fight hard, but they are not necessarily fatalistic suiciders. Nevertheless it is clear that the Japanese high command does not like its men to be captured. Fighter pilots have parachuted and reached the safety of a prisoner of war camp, but they believe that by preserving their own lives they have given up forever all hope of returning to Japan when the war is over. Japanese pilots are instructed that if they can't bring their machine home they must crash it so that it is totally destroyed. Some do and some don't. Some bale out and some don't.

I can't help thinking of Peter Turnbull's story of the Zero pilot who was swimming ashore from his crashed plane when he was machine-gunned and killed by a fellow Japanese pilot. The Japs are not only brave and clever. They are thoroughly ruthless. To beat them we must realize that they are ruthless, as well as brave and clever.

The fighter pilots up here don't make the mistake of underestimating them. They know, in their job, that the penalty for error is usually death.

### Hot Water

Everybody tells me that I am in very hot water and that Lieutenant-General Brett, Commander of Allied Air Forces, considers that my license as a war correspondent should be cancelled because of a story which my papers published yesterday under my name. The story happened to be one I felt *should* be written. With a few minor deletions it was passed by the censors, anyway. Here it is, exactly as it appeared under the headings: "No Fighter Escort for Bombers. Allied Pilots at Disadvantage."

"Japanese fighter superiority in the New Guinea air war is an ugly fact which must be faced and overcome if we are to win the vital battle for command of Australia's northern approaches.

"We will continue to suffer losses and still heavier losses until we realize we are fighting a skilful, implacable enemy right on our northern doorstep. Australians and Americans are tough enough and determined enough to take bad news with good if they know that a realization of our mistakes and setbacks will help us overcome them.

"The bad news is that the Japanese who have consistently had numerical air superiority in northern battle zones, are now rapidly building up tactical superiority. This is not giving away military secrets. The Japanese certainly know it. We still believe the Japanese are copyists, that everything they do falls short of perfection. The fact remains that in the New Guinea area alone they are employing large numbers of some of the finest aircraft in the world. These aircraft include a crack new model Zero fighter which in its class probably has no peer.

"It's the old, old story of brave men facing unnecessary dangers simply because they have not got what they deserve—as much protection as possible from air attack. Yesterday our force of allied bombers went out over Lae to attack Jap positions, and they went without a single fighter plane to support them, despite the fact that over the target area they were intercepted by 15 Zeros.

"It is significant that the Japs when raiding Moresby never send bombers over without fighter support. They usually work on a rough basis of having a screen of half as many Zeros as there are bombers, but often they put over a heavy fighter screen consisting of more support planes than bombers.

"Singapore had its guns facing the wrong way, and this was not found out until it was too late to remedy the fault. Penang had no camouflage until there was no further need of camouflage. Rabaul relied on a few Wirraways for air defense against a Japanese air armada. Are we to continue finding out our mistakes only when it is too late to rectify them?

"While our bombers were attacking Lae yesterday another force of heavy bombers struck at Rabaul, shooting down two Zeros and causing large fires among grounded aircraft on Vunakunau aerodrome. Our bombing force, also unsupported by fighters, was attacked by 17 Zeros over Rabaul. Thus in both raids we had 32 Japanese fighters against our bombers and not one of our own fighters in the air."

I am still glad I wrote this story.

By next day I was more glad than ever that I wrote my piece. I'm told that the matter will be allowed to drop in my case, and also in the case of Pat Robinson (who writes for International News Service, New York, and who, it seems, also got into bother for a story on similar lines).

That doesn't matter a damn. The important thing is that our bombers which went over to attack Lae yesterday all had considerable fighter support! And they did their job and came back without loss.

The war in New Guinea is utterly a war in the air now. I'm getting fed up with writing (and I've no doubt the newspaper public is getting heartily fed up with reading) stories of bombing attacks and air combats. One air raid is very much like another. One dogfight is very much like another, and in any case a dogfight is the most disappointing of all spectacles to watch, because you never seem to be able to tell which plane is on your side, and which is on the enemy's.

I have applied to the Royal Australian Navy for permission to spend a couple of weeks in the Coral Sea with an Australian corvette doing convoy work and anti-submarine patrols in the waters between New Guinea and the mainland.

### Moresby Convoy

Astern of us the tropic sun was going down in a purple sky streaked with green and pink and gold. The mine-sweeping otters on the corvette's after-deck bulked blackly in the foreground and beyond were the silhouettes of two ships, one a Dutch liner carrying American and Australian troops and the other an American tramp laden with war materials. Aldis lamps winked from the corvette to the two merchantmen, which winked back in reply. The convoy moved out, bound across the Coral Sea to Port Moresby. The corvette rose and dipped as she felt the swell at the harbor mouth. Behind, like ponderous cattle following a heeler, came the convoy.

"Come an' get it!" yelled a voice from the darkening deck. And the two ship's cats, Smoky and Bombo, streaked up for their evening meal. Bombo had been born during an air raid in Singapore. They both knew how to take cover in an air raid. And they both walked wide-legged, like seamen, to the rolling of the ship.

I looked around the little craft that was to be my home for some days to come. About the size of a whale-chaser, compact, sturdy, built at Sydney, and (I was told by some of the ratings) the most bombed corvette of the Australian navy, fresh to the Australian patrols after months of hazardous adventure in Malayan and East Indian waters. Only 32 feet wide, 185 feet long, 870 tons of camouflaged steel and hidden mysteries, she had been chasing submarines and fighting aircraft, sweeping mines and escorting other ships. Now it was her job to safeguard the convoy behind us—a thousand men and hundreds of thousands of pounds' worth of war materials. Completely blacked out, the ships moved out from the dwindling purple line of the shore.

I was thinking how strange it was that war had come so close to Australia that shipping off the coast had to be escorted in convoy when I was shown my accommodations by a cheerful young officer who, when last I had seen him, had been second mate aboard a lighthouse tender. My bed was the settee in the wardroom—for there are no guests' cabins or spare accommodations of any sort in a corvette, where every square inch of space is needed for some purpose more useful than providing soft beds for itinerant war correspondents. And the wardroom was about the same size as the average kitchen in a suburban home. Ahead of the wardroom was the engine-room for depth charges. I was given facts and figures that cannot be published, but as I rolled and lurched on the settee that night my mind kept turning and turning again to one interesting fact—that round my couch, stored neatly only a few feet away, was a total of 16,000 pounds of amatol high explosive capable of making an explosion equivalent to that of forty 1000-pound bombs hitting simultaneously. I remember wondering whether, after such an explosion, there would be any solid pieces of the ship or whether only smoke and a stain would remain. And then it was daylight and the wardroom steward was shaking me and in his hand was the most enormous cup I have ever seen filled with very hot, very strong, and very sweet tea.

Outside the slanting rays of the early morning sun were bathing the ships following in brilliant orange light. Flying fish skimmed and darted across the crashing white caps. One of the seamen was cursing the ships astern because one was squirting out a great stream of black smoke and the other was lagging miles behind. He pointed to the smoking funnel astern.

"What the hell does he think he's doing?" he muttered. " 'Struth, they could see that in Tokyo!"

Lookouts, with binoculars to their eyes, seemed to be everywhere. Only a fortnight before two enemy submarines had been sighted and bombed in these waters by R.A.A.F. reconnaissance planes. And you never knew when the Japanese planes might come. So the lookouts searched the horizon, and the men on duty at that miracle submarine-detector, the Asdic, searched beneath the seas. Then a sudden shout from the bridge lookout: "Aircraft, sir!" Everyone was at action stations in a flash. Covers were whipped off the muzzles of A.A. guns as the black specks of the bombers came closer. Then the flash and wink of an Aldis lamp from the leading plane—recognition signal—Australian-built Bristol Beauforts on some job or other. The convoy ploughed ahead, but the vigil was never relaxed for a moment. The rattle of machine gun fire from astern indicated that the rear ship was practicing gunnery. The corvette, too, roared off a few rounds to keep the gun crews on their toes. For every minute of the day and night there was an atmosphere of preparedness aboard the ship—exercises in "repel aircraft," "action stations" and "abandon ship." These men knew the value of preparedness. Their ship had been the last to leave Palembang only one jump ahead of the Japs, the second last to leave Singapore.

That night an enormous moon lifted above the black rim of the sea—a bomber's moon. The convoy, bathed in revealing light, steamed silently through a sea of flashing silver. And on the wing of the bridge a petty officer stared at the huge silver disk and cursed it softly in unmentionable words.

Some time before dawn another warship joined us—one of the Australian sloops—and fell into position without fuss and with the minimum of signals. By midmorning the sparkling tropical seas of the day before had gone. A heavy swell moved sullenly beneath a gray sky and thick rain squalls marched across the whitecaps. In everything except the temperature—for it was still warm—the scene resembled the North Atlantic more than the Coral Sea. But the gray picture—gray seas flecked with white, gray clouds right down to the horizon, gray ships plunging ahead—had more affinity with war than yesterday's picture of sun-dappled waves and flying fish. Today it was possible to realize that warships had fought in these waters only a few weeks before, that the mangled wreckage of Japanese warships lay below us on the seabed, 2400 fathoms down, 14,400 feet below our sharp bows. In the wardroom the gray light changed every few minutes to an unearthly aquarium-like green as the corvette rolled her ports beneath the lashing waves. White foam was bursting at the sides of the ships wallowing astern. The sloop to starboard dipped every now and then below the wave-crests. A seaman turned to me as a squall slapped rain against the bridge and pushed the little corvette down even farther into the rushing white water.

"This is what they call the glamorous tropics," he said, and spat contemptuously into the sea. He stood swaying for a moment and then waved his hand along the deck. "She's a dandy little ship though, isn't she? Takes the seas like a bird!" He probably didn't realize that there was a very real light of pride in his eyes as he spoke.

The sloop had left us outside Moresby Harbor when the Japs came over today. The "rattlers" (alarm gongs) had gone and everyone was at station. Overhead was the drone of aircraft. Fighters were making weird vapor trails so high in the sky that the planes themselves were invisible. Then a rattle of machine gun fire signified that the fun had started. Allied fighters were up, too, to tackle 18 Japanese naval bombers and 12 Zero fighters. A fighter plummeted down with a long-drawn, snarling whine, smoke pouring from its tail. For a second it seemed that it would crash on our ship. Then it burst into flames and crashed into the sea just ahead of our bows. We saw a man falling, but his parachute didn't open. The noise of aircraft overhead had become a roar punctuated with the snarl of diving fighters. Over the quarter a big Jap bomber exploded in the air. Tiny black pieces of debris spiralled down. Another bomber was hurtling down with a fighter on its tail pouring out a stream of tracer bullets. The bomber crashed into the sea astern of us. A second or two later the silver fuselage of a Zero fighter glittered in the sun as it came down to port. In less than two minutes four planes had crashed near our ship. Then we could see the bombers coming over. They were directly above the ship—a packed formation of silver shapes difficult to see against the midday sun. Right over the ship. They couldn't miss. And then the shout of the lookout: "Bombs released, sir!" We hit the deck and pulled steel helmets more tightly over our heads. Above the soft hissing of the seas you could hear the bombs whistling, then the running crash of bomb after bomb falling. The little corvette shuddered with each explosion but the salvo had fallen over to port. Huge waterspouts and great clouds of brown smoke blotted out everything. Then, through the curtain of smoke and falling water, came the bow of a ship and a rust-streaked hull settling back gently from the roll caused by the blast of bombs. It was the American freighter we were convoying. She came through with only a few splinter marks and a shrapnel hole above the waterline through which you could put your fist.

The American ship is a 5000-ton chunky-looking freighter, the *Coast Farmer,* which recently carried out one of the most astonishing blockade-running feats in modern history. On New Year's Day she left Brisbane under the command of Captain J. Matheson with instructions to head north and then west, through waters infested with Japanese naval craft, to take a full cargo of food to the beleaguered American garrison at Corregidor.

Slowly, and with infinite caution, Matheson took his ship along the allotted course and into the harbor at Corregidor under cover of darkness. Deep water ran right to the edge of the rocks and the *Coast Farmer* was anchored in the lee and under the shadow of a vast cliff. Japanese reconnaissance planes were over in the morning and the evening but their observers failed to see the ship. At night she went in to discharge her cargo and before dawn returned to her anchorage to shelter under the cliff throughout the daylight hours. After three nights of this hazardous work the *Coast Farmer's* holds were emptied and she headed south. She returned to Brisbane twenty days after her departure. Since then the grand old ship has been transporting urgently needed war supplies from the mainland to Moresby. Everybody is delighted that she has escaped again.*

Tonight we are heading into a gray squall. On the beam the *Coast Farmer* is flinging spray over her fo'c'sle-head. The corvette is rolling her lee rail under and spray is pattering over the bridge. I think of the bombs dropping on our port beam. The Japs, we hear officially, lost seven bombers and two fighters at the cost of only two of our fighters and a small shrapnel hole in the *Coast Farmer.* Which makes it a good day for us.

But I can't help thinking, as I stretch out on the wardroom settee, of the explosives packed in the tiny ship, and particularly around this very room—the equivalent of forty 1000-pound bombs exploding simultaneously.

* The *Coast Farmer* was torpedoed and sunk by a Jap submarine off the east coast of Australia within a month.

*"It's Only the Cats"*

American planes are pouring in—Kittyhawks, Airacobras, Douglas Dauntless dive-bombers, Flying Fortresses, Lockheeds, Marauders, North American B-25 Mitchell bombers. Not as many as any of us would like, of course, because you can't have too many fighting aircraft, but an enormously greater number of planes than we've yet become accustomed to seeing.

American planes and American pilots have been monopolizing the news. This isn't the fault of the Americans, because they know well enough that the R.A.A.F. has done, and is still doing, a grand job. But there's a stupid censorship rule in operation that allows us to interview American air crews and quote them, if we want to, by name; whereas names in R.A.A.F. stories are taboo, and interviews are technically illegal. "Names make news" is a truism, and so the Australians have been left rather out of it. We are fighting hard to have the rules altered, because if this sort of thing goes on people will think that the R.A.A.F. has packed up and gone home since the Americans came.

It might be a fitting time to write some stuff about the Australian Catalina pilots, who did such a magnificent job in holding the fort almost unaided in the weeks and months when we were waiting for air support.

I remember a night two months ago in Moresby. It was a still night with half a moon and a light rain falling among the broad-leafed trees. In the tent alongside me a man stirred uneasily, sensing, even in his sleep, the faint droning noise of aircraft. It was a noise that, in the Moresby of those days, usually spelled trouble. He awakened and turned questioningly to his tent mate, who was sitting at a kerosene case writing letters by the faint light of a blackened hurricane lantern.

"It's only the Cats," said the writer, without looking up. "You can go back to sleep. No raid tonight."

"It's only the Cats!" How often did we hear and speak those words in those days? The drone of approaching planes, the noise of engines louder and louder, and then dying away as the Catalinas climbed over the range heading for Rabaul. Catalina flying boats, built for ocean reconnaissance, but used in those days of alarming air inferiority for almost every duty from carrying mails to active bombing.

Their squadron leader, when I knew the Catalina men, was lovable, laughing, handsome Dick Cohen, who earned the D.F.C. as a Sunderland pilot when he rescued Lord Gort and Mr Duff Cooper at revolver point from pro-Axis Frenchmen in the Moroccan port of Rabat.

Cohen became a hero in the minds of all the troops one night late in February. There were many ships in Rabaul Harbor, and the searchlights were sweeping the night sky and the bursts of anti-aircraft fire were flowering like dazzling rockets as the Cats swept in toward the smoking cone of Matupi. Gun flashes were a brilliant yellow against the blackened earth. Sticks of bombs carved strips of flaring light from the darkness. Tongues of flame leaped among the wharves and warehouses as the great, lumbering, slow Catalinas moved through the barrage. From 7000 feet the ships at the wharves looked like toys. It was too high for accurate bombing in these planes.

Cohen, who had kept his bombs, swung his plane out of formation, put her into a steep power dive, and lunged down through the barrage. In a dive-bomber, specially built for the job, the suspense of that dreadful screaming descent is nerve-wracking. In a Catalina flying boat it's a nightmare. Down through the red curtain of the bursting shells plunged the cumbersome machine, almost pulling off its square-tipped wings with the velocity of its 7000-foot dive. When almost over the mastheads of the ships Cohen released his bombs. The plane rocked wildly with the blast. All around were the vivid flashes of bursting shells, the phosphoric streak of tracers, the ruddy orange glare of flames. The Catalina shuddered and strained as Cohen pulled her out of the dive, went skimming across the water with the A.A. bursting far above, leapfrogged over the volcano, and was heading homeward. From 50 miles away the ruddy glow of Rabaul's fires could still be seen.

A few nights later the Cats went out again on a raid to show the temporary residents of Rabaul a pyrotechnic display with incendiaries. The flying boats bucked and kicked through the fury of monsoonal gales. They came over Rabaul with a thunderstorm raging below them, and the cold light from a gibbous moon shining on the solid-looking slate-colored wall below. For an hour and then for another hour the Cats droned overhead, probing and seeking some way through the blanket of weather. No luck at all. So the squadron leader made his signal, put the plane into a steep dive, came through the clouds right into a red fury of anti-aircraft fire, and dive-bombed the target before climbing back into the wet security of the clouds. He cruised around for a few moments. Everything was quiet. So down he went again in that hair-raising descent, this time with machine guns pouring streams of bullets into the Japanese positions.

And the enemy fire faltered and died away against the dive of that roaring, terrifying monster of a flying boat, unseen in the blackness except for the streaming silver morse of the tracers and the orange flickering at the gun muzzles. The amazing thing with the Cats was not so much that their method of attack was so un-orthodox, as that they all came back safely!

These planes—except for long-range ocean reconnaissance, which is the job they were meant to do—never did measure up to 1942 standards of aerial warfare. Yet I often wonder just how much those crates checked the Japanese, how much they contributed to the "New Guinea Hurdle" that held the enemy up long enough for our American allies to come to our aid.

The first Japanese raid on Rabaul was made on 4 January. The first *allied* raid on Japanese-occupied Rabaul, in which United States bombers participated, was on 22 February. In the intervening span of forty-nine days Australia must have been, to a large extent, saved by the courageous activities of a handful of Australian pilots, gun-ners, observers and navigators, who harassed the enemy day after day, night after night. Many young Australians gave their lives, many were posted missing, a few won, and all earned, gallantry decorations. I feel proud to have known these men in the days when we regarded ourselves as wishful thinkers if we spoke of "future air support."

It seems a long time now since I yarned to them when, tired and unshaven, they returned from patrols and grinned as they lied: "We've just been scaring hell out of the Zero fighters!" Repeatedly I saw men come in after thirteen-hour patrols, snatch a bite of food and a few hours' sleep, then roar off again over the reef on another "job" that would keep them in the air for fourteen hours. I saw them, almost staggering from want of sleep, falling into bunks while the squadron's incomparable ground staff "bombed up" for another trip scheduled for take-off a few hours later.

There were never any distinctions of rank in these flying boats. In the confined fuselages there never was enough room for "sirs" and salutes. Men fought together, flew together, slept together, and often lived together for days on end in some remote, fever-infested lagoon.

Many of the pilots had served in Sunderlands with the R.A.F. in England. I once asked one of these "veterans"—for in the air force you can be a veteran at the age of twenty-six—what was his toughest assignment. He smiled and replied: "The day I came to New Guinea. The Sunderland job on the other side was a picnic compared with this."

There were also special sorts of hazards because of the fragile fabric of the big hulls on the flying boats. We were warned against tossing empty beer bottles into the sea. "Coming in to put a Cat down takes some doing," they told me. "Floating coconuts or a floating beer bottle will rip the hull of the boat, and they've even been known to sink just because of a tide-borne coconut!"

Shrapnel holes, of course, could produce the same result. The pilots called it "fretwork." You could climb through some of the pieces of "fretwork" that came back from Rabaul and Gasmata and Bougainville! How some of the Cats ever got back is still a question that tantalizes my imagination. But they were patched up, and out they went again, plastering the enemy positions with such persistency that the Japs must have thought we were using a veritable aerial armada of Cats.

And if they couldn't be patched up sufficiently for combat operations, they were repaired temporarily and sent back to the mainland with wounded.

I once went down on one of these flights. Patchy moonlight came through the bullet holes in the fuselage. The control panel was a mass of shattered dials and broken glass and snarled wires. The altimeter didn't work any longer, the air speed indicator was "out," the turn-and-bank indicator no longer functioned, the efficiency of the compass was extremely questionable. Lashing rain smacked the portholes and splashed in through the jagged holes. The pilot was flying blind, with no instruments to help him. The boat dropped and soared sickeningly in the air currents.

Australian wounded were lying on stretchers behind the pilot. One man had a broken pelvis, strapped into place temporarily by a wide bandage. With every lurch of the plane the broken bones grated. Beads of perspiration speckled his forehead; his lips were white and tightly pressed together. No sound came from him. Once the pilot left the machine to the co-pilot and went back to him, picking his way carefully between the stretchers.

"How are you making it?" he asked.

The patient, who must have been suffering indescribable agonies, took a deep breath and grinned. "Right as rain!" he replied.

"Sorry about the bumps, old man," said the pilot. "It's lousy weather, but it'll probably improve."

The patient grinned again. "You're doing all right. Haven't felt a bump yet." But he couldn't control an involuntary grimace of pain as the Cat gave a nauseating lurch.

The pilots of that battered Catalina groped southward through the thunderheads, without instruments, without even a map to guide them. Dawn, by dead reckoning, should have given them a position off the Queensland coast, out to sea. But the gray wetness of 5:30 A.M. merely disclosed great mountains and rolling plains beneath—strange territory for a flying boat to be crossing.

"The pilot used to work on a sheep station," explained the observer, without the flicker of a grin. "He's going home for the week-end."

"What's worrying you?" retorted the man at the wheel. "The sun came up on our port side. We must be flying south. So all we've got to do is to turn to the left and keep flying until we hit the sea!"

We were 300 miles inland, and it wasn't until three hours later that we did hit the sea! But the plane got home, and the wounded went to hospital, and, in due course, the plane returned, patched and titivated, to get on with the job of hammering the Jap.

### Try This On Hollywood

The things that happen to men in time of war sometimes don't make sense. That applies more than somewhat, as Damon Runyon would say, to this particularly screwy war in New Guinea. Adventure is no longer unusual, but sometimes the adventure is so fantastic that the story is worth telling, if only to prove that Hollywood movie producers, even in their wilder flights of fancy, can't beat the true experiences of some pilots.

I heard this story today. A North American B-25 bomber was out on reconnaissance over the north coast when it ran into thick weather and had to make a forced landing in the jungle, being out of fuel. The pilot, Captain John Feltham, put the plane down carefully enough to enable the crew, if not the plane, to survive. The young Americans got out their jungle knives and started heading toward the coast. They cut and slashed for several days and eventually stumbled into a clearing—a deserted trading post, alongside which were parked the remains of two ancient old biplanes. One—of a type in use in 1914—was standing on its nose with its propeller shattered. The other—a comparatively modern model of 1919—had been badly burnt.

The Americans looked at the relics for a while. The older plane was in the better condition. But there was a lot of work to be done. The propeller was taken out of the burnt plane and fixed to the veteran. Struts which were almost powdering because of the white ants were replaced by cut bamboo. The canvas from a camp stretcher and a couple of bedsheets were used to patch the holes in the fabric. There was no aviation fuel, but there was a dump of motor car petrol in 44-gallon drums. Within a week the old plane was airworthy (if you didn't place too fine a definition on the word!) and Captain Feltham taxied her down the rough floor of the valley. Pieces of string and wire fluttered from the struts. To get out of that valley you had to climb across a mountain range with peaks up to 8000 feet. The old crate wobbled and lurched and took to the air. It circled twice and then disappeared over the wall of jungle.

Feltham climbed to within fifty feet of the mountain top, but the engines were wheezing and coughing and the plane would go no higher. The precious petrol was rapidly running away as, for half an hour, the pilot tried to gain that extra few feet of height. He had almost succeeded when a fierce down-current took the battered old museum piece, whirled it down like a leaf, and dashed it into the mountain side.

"The plane went in nose first just before dusk," Feltham explained to me, "and both my legs were jammed underneath the engine. It took me just six hours to work myself free and I just lay there through the night hoping that they'd seen the crack-up from the trading post I'd just left. Luckily they had, and next afternoon the boys came along, correctly diagnosed that both my legs were broken, strapped them up with splints made of bamboo and carried me down the mountain side in a litter.

"A couple of days later a little Australian Tiger Moth spotted our signals and the pilot dropped a message telling us where he would be able to make a landing. It took us three and a half days to reach the clearing he had indicated, and sure enough, down came the Moth in a bumpy landing in a small patch of kunai grass. He took me out first and then went back for the rest of my crew. It took us 20 minutes to fly over the country we had taken nearly four days to walk across."

Thinking it over, I feel that the Hollywood director would have bettered my story. Feltham would have reached Port Moresby in that queer Great War biplane. Well, but for that sudden blast of wind, he probably would.

The Australian who rescued him was dear old ageless Jerry Pentland, whose "Flying Circus" of tiny Moths and strange biplanes has been the laughing stock of New Guinea for many weeks, but who has saved more lives in a month—soldiers, pilots, and even sick natives—than I can attempt to count.

*Independence Day—with Fireworks*

Today has been what the American bomber and fighter pilots are still—at 11 P.M. with the last bottle of Scotch gone—describing as "a day and a half." Both sides tried to celebrate Independence Day. They broke even. We've just been totalling it up and the day's tally is twelve each. The Japs lost five Zeros for certain, another one almost certainly, and had six badly damaged. We lost two Marauders and three Airocobras and had seven planes damaged.

The day began, as most days do now, at breakfast time, when 20 Zeros came over for the sixty-seventh raid on Moresby and ran into a small screen of Airocobras. Our boys were outnumbered and out of position. We got one of the Zeros and smacked a few bullets into three others, but three of our fighters came plummeting down in flames and three others were damaged. Progress score: Japan, 6; U.S.A., 4.

A formation of Marauders had just taken off to paste Lae airfield. They had released their bombs on the first run when the Zeros coming back from Moresby attacked them. Even by talking to the pilots you can't sift out what actually happened in that whirling dogfight, but one incident is clear to most of the pilots and it's worth telling because we don't often have a bomber brought down by a dead Jap!

One Zero turned in above a Marauder piloted by Lieutenant Walter Krell, and as he nosed down, Private Pat Norton, in the turret, ripped a hundred rounds into his left wing and cockpit. Lieutenant Gene Grauer, the navigator, had the best view of what happened and tells the best story:

"The Zero seemed to jerk downward and the pilot to jerk upwards. Then the Jap slumped down at the controls. I could see him clearly, and he was surely as dead as he could be. The Zero spun crazily and would have hit us if Walt hadn't banked sharply. It swooped under our belly a few feet away. Pieces of its wing were falling away like butterflies. Then its nose went up and it went straight up into the sky, hung there for a moment, and then nosed over and began to come down in a steep dive. We yelled a warning over the radiophone to the rest of the formation, but I guess the last plane either didn't see the Zero or didn't have time to get out of the way. The Zero dived straight into the fuselage of the bomber, cutting clean through the tail. The Japanese plane was smashed to pieces by the impact and went toward the ground like a spray of shrapnel. Our bomber kept on its course for a few seconds, then wobbled and went into a spin. It plunged into the sea off the end of the airfield. We were too busy warding off attacks by the other Zeros to take much notice of what happened afterward."

Altogether four Zeros were shot down and one went into a spin, smoking, but was only claimed as a probable. We lost two Marauders but four which were damaged got home to make crash landings. The Marauders went over again this afternoon, shot down one Zero and damaged two others. Total score for the day: U.S.A., 12; Japan, 12. It might not be the Independence Day celebration that some of us expected, but it didn't lack fireworks.

# IV. RETREAT TO VICTORY

*July 22, 1942—September 27, 1942*

---

*Invasion Day*

**K**APUA, as distinct from the mandated territory, has been invaded for the first time. At dawn today, July 22, a Japanese invasion force, very tentatively estimated to number between 4000 and 6000 troops, made a successful landing near Gona Mission. Curiously, we had no land defense. Last March I was told that one of the main threats to Port Moresby was the Buna-Gona area (Buna is only about ten miles to the eastward of Gona Mission) because it was the northern terminus of the one "good" track through from the north coast to Port Moresby, by way of the inland hill station of Kokoda. Yet the area was undefended. A strong Australian garrison was to have been pushed in there in the next few days. The Japs have beaten us to it by about a week.

So our defense against this landing has to be made by planes. Bad weather has been a hampering factor, but altogether we've done a good job today . . . or as good as one could have expected. The bombers wiped out an 8000-ton transport. Unfortunately the Japs had been taken ashore, but Airacobras strafed the landing barges and killed a good many of the troops.

An unusual feature of the landing was that the Japs made it without air support except that provided by two floatplanes from an escorting cruiser, one of which was shot down. Our planes kept attacking in waves throughout a day of more intense air activity than at any time since the Coral Sea battle; but tonight the Japs, although they have lost many men and a fair quantity of stores, seem to have established their beachhead. At the moment the reason for the landing is a matter of pure conjecture, and, believe me,

106

there's plenty of that tonight! At least this ends the seventy-day period of checkmate.

In that time we have seen nothing but aerial warfare, with the exception of one attack on Salamaua by our jungle guerrillas in the Huon Gulf area. They went into the town of Salamaua under cover of darkness early this month, and completely surprised the Japanese garrison with the audacity and daring of their attack. Our casualties were two men wounded. The Japs lost 60 killed and more than 40 wounded. In retaliation, next day they bombed the little native villages of Mubo and Komiatum. Those bombing attacks are significant. They show very clearly how the Japs have been pinned down to the narrow coastal fringe by the ceaseless watchfulness of Australian jungle fighters, because Komiatum is only two miles from Salamaua. When you have to bomb a village only two miles inland from your main coastal base it indicates that you haven't maintained a very firm grip on that area.

Apart from that one raid, nothing of very great importance happened anywhere until today. The significance of the Gona landing will no doubt become clearer in a few days. Buna is almost due north of Port Moresby (120 miles by air) and is a small but fairly important native administration and mission centre. A good foot track leads through undulating jungle country to Kokoda, 60 miles to the southward; and then a much tougher foot track leads over the Owen Stanley Range, through a wide, 6000-foot pass known to New Guinea air pilots as "The Gap," and on through terrible mountain jungles to Moresby. With the exception of a small stretch between Buna and the Kumusi River (less than half way to Kokoda) the track is impossible for mechanized transport, and so it seems unlikely that the Japs can hope to attempt any overland invasion of Moresby by pushing southward through the mountains, with Buna as a supply base. It is true that Buna has what Lae and Salamaua have always lacked—a *direct* link with the main Australian base; but it seems more logical that the landing has been made to gain control of the comparatively flat north Papuan coast, with its limitless possibilities for the establishment of many good, large airfields and landing strips over a wide area of dispersal and within thirty minutes' flying time of Moresby.

This new move by the enemy might be the curtain-raiser for almost anything. Perhaps, even, the long-expected Battle for New

Guinea. The thing that sticks out most tonight, however, is that the campaign still depends enormously on air power. The side with command of the air will win. It will be interesting to see which side has that command.

*War in the Air*

While the Japanese in north Papua are fanning out into the jungles and kunai patches and sago swamps north of the Kumusi River, the Papuan sky is filled with aircraft. We are seeing something that we haven't seen before in New Guinea. We are seeing the United Nations inexorably wresting air control from the Japanese. It is a mighty heartening sight. Most of the planes in the air are ours—Fortresses, Marauders, Kittyhawks, Airacobras, Mitchells, Bostons, Douglas dive-bombers. There are thousands of men in New Guinea today who are giving thanks to the United States for these planes which, hour after hour, are smashing the Japanese positions 120 miles to the northward.

The Japs have hurled into the battle far fewer aircraft than we had expected. It was not until two days after the Gona landing that they gave indirect air support by attacking Moresby's airfields (our seventy-third raid) with 18 bombers and 16 Zeros. They are scared of our interception, and scared of our anti-aircraft guns. They're giving almost 100 per cent fighter support to their bombers now.

While their planes were over Moresby American bombers were dropping 23 tons of high explosive on the Buna-Gona positions.

The day before yesterday the Japs for the first time attacked a mainland town on the eastern seaboard of Australia—three Kawanisis bombing Townsville, 675 miles south of Moresby, by moonlight—without any damage at all. Our bombers over Gona were at various times on the same day attacked by eight, six and fifteen Zeros. Most of the attacks were aimed at our Flying Fortresses. These big, four-engined bombers have actually been even more effective against Zeros than our fighters. Some of the Fortresses are based on Moresby, some on the mainland, but there are so many of them now that it's difficult—in fact, impossible—to keep track of their exploits.

The men who fly them live in tents scattered through the scrub and stunted gums, always within earshot of the roar of powerful engines. They come from America's big cities and "whistle stops" and they seem to represent most of the forty-eight States. In each squadron you will find quite a number of Australians—ground mechanics, co-pilots and observers—who eat and sleep with them under canvas, play volley-ball or badminton with them under the tropic sky.

Yesterday I was out with one squadron which has been whacking Japanese shipping for days. Many of the men and crews were in the bitter air battles of the Philippines and Java, and since then they have been fighting for months over New Guinea and the Solomons, the Bismarcks and the Admiralties. In almost every tent you will find two or three men who have already been decorated in six months of war. Every man has seen friends go out with a cargo of bombs for the enemy and never come back. The squadron has a magnificent record of ships and planes destroyed, but that record has not been gained without losses. A good illustration of their work was given to me by a young first lieutenant from North Dakota:

"My toughest assignments were a couple of jobs done over one week-end more than a month ago. The first was on Saturday, when we went out in a formation of five ships. It was a low-altitude raid, carried out in daylight, about three o'clock in the afternoon, and without fighter support. We ran over the target in formation and all let go our bombs over the area. Ack-ack was coming up very heavily around our ships, and the captain, who was leading, took us into a dive to dodge it. While we were pulling out about eight to ten Zeros came at us.

"They made a couple of passes while our gunners worked top speed keeping them away. We were pulling off when one plane called up the leader and said he was hit and losing speed. We slowed down to give him some protection, and the Zeros got in a couple more passes. Then the ack-ack blew one of his motors out and he went down in the sea. We watched the men get out and we watched a couple of Zeros flying up and down strafing them in the water.

"We made a tight formation then so that we could protect each other by concentrating our fire power. If one plane drops behind the Zeros all pounce on him and tear him to bits. The Zeros were hanging behind, but when we turned inland from the sea they got ahead and knocked out one motor of our number two plane in a head-on rush. The co-pilot was killed by another burst in the cockpit. We slowed down to protect the plane and went down to 1500 feet. The Zeros climbed 1000 feet above us, and one of them dropped an aerial bomb right in front of my ship.

"The leader made a quick turn to save the formation, and we got through, although I don't know how. The wing of my plane went right through the smoke made by the bomb when it exploded. After that we got clear away. Several of our gunners made hits, and we saw one Zero chopped to bits by our guns when they made their head-on attack.

"That was on the Saturday. We picked up some more planes and went over again on Monday, with the same captain leading. There were eight of us this time, and the weather was so bad that we had to come along the shore and run in from the north at 3000 feet. They spotted us this time, and 10 miles out we could see their fighters coming off the runway like peas out of a pod. By the time we got in they had about 20 up waiting for us.

"They hit us before we reached the target, but we went right on and dropped our bombs where they were needed. One of our ships caught fire. We made a steep turn and dived—and then all hell let loose. We made a couple more turns, but we couldn't shake them off. They got the captain and slowed us up. I hung on to him until he went down, but the formation was broken and we just couldn't get back, so I dodged into a cloud, picked up another ship, and went home with it. As we ran into the cloud I saw four of our planes going down the coast, fairly low, fighting off a swarm of Zeros. They followed us and even made passes at us in the raincloud, but we shook them off."

Luckiest men that day were the crew of a plane piloted by a lieutenant from Georgia. "We were flying on the captain's wing that day," he said, "and both planes were thoroughly shot up together. I got a hole in the gas tank, my hydraulic landing gear was shot up, and the plane was like a sieve. But nobody was hurt and we kept on flying. I souvenired a 25-calibre shot that broke the window beside me, broke the skin on the back of my head, missed the co-pilot and lodged in the cabin. Luckily I was leaning forward when it happened.

"When the captain caught fire the Zero came on over the top.

The captain's gunner and mine got him together, and he just disappeared. I got my ship home and put her down, and I figure I'm lucky. That was the toughest raid I've seen, but we dropped our bombs and we got several Zeros between us, so they didn't have things their own way."

They are not the only lucky men in the outfit. There is an Irish corporal from Connecticut who had the sight knocked off his gun by a Zero, but kept on firing until the pilot had brought the plane down in the sea. Four Zeros kept up strafing runs against the stricken plane, so the pilot ordered the crew to separate. The corporal deflated his life jacket and swam under water whenever the Zeros dived at him. A bullet nicked his thumb, but did not even draw blood. At nightfall they turned home, so he inflated his jacket and made for the shore. For nearly forty-eight hours he was struggling in the water—from early on Saturday afternoon until noon on Monday. After that he hiked many miles through the jungle, living on coconut milk and fruit. He turned up a few weeks later, full of malaria, but still full of fight.

There is another enlisted man, now in the hospital, who was operating the lower turret when his plane was cut out of formation by eight Zeros, which circled and dived around, pouring fire into it. A cannon shell exploded in his compartment, and a fragment cut his head. The blood poured into his eyes, and interfered with his sighting. A machine gun bullet smashed the bone of one arm, and another hit him on the foot. But he kept firing with one hand, sent the Zero down in a plume of smoke, and drove off the others after a five-minute duel. The ship came home in one piece.

Dozens of men up here could tell stories like these. There are some who have struck it lucky, coming back from half a dozen successful missions with nothing much to report except the targets they hit and the weather they had to fly through. But men who enlist for air crews are not trying to dodge trouble, and a man with a fair tally of operational flying hours has usually made his way out of some tight corners, and expects to find himself in more before he is much older.

Most of us are beginning to realize how much we depend on these youngsters from the States—and how much more we shall be depending on them if the Japs decide to go all-out in the Battle for New Guinea.

Today, with the Japanese ground troops already nearly 40 miles inland from the coast, at Oivi village, some of our bombers were chased all the way back from Gona to Moresby by 15 Zeros. Two of the bombers did not get home.

In this war that is a trifle. But back home in the United States there are 18 American families for whom the great personal disaster of the war has occurred. They won't know about it yet. We know about it. We can visualize the charred and crumpled wreckage of two bombers littered along the slopes of some jungled mountain, the shattered and unrecognizable bodies of the two crews. But—such is the callousness and forgetfulness of modern war—it doesn't mean anything very important to us. It is a pity that we have become used to thinking in terms of machines. Two bombers lost means two less machines of steel and duralumin and rubber and plastics. We are already beginning to forget that machines have to be flown by men, and two bombers lost also means that eighteen young Americans have died.

### "They're Coming in Hundreds!"

It is obvious now that the Japanese mean to do more than establish a beachhead and airfields in the Buna-Gona area. They have advanced half way into Papua and are now fighting the Australian Militia at Kokoda village, strategic key to control of the Owen Stanley's.

The first land fighting in Papua began a week ago, when a handful of native troops of the Papuan Infantry Battalion, under the command of young Australian officers, attempted to stem the Japanese advance at Awala, 25 miles inland, along the Buna-Kokoda-Moresby track. They were outnumbered ten to one and they could do nothing. After a few bloody skirmishes they were forced to retreat, establishing road-blocks as they went.

It's believed now that the Japs have 6000 troops in the area—first-class fighting men mainly from specially trained marine landing detachments. That makes the position pretty serious. We have less than 1000 men, mostly of a Militia battalion, up in the mountains. They have never been in action before. They are not equipped or supplied as well as the Japanese, and we can't hope to give them the help they need for a considerable time. Their job is to hold the Japs north of the range, while we build up reinforcements, and attempt to cut some sort of supply line through the incredibly wild country of the southern Owen Stanley's.

Four days ago the Japanese, who had pushed more than 60 miles inland in a week, reached Kokoda. Since then the little village sheltering beneath the towering green hills of the main range, has been a no-man's-land. It is a tough battlefield, with its green mazes of rubber plantations and humid jungles and snaking tracks through solid walls of bottle-green foliage. But if we can't hold them at Kokoda the battlefield will become infinitely tougher.

The Australians are lucky to have among their officers some men who have had experience of the jungle. Some of them have fought the Japs before. Major Cameron (who, as a captain, fought the enemy at Rabaul, and was the only A.I.F. officer to oppose their landing at Salamaua) is one; Major Bill Watson, one of the "old hands" of New Guinea, is another. Lieutenant-Colonel W. T. Owen, who was with the A.I.F. at Rabaul, and who commanded our Kokoda force, has already been killed in action leading his troops in an attack at Kokoda. He died almost on the steps of the administrative building, shot through and through by Japanese bullets.* Many other Australians have died, but even more Japs. Watson has taken command of the little force.

Fighting, by all the standards of the Second World War, has been on a very small scale. But it has been tough. When the Japanese began to push ahead to take Kokoda, the Australians dug themselves in on a tiny plateau. The Japs came in overwhelming numbers from the front and from both flanks, using heavy and light machine guns and many mortars. The Australians replied with brisk machine-gun and mortar fire. Colonel Owen was in the forward Australian trenches when he heard the clank of metal over the lip of the plateau. He climbed up to the steps of the government building to investigate, carrying a private's rifle and a couple of grenades. For a few moments he stood there. Then there was the *brrrrrp-brrrrp* of many machine guns. Owen fell backward, staggered to his knees and crawled back to the trench. His last words were: "Look out! They're coming in hundreds!"

They were. The Battle of the Owen Stanley's had begun. Over

* Lieutenant-Colonel W. T. Owen was posthumously decorated by General Mac-Arthur with the Distinguished Service Cross, thus becoming the first Australian to receive an American gallantry decoration.

the lip of the tiny plateau swarmed hundreds of Japanese. Many of them were big men, some six-footers, with magnificent physique, and all were clad in the green jungle uniform that blended with the background of jungle far better than did the Australian khaki. The first wave fell, ripped to pieces by Australian mortars and machine guns. The second wave climbed over the bodies of the fallen. On the tiny, flat-topped hill, less than an acre in extent, Australian soldiers and Japanese died, in bloody, hand-to-hand fighting. As fast as the Japanese were killed others scrambled over the plateau rim to take their places. There were no other troops to take the places of the Australian dead. Men lunged with bayonets and sought each other's throats with bare hands in that grim battle which raged above the bodies of men who had been trampled underfoot. One of those bodies was that of the Australian commander.

The Australians were forced to retreat, leaving their dead and some of their wounded behind. But on Saturday they counterattacked, under cover of powerful air support from American fighters and bombers which hammered the enemy's Kokoda position, and drove the Japanese out of the village despite the fact that they were outnumbered four to one. Major Watson, the new commander, had only one order for his men: "Stand and fight!" Near the torn, bomb-blasted plateau they found the body of Colonel Owen, tossed into a ditch. He was buried with full military honors near a line of Japanese graves marked with wooden sticks covered with ideographs, and with a bowl of food before every grave. All day yesterday we held Kokoda, against furious Japanese attacks. The government buildings were shattered, the village almost demolished in those fierce exchanges. But men cannot do the impossible. Today we were hurled out of the tiny village in the foothills. But we are standing firm in the hills behind, guarding the villages of Deniki and Isurava that lead to the vital pass through the range.

Far beyond, in the territory which the Japanese have conquered, our patrols of the Papuan Infantry Battalion are still continuing the fight. In Moresby troops of the A.I.F., who have already won splendid battle honors in Libya and Greece, Syria and Crete, are being poured into the garrison. Troops are rumbling in lorry-loads up the twisting road that leads beyond the Laloki gorge and ends where the terrible foot track across the range begins. Far away on the other side of the range the remnants of a gallant Militia battalion are trying to stem the avalanche of thousands of Japanese simply because they have been given an order—"Stand and fight!"

### *"The Situation is Well in Hand"*

Today is the fifth day of the first counter-offensive yet undertaken by the United Nations in the south Pacific. After five days it is still notably successful. It is, according to the division of command and the requirements of geography, outside our own particular little theatre of war—in the islands of the South Solomons; but there can be no question about its importance so far as New Guinea is concerned. Since Japan first brought war to the Pacific south of the equator the Solomons and the New Guinea area have been woven into one pattern of war. The activities of our planes, now that the United States marines have struck a devastating first blow in the Solomons, is sufficient proof of that. Fortresses from the MacArthur command are streaming over to Rabaul almost every day and night, blasting the Japanese airfields and hitting the concentrations of shipping. Every move by air is now designed to help the Solomons campaign, because, indirectly, it is a blow to relieve our force struggling at this moment in the Owen Stanleys. The marines have opened up a second front for us.

It is just as well that the attack was made. There is plenty of evidence that the Japanese had intended to build up the south Solomons as an air and naval base of paramount importance—for attacks on New Guinea and the Australian mainland, no doubt, as well as for possible future moves against New Caledonia, New Hebrides, Fiji, even, perhaps, New Zealand. Guadalcanal, with its flat coastal plain, was to become the major air base; Tulagi, with its magnificent harbor, was being prepared as a first-class naval base. Japanese garrison and labor units have been busy on both islands for almost two months.

The marines struck at first light on Friday, August 7, in an operation that had been skilfully planned, and that had all the elements of faultless timing and complete secrecy. The Japanese were utterly surprised. At Tulagi the first knowledge given to the enemy of the attack was the fall of shells in Tulagi harbor, the crash of bombs from carrier-based dive-bombers and land-based heavy bombers and the roar of naval gunfire in the bay. Eighteen Japanese floatplanes were sunk before their engines could be started. At Guadalcanal carrier-based fighters and dive-bombers smashed any large-scale Japanese resistance and the marines landed, annihilated the Japanese parties who attempted to obstruct them, and seized the vital airfield beachhead. By dusk they had a firm grip on Guadalcanal, had captured Tulagi and Gavutu islands, and had established a bridgehead on the island of Florida. By dawn the Japanese had recovered from their first surprise, and the marines who had landed on Gavutu had some tough fighting before they were able to conquer the adjacent island of Tanambogo.

The Japanese used a few planes in the afternoon of the landings, more during the night, and almost every plane they had available on the following day. As many as 80 Japanese bombers, Zeros, torpedo planes and dive-bombers were in action against the American ships. Many were shot down into the sea by anti-aircraft fire or by pursuit planes from American carriers.

On Saturday night the Japanese navy was thrown in to smash our ships, but they were met by American and Australian warships in hard-hitting duels and driven off, despite the fact that the initial advantage lay with the Japanese, who surprised the allied cruiser screen on patrol north of Guadalcanal and sank the Australian heavy cruiser *Canberra*—flagship of the Royal Australian Navy—and the United States cruisers *Astoria, Vincennes* and *Quincey*. Despite this blow to our defending naval force the Japanese were unable to penetrate our line of sea defense and failed in their objective, which was to smash our transports and supply ships and stage a large-scale bombardment of the beachhead we had established. During the naval action three powerful air attacks were made on our positions by Japanese aircraft, but they were driven off with heavy losses by army and navy fighters, already using the airfield on Guadalcanal which the Japanese had obligingly built but had not been given time to use.

By midday yesterday the marines had crushed all major enemy resistance on Guadalcanal, Tulagi, Florida, Makambo, Gavutu and Tanambogo.

The effect of this United States victory on the campaign in Papua may easily prove considerable. It depends on how much the face-saving Jap is prepared to gamble in his attempt to win back these six islands which have so suddenly and so dramatically been lost to him.

Even now, his carefully prepared plans have suffered considerable dislocation. He cannot afford to allow the marines to sit down and consolidate their new conquests in preparation for further drives into the north Solomons toward Rabaul. He is in danger with a strong enemy on each of his southern flanks. He must divert to the Solomons bombers and fighters and warships and trained troops which were, no doubt, being built up into a formidable force for attack on Papua.

The important thing is that the initiative has at last been wrested from the Japs. For the first time in the Pacific war the time and place for battle have been dictated by the United Nations. Most of the war correspondents here feel that the curtain has at last gone up on the battle for domination of the scattered islands and tenuous sea lanes of the mightiest ocean in the world. Now that it has begun on a big scale it is difficult to see how it can end before one or the other of the adversaries takes the knockout.

Admiral Ghormley struck the first blow according to principles of warfare that are as old as time. He relied on the element of surprise and confusion, and struck according to classical military precept at the exposed left flank of the enemy. Now the advantage must be held, and if it is held it must be exploited to harass the Japanese all along their southwest Pacific defense line.

It is interesting now to look back on the early months of this strange island campaign. None of us thought it could be more than a tropic sideshow. But the thing is getting out of hand completely. It shows all the earmarks of developing into a first-class war. Which simply goes to prove that *both* sides must agree if you want to make a war big or small.

Some of the newspaper writers in the United States have been urging the authorities to decrease the war supplies to the south Pacific areas. Most of them use that lovely term, "global strategy." We Australians are truly thankful for the assistance that America has given us. I have no doubt that without the American planes and American ships that have been assisting us in recent months we should have been defeated in the islands, and the heel of the Japanese invader would now be firmly set on our continent. But none of us will bolster up the popular misconception that Australia has been fed by an inexhaustible torrent of American men, aircraft, ships and material. America, apart from aircraft, has given us just enough to fill the gap created by the Australian men and the Australian ships that are fighting for a democratic way of life thousands of miles away on the other side of the world. By far the greater part of the defenses of Australia are still Australian.

Some of the American writers say that the assistance given to Australia has dislocated "global strategy" and drained more important fronts—which is all complete eyewash! In comparison with the American potential, the supply to Australia has been little more than a trickle, though a very welcome trickle! The entire amount of material, including aircraft, that has come to Australia represents only three days' output of America's annual production.

If they want to talk about "global strategy"—and who am I to stop them?—let them remember that so far as a global war is concerned Australia is carrying its own load. This may all sound parochial and selfish and bad-tempered; but isn't meant like that. After all, we are allies fighting against the one evil, and we will fight better without bickering.

### Curtain-Raiser

Until today even the campaign in the Owen Stanley's had looked like another of the "phoney" phases that have been such a feature of this south Pacific war. Nothing much has been happening. We are not permitted to speculate on possible future moves (which would certainly give us a lot to write about) and this limits us to subjects that are disconnected and, to some extent, almost meaningless.

Since the U. S. marines made their spectacular landing on Guadalcanal the Japs have tried repeatedly to retrieve the position, without any success, and the marines are consolidating and building up a fine, strong base.

The Japanese planes have been showing a decided interest in Milne Bay, where we have established a strong garrison of the A.I.F. and the R.A.A.F. (two Kittyhawk fighter squadrons, as well as bombers and general reconnaissance planes). Our bombers have been plastering Rabaul and Lae and Salamaua and any signs of movement among the Japanese ships scattered round the enemy's island bases. Allied fighters have seldom stopped strafing the track between Buna and Kokoda, and this dislocation of the Japanese Papuan line of communication has undoubtedly kept the enemy nailed down at Kokoda—even if that nailing down is only temporary. The Japanese air force has been singularly inactive, with the exception of a big raid on Moresby a week ago yesterday, when they destroyed or damaged a number of our bombers and transport planes. An attack on Milne Bay yesterday was driven off with heavy enemy losses by our Kittyhawks. Farther afield Nauru and Ocean Island, in the Gilbert group, have been bombed by Japanese aircraft and shelled by Japanese cruisers and it looks as if Japanese conquest is contemplated.*

Our reconnaissance planes are out day and night, in dreadful weather conditions, trying to check up on ominous enemy shipping movements in the Rabaul and Solomons area. Tonight, with reports of another enemy convoy moving south from New Britain, almost every plane we have is grounded because of appalling weather. The Japs are amazingly clever in exploiting weather conditions to move ships, to transport reinforcements and shift aircraft from base to base. And up in the Kokoda area thousands of Japanese troops are massing for a large-scale attack. Two A.I.F. battalions are being rushed up—if you can use the word "rushed" in describing the movement of troops across that terrible track which is known now as the "Kokoda Trail." Until they get there we shall have to depend on two Militia battalions, one already badly mauled from the earlier fighting near Kokoda. In the Salamaua area a powerful Japanese force has captured Mubo, nine miles to the southward, and is building up for what is believed to be a big attack aimed at conquering the rich Bulolo Valley and the important mountain airfield of Wau, in the goldfields. The balloon should go up at any time now. If the Japanese raids on Milne Bay are interpreted as their usual softening up before attack, it would surprise none of us to see a concerted three-pronged land assault beginning this week—one prong thrusting from Mubo toward the Bulolo area, the central prong hitting into the Owen Stanley's, the easterly prong striking at Milne Bay. We have airpower and some force of ground troops to counter each move. The Japs also have

* All communication with Nauru and Ocean Island ceased on 2 September.

seapower. If they strike simultaneously on all three fronts the splitting of our airpower might earn them some success. If their timing is not perfect, however, they should receive something of a shock.

From all reports, people on the mainland are more jittery than the troops. There was the usual political howl about unpreparedness on the north coast of Papua (some of the loudest howlers were the men who themselves had had the opportunity of seeing that the job was done) and the statement which MacArthur's headquarters issued only partly allayed the general anxiety. It was:

The defense line of the Allies in New Guinea is along the almost impassable range of the Owen Stanley mountains, beyond which lies the north coast. With the enemy in partial control of that coast and in control of the sea lanes from Rabaul leading thereto, it would have been impossible to defend this advanced position in the main only from the sea, with little hope of success, and any garrison there would undoubtedly have been overwhelmed in case of serious attack. Isolated positions subject to enemy envelopment are invariably doomed, with no commensurate advantages. They represent nothing but forlorn hopes. No special threat exists by its occupation by the enemy, and the establishment of an air base there would be difficult indeed in the face of our air opposition. Similarly, in case of any Allied attack on New Guinea, the Japanese in the isolated Buna-Gona area would find themselves in a most exposed position.

There was a lot of sound common sense in that statement. There was also much that can be proved right or wrong only by the events now building up.

### They Died in Hundreds

For some weeks many of the troops up here have been singing a parody, one verse of which is:

> Down to Milne Bay we did go,
> To beat the twirps from Tokyo:
> Hardships, you bastards, you dunno what hardships are!

That verse, at least, has been proved correct. Last Wednesday, August 26, the Japs invaded Milne Bay. Today the laconic report from Major-General Cyril Clowes, commander of the Milne Bay garrison, is: "Only mopping-up of remnants of Jap landing force remains to be done." In less than a week picked Japanese jungle fighters have suffered their first major defeat of the New Guinea war. The "surprise" invasion was no surprise, and the enemy walked right into the trap we had prepared for him. That isn't to say, of course, that it was easy. For a time, indeed, it seemed that we might suffer a disastrous reverse, when Japanese warships were in Milne Bay, pouring shells into our positions, and the Japanese marines, fighting like fanatics, had driven right up to the edge of the airfield which was the strategic key to command of the area. But they never advanced a single yard on to the cleared area of the airfield. They died there in hundreds. Eventually their bodies had to be buried with a bulldozer!

This is our first big success against the much-publicized Japanese *tadori*, and it deserves to be set down in some detail. Exactly a week ago a Japanese convoy was sighted in the Trobriand Islands, heading for Milne Bay. Australian bombers and fighters went out in shocking weather, blew one small gunboat to pieces, but could not take any effective action against the transports. Soon after midnight the convoy reached Milne Bay and landed extensive numbers of specially trained marines on the north shore. The Australian planes, assisted by American Flying Fortresses and Marauders, went for the ships, and although they scored hits they could neither prevent the Japs from getting ashore in their landing barges, nor could they greatly interfere with the unloading of supplies, which included light tanks.

The Japs stepped lightheartedly ashore into a morass of flowing mud and a tangled wilderness of coconut plantations (the Milne Bay coconut plantations are the largest in the world) through which swollen streams rushed down to the muddied waters of the bay. They could not have expected much more than token resistance. The first party of 500 marines chattered and laughed and sang as they made inland along the tracks leading from Gili-Gili. They had walked 400 yards when the Battle of Milne Bay began. A small force of Australian militiamen were the first to oppose the invaders. The Japs scattered in the first burst of machine gun fire, but the enemy tanks came on, their searchlights blinding the Australians.

It had been raining almost without a break for a fortnight. Tracks deserved the name only because they were merely four feet deep in mud as compared with the six feet of sinking, slow-moving ooze that covered every other square foot of land. Over 10 square miles of that sort of country the Battle of Milne Bay raged for the next six days.

At dawn the Japanese transports and warships steamed away, leaving behind the blazing hulk of a shattered merchantman. Japanese marines, almost invisible in the jungle, pushed forward toward the airfield from which Kittyhawks piloted by exhausted, bearded Australians constantly harried the Japanese, strafing the tops of coconut palms to bring enemy sharpshooters toppling to the ground, hammering the tanks that had finally bogged down in the mud, smashing enemy landing barges and supply dumps on the beach. And the rain came down unceasingly.

Tongues of flame leaped skyward from the burning store dumps. Through the dripping wilderness, patrols of Australian A.I.F. men, who had last fought in the ravines of Syria, moved forward to meet the enemy. They found, in that first day, new problems of fighting to overcome—the silence and stealth of the Japanese jungle fighters, the accurate marksmanship of snipers lashed into the tops of coconut palms, the difficulties of infiltration in a battlefield where it was impossible to see an enemy 10 feet away.

Japanese troops groped their way behind our lines, then shouted "Forward!" in perfect English in attempts to get our men to push ahead into skilfully prepared ambushes. Enemy snipers threw themselves among the heaps of Japanese corpses already littering the tracks, opening fire on our men when they had passed. The Japanese were skilfully camouflaged. Many had gone to the extent of shaving their heads and painting their scalps and faces green. The Australians, covered from head to foot in stinking mud, scarcely needed camouflage.

Japanese sniping was amazingly accurate, but the marksmanship of the rank and file was fortunately poor. They were using light-calibre automatics (.256), three-inch mortars, light and heavy machine guns, and grenades. One Australian party of four men was ambushed in the centre of a clearing 200 yards across. As the Australians reached the centre of the clearing more than 50 Japs opened fire from the surrounding jungle. The Australians had no chance to break through to the edge of the trees, so they fell to the ground and took what cover they could find. The Japs blazed away at the four men for three hours, and when they were finally cleared out the Australians were still untouched!

Nevertheless in the first advance the Japs rolled the Australians before them as they struck toward the air strip. A.I.F. troops were thrown in, with the order that the airfield must not fall into enemy hands. The Australians went to their positions and dug funk-holes in the mud with their tin hats. The first wave of Japanese came to the edge of the clearing. Machine-gun fire roared and echoed through the trees. The Japanese went down like corn. Again and again they came, but not one Japanese stepped a yard inside the clearing. They were forced to withdraw when the line of Japanese dead at the edge of the airfield was almost six feet high.

Elsewhere the Australians were attacking desperately against a strong Japanese position established near an abandoned mission. They moved forward with Kittyhawks, almost invisible in the low rain clouds that hung just above the trees, roaring overhead and pouring bullets into the feathery tops of the palm trees to catch the snipers who were picking off dozens of Australians. The Japs retreated cunningly. While the main body withdrew, small parties were left on the side tracks and in the jungle with light machine guns, which opened up on the Australians from behind. Once the Japs counter-attacked in force, badly mauling one Australian battalion. They attempted to continue the advance, under cover of two tanks, but the Kittyhawks went down to the tree-tops and put them out of action. It cost us one Kittyhawk and the life of a gallant Australian, the leader of the squadron, Peter Turnbull, who was killed on his 116th operational flight when his plane wing caught the top of a coconut palm.*

Almost every night Japanese warships were in the bay, sometimes shelling the Australian positions, sometimes landing reinforcements and stores, sometimes evacuating wounded. Japanese dead were huddled all over the battle area, some killed by infantry attack, some killed by air strafing. One stormy day the Japs attempted to give air support to their invasion force. They struck with 15 dive-bombers and fighters, but they came at a time when the Australian fighter squadrons were operating with a fierce spirit and a deadly skill that could not have been countered by any enemy. To the loss of one Kittyhawk, nine of the Japanese planes were shot out of the storm clouds in flames.

* The airfield near by has since been named Turnbull Field.

On Friday and Saturday the Japs launched their fiercest attacks in the sodden jungle, with machine gunners in the coconut groves covering their thrusts with accurate fire down the lanes between the palms. The Australians fixed bayonets and charged with piercing yells that routed the Japs and forced them back again. The Australians reached a creek bank and dug in, but at dusk 400 Japs counter-attacked again in close formation. All night intense fire was exchanged across the creek. Luggers that had been used to take off our wounded were unable to come inshore, so experienced lifeguards from Queensland and Tasmania courageously swam out to the vessels with the wounded. There never was any lack of courage at Milne Bay.

An engineer unit of a sergeant and three sappers was sent out to clean up a road-block. They had partly completed the job when 20 Japs attacked them. The sergeant and two sappers held the enemy off for thirty minutes with rifle fire while the third sapper completed the job.

A youngster who had been shot through the foot dragged himself to a palm tree against which he propped himself up. Although he had used all his ammunition he retained his rifle and bayonet. A Japanese stalked him, armed only with a knife, but all night the Australian, lying against the tree and unable to stand, kept him off with a bayonet. He was found by his comrades at dawn and the Jap was killed.

The Japanese never gave up the fight. One Australian was walking through a coconut grove when a Jap dropped on him from the trees. He was impaled on the Australian's bayonet, and the Australian promptly finished him off, as he thought. As he walked ahead the Jap, with a dying effort, raised himself on his elbow and emptied his tommy gun into the Australian, seriously wounding him. Although severely wounded, a twenty-year-old Queenslander who had been stabbed in the back by a stalking Jap wrestled with his assailant and strangled him to death with his bare hands. It was bitter, bloody fighting in which no quarter was given and no prisoners were taken.

Some of the Japs were without firearms, all their weapons and ammunition having been destroyed on the beach by fighter strafing. Completely naked, and armed only with long knives, they raided inside the Australian lines at night, or swam along the foreshore to get behind our positions. The awful bubbling scream of a man whose throat had been cut was often the only evidence that these night-prowling killers were in the Australian positions. Small grenades and even firecrackers were employed at night to confuse the defenders. Shouted orders in perfect English—"Hey, Bill, is the corporal there?"—cost several young Australians their lives until our troops became aware of the trick.

Even when the bulk of enemy resistance had been crushed, and more than 700 Japanese corpses scattered through the coconut groves and swamps afforded grim evidence of the Australian triumph, small Japanese patrols continued to give battle, and snipers were constantly in action from tree-tops and cleverly concealed funkholes.

The most tense period of the battle came on Saturday night, at about 9 p.m., when a Japanese cruiser and eight destroyers nosed into the bay during a torrential downpour and turned their guns toward the shore. Until dawn no sound was heard from the land, except the occasional chatter of a machine gun in the jungle. Not a single light showed from the Australian positions. Smoking was forbidden. Men stayed where they were throughout the pouring night. In any case it was almost certain death to wander in the darkness.

When daybreak came the Japanese naval force had gone without firing a shot at the shore positions. The original belief was that the warships had landed extensive reinforcements. It seems more likely now that they evacuated Japanese wounded and those parties still surviving which naval landing parties were able to contact in the jungle.

That morning the Australians began to counter-attack along the whole scattered front. Except for mopping up—an operation which might go on for many weeks—the Battle of Milne Bay was virtually over. Japan's crack Kure No. 5 landing force had been smashed and cut to ribbons.

It was at Milne Bay that American soldiers—light anti-aircraft gunners and engineers—had their first battle with the Japanese in New Guinea, sharing with the Australians the successful defense of the vital airfield. How vital that defense was is now very obvious to everybody. Without the air support which the Australian Kittyhawks provided it is possible that we could not have held Milne

Bay. In a few days the squadron that began its exploits as the first fighter defense force of Port Moresby has added many laurels to its already splendid record of achievement.

There hasn't been much time for jubilation about the Milne Bay victory. The full-scale Japanese assault on our positions in the Owen Stanley's began six days ago. Things are not going very well. The Japs are pushing us back into the pass through the range. A large enemy force based on Mubo, south of Salamaua, is moving south cautiously. Our guerrillas are continually harassing the enemy and his thousand native carriers. We've smashed one of the three prongs, but the other two are still very menacing at the moment.

NOTE: Australian troops at Milne Bay were still mopping up scattered enemy parties more than two months after this entry was made. For some days after the failure of the landing, Japanese warships continued to shell the garrison under cover of darkness. One naval force arrived when the Australian hospital ship *Manunda* was alongside the jetty evacuating wounded. The Japanese warships trained searchlights on the hospital ship and kept them there while they shelled the shore positions. The *Manunda* was not fired upon, although shells were hurled right over the top of the ship, which was within point-blank range of the warships. A.I.F. nurses aboard the hospital ship continued their work with cool courage, although they later admitted that they were "as scared as the dickens." Ashore, doctors from the hospital ship displayed great heroism. For 36 hours, without a single break, they worked in rain and mud and slush, sometimes under fire. They performed critical operations in tents with floors of mud that squelched over the tops of their ankles. At the end of 36 hours one South Australian doctor collapsed at the side of the operating table.

During mopping-up on 4 September, a series of strong enemy machine gun posts was found by units of an A.I.F. battalion. One section led by Corporal John French, a Queenslander, was held up by furious machine-gun fire from three enemy weapon-pits. French ordered his section to take cover, crawled along the ground and silenced the first of the posts with grenades. He came back for more grenades, advanced again, and wiped out the second post. He went for the third post with a tommy gun firing from the hip. His men saw him reel, but he went on again with hisgunstill firing. French's section attacked when fire ceased from the third machine-gun post. They found that every man of the three enemy positions had been killed. French was dead in front of the third pit.

In January 1943 the King agreed to the posthumous award to French of the Victoria Cross—the first award of the world's most coveted gallantry decoration to a soldier in New Guinea.

### World's Worst Battleground

Our wounded are beginning to come back from the Owen Stanley's—thin, bearded, gaunt men with hollow cheeks and the marks of strain and pain around their eyes. Their uniforms are ripped and covered with dried mud. Their slouch hats are pulpy and shapeless. Stretcher cases are jolting back on crude log litters on the shoulders of brawny Papuan natives. The others have walked all the way along the terrible track that links Moresby with Kokoda. They don't try to conceal what they've been through. It's only by realizing the difficulties our troops are facing that we shall be able to overcome them.

"Up there we've been fighting on the worst battleground in the world," one man said. "Before I was hit I spent forty-six hours without shutting an eye. There are mists creeping over the trees all day, and sometimes you can't see your hand in front of your face under the cover of the jungle. Most of our chaps haven't seen a Jap! You don't even see the Jap who gets you! It's like fighting the invisible man. Those Japs are tough, hard fighters and their camouflage is perfect. They can move through scrub or tall grass without making a sound and without showing a sign except—if your eyes are good—an occasional stirring in the vegetation.

"My unit made two attacks on Japanese positions. We got to within 15 feet of them, but we still couldn't see them. When they were attacking we could hear a voice shouting from some distance back. We soon learnt that trick. The voice always comes from a long way back, but the real danger is the Jap force right up close to you. The Japs have amazing patience. They will lie on the ground or stand in a creek up to their necks in water all day without moving, just waiting to catch you off guard. They use the old trick of calling out false orders, and sometimes they begin jabbering to you from only a few yards away. If you stood up to cover them with your rifle a sniper would take a crack at you from a different direction. At the moment they're all over us, but they've got five times the number of men we have."

Another Victorian (he had celebrated his nineteenth birthday in the Owen Stanley's) had been out with our scouting patrols. "The Jap patrols travel much lighter than we do, and they don't stick to the tracks," he explained. "It's nerve-wracking work. You mightn't see a thing for hours and then suddenly two patrols meet on a narrow twisting track through the jungle trees. Most of the fighting is done at a range of a few yards, and the man who is quickest on the drop is the man who comes home."

Unfortunately there's going to be a great deal of hard fighting before we get them in the open. The militiamen under Major Bill Watson did all that could have been expected of them in holding the Japs at Kokoda for nearly a month. Watson told them to stand and fight, and they did. Many were killed, many more wounded, and when the Japs finally assembled their striking force and pushed into the mountains we could not hold them. For a day or two the Australian line held, but the other Militia battalion up near Isurava Ridge couldn't resist the pressure and the Japs broke through. It's been chaos ever since. One of the A.I.F. battalions which reached the danger area after a bitter forced march up the slimy, precipitous trail over the southern flanks of the Owen Stanley's, had to be thrown in without rest or food to try and stem the rout. The Japs attacked them from the front and two sides and infiltrated behind them. The whole battalion has since been cut into small sections and scattered over the dripping mountain jungles. Our casualties must have been heavy. On the track back to Moresby there are long lines of loyal Papuans, slipping and stumbling back with crude stretchers on their shoulders. It will take the wounded at least a fortnight of agony to reach the safety of a base hospital.

Today we are retreating through the pass in the mountains, fighting a desperate and bloody rearguard action six and a half thousand feet above the sea. Reinforcements are attempting to struggle up the track, but supply is the big problem. The Japs are advancing, with good equipment and sufficient troops, from a firm supply base established at Kokoda. Our supply has almost reached saturation point. It is very doubtful if we can feed and provide ammunition for a force numerically greater than the one we have up there near Isurava. And much of that force is exhausted by long weeks of constant battle and unbelievable fighting conditions. The survivors of one battalion have been in action for forty days on light rations—and on every day but four it has rained, real tropic rain that soaks clothing to the skin and never dries out at night. While these men were fighting larger forces of our most experienced A.I.F. infantrymen were struggling up through the mountains to take the battle over from worn-out men who had fought the Japs through the rain-sodden forests for more than a month and who had killed more than 700 of the enemy. They lost the race. Fresh Japanese troops, coming on in waves, and slipping through the jungle tracks like phantoms, had made the critical break-through before our men could be relieved. The survivors of the Militia force —wounded, riddled with fever, tropical ulcers and dysentery—stumbled back through the Gap, but they had taught the Jap that he would have to fight men who also could fight in the jungle. Already the Japs have lost 1500 killed and an unknown number wounded since the first fighting began at Kokoda. But they are pushing on. Today a couple of A.I.F. companies are doggedly holding the track through the pass at Templeton's Crossing while the rest of our troops withdraw to make a stand at Myola.

The Japanese are using the same tactics that won them such swift and easy success in Malaya. The basis is movement, which is closely and scientifically adapted to the terrain. In these dripping, shadowy mountain jungles the foot soldier has to do the work of the tank and the reconnaissance plane. He has to find the enemy, feel for the weakness in his position, break through and cut up his supply lines. That is exactly what the Jap has been doing. If we had the numbers—and the supplies—perhaps we could hold him. The Japs are disregarding their losses—we estimate that they have more than 5000 men in the mountains—and they are burrowing into the scrub and nibbling their way forward like beavers. They are just as hard to find. The troublesome factor for our troops is that they are fighting an enemy they can't even see. Seventy-five per cent of the soldiers who have been constantly in action—including the wounded —have never seen a single Japanese soldier! That seems to be their greatest complaint.

According to the calendar it must be spring in New Guinea. The calendar is never wrong, but it is a curious spring. Each morning the sun burns as dully as ever through the overcast. Late in the afternoon the southeast trade wind rises and the mosquitoes take shelter in huts and tents for the evening meal.

The only difference is the rain. A month ago the Moresby area was a small but realistic imitation of the Middle West dust bowl. A few downpours have kneaded the thick surface dust into a paste which is hammered into concrete by the chained wheels of hundreds of army lorries. All night you can hear the jingling of the chains as the trucks rumble along the first stage of the road up into the mountains, the road to the battlefront.

You only hear these sleigh bells along the first stage. The bitumen does not last very far. It is an earth road that winds through the scrubby hills inland from Port Moresby and climbs laboriously through the river gorge to the rich rubber country. As you climb the clouds close in, the country becomes richer, as rich as an English parkland, and the track grows soggier. By the time you have reached the forests on the south side of the Owen Stanley Range, it is a long mud trail where lorries choke and struggle up the hillsides and slither down like crabs. Small, heroic bands of soldiers labor, stripped to the waist, in the moist semi-darkness to keep the trucks moving through to the roadhead, where mules or porters will take over the traffic and lump the precious supplies farther on towards the front.

There is very little in common between this country and the yellow grass and shaggy, stunted gums of Moresby. Down on the coast the few early showers do not mean very much. They are a foretaste of the rainy season to come, but if the seasons hold to their routine, the real wet should not begin before November. Then the clouds press down on the hilltops, the rain teems over the brown land, and the months of mildew, mosquitoes, and tropical sores have to be faced.

Farther up it rains for months before this season. Over the range the high country is covered with rain forest, a sodden, fungoid vegetation far different from the riotous matted jungle of the lower slopes. It is colder country, free from mosquitoes and more easily penetrable, as the Japanese know. Over large areas of New Guinea now it rains almost daily. At Milne Bay our troops had to wade through feet of mud kept soft by a daily downpour. An airman who walked across New Guinea from a point near the north coast, where he made a parachute landing, told me that it rained without stopping for six days. At night he used his parachute as a tent, and painfully dried himself out in sections. A few minutes after he had started hiking again he would be soaked to the skin.

It has been called the world's worst battleground, and this is probably not an idle boast. As the rain spreads to the drier areas it will make movement still more difficult, and maintenance of troops will be a greater problem. Air war will be further cramped because it is impossible to come down through the perpetual overcast and search for targets in steady rain when a deviation of a few miles from a true course might mean a crash into a mountain.

An extension of the rainy areas is not going to make things easier for our ground troops or our air troops in New Guinea. They are not easy now. A.I.F. troops accustomed to fighting in the open country of Syria or the dead wastes of the Western Desert have faced a new test in the rainsodden, tangled vegetation of New Guinea. I have seen A.I.F. men back from the fighting on one of New Guinea's battlefronts who spoke wistfully about Cairo and Tel-Aviv.

"The Middle East was a cinch to this," one of them told me. "You could move there, and you could see whom you were fighting. Out here it's a hell of a job walking a couple of miles. And finding the Japs in this blanky jungle is like looking for a needle in a haystack. Don't let anybody fool you. This is the toughest place we've fought in yet."

This is the country where Australia's Army is fighting its first battles against the Japanese advance guard. Make no mistake: they are still fighting the battle for Australia up in the rain forests of the Owen Stanley Range and in the matted slush of Milne Bay. These are the pinpoints where the vast Japanese war machine is drifting against the outer crust of Australia's defenses. Australians are fighting in these appalling conditions because if they do not fight in front of Port Moresby there will be no positions to fight the battle for Australia outside of Australia itself.

All through the winter months the land war hung fire in New Guinea. The war was going on in the air; the ack-ack men had plenty to do, but the infantry took part in the war only when Japanese fighters and bombers unloaded iron-mongery on them. In the last two months the position has changed. The main enemy is no longer monotony: the Japanese thrust against Moresby is real and tangible. The battle for New Guinea is on, and everybody knows it. The Japanese shock troops who fought through the Malayan jungles in the summer months have been toughened and experienced in jungle fighting. It suits them well to fight the next round in tropical New Guinea, but the knowledge that they are facing a tough and well-prepared enemy has never before reduced Australian armed forces to defeatism, and it is not doing so now.

The calendar says it is spring in New Guinea, which means about two months to the rainy season. Those two months are not going to be wasted by either army. They may well decide the fate of New Guinea and the whole character of the next phase in the Pacific war.

The troops have sensed this, and it has changed their attitude already. The minor irritations seem less important than before, and there is even a curious affection creeping into their remarks about the much-cursed shantytown of Moresby. I met a young Victorian from a signals unit who was coming down the road, grimy and bearded, after three grueling weeks in the front line on the Kokoda sector. He was obviously worn out, but was making a pretense of being cheerful and hardy, a pretense that deceived only himself. He kept leaning out of the rattling truck that was jolting us down the road. As we rounded a bend that showed a steep valley running down through the foothills toward Port Moresby, 19 miles away, his eyes lighted and he smiled.

"My oath," he said, "it's grand being back in civilization again!"

I never thought I'd hear that said about Port Moresby. But everything, as I think I've said before, is a matter of relative values.

### The Generals Talk

I have been trying to sort out the bits and pieces of this strangely tangled campaign. There has been the periodical clamping down by censorship. It isn't that the censorship tries to stifle truth in order to permit the release of news which is false. It merely crushes everything in these periodical outbursts, for no apparent reason, and limits release of news to the bare terms of the official communiqués, which are often about as loquacious as a deaf mute with both arms cut off.

I've had a long talk with Major-General George Kenney, new Commander-in-Chief of Allied Air Forces in the southwest Pacific. He took over from Lieutenant-General Brett on 4 August, about two weeks before Brett went back to the United States. Kenney has impressed all of us as exactly the right man for the job.

He is very short, very chunky, very bristly about the hair, very scarred about the face. He knows flying and he knows fighting, because he flew long range reconnaissance planes for the French Army in the last war. He is dynamic, and he *thinks,* and the sentence he hates more than any other is, "It can't be done!" What is more important is that he has the rare capacity of being able to convey his own outlook to his men—and the spirit of the Allied Air Forces is all the better for it.

The High Command is pretty anxious to get large numbers of reinforcements and heavy supplies up to New Guinea to stop the Japanese advance. Kenney said he'd fly the whole lot in with his aircraft. Everybody said: "Oh, but it can't be done!" That got Kenney's back up. He snapped: "Give me the planes and a few days to make arrangements and I'll fly in the whole goddam United States army!"

At the present time he has every spare bomber and every spare transport plane flying troops and war materials into New Guinea in one of the biggest air transportation feats since Crete. Kenney thinks it will be 100 per cent successful, and if he thinks that, then I feel that it will be 100 per cent successful. He inspires you with just that sort of confidence.

Kenney took over the air job at a difficult time, and since then we have built up a staggering record of achievement. In the Papuan skies our planes have won an outstanding air superiority. Repeatedly the Japs have tried to establish an air base in support of their advancing ground troops at Buna. Each time the Allied fighters and bombers have roared into them and brought them down like ninepins. In the first three days the Japs lost 19 Zeros over Buna, to the loss of one of our fighters. The figure now is 36 Zeros down to two American planes! And the Japs still haven't been able to make the slightest use of the Buna air strips, now littered with the debris of crushed and burnt-out Zero fighters.* In addition the

---

* Eventually 100 Japanese planes were destroyed on Buna air strip. The planes were caught on the ground, and the Japanese were *never* able to use the field operationally.

bombers and fighters under Kenney's command have kept up a non-stop blitz on the Japanese supply dumps and lines of communication from Buna to the Owen Stanley's. It's too early yet to assess the effect of this constant hammering, but Kenney is confident that it will defeat the Japs in the mountains. In the densely covered jungles outright attacks on fighting troops rarely do much good, but the hamstringing of their supply lines will have an incalculable effect now that the Japs are in the lonely, hungry, incredibly tough country of the southern Owen Stanley's. And don't forget that in the last two days—quite apart from fighter strafing—fifty tons of bombs have been dropped on the Japanese positions north of the range.

Kenney believes that in the last month Japanese plane losses in New Guinea, New Britain and the Solomons exceed total Japanese production for that period. "But we have to shoot down three Japanese planes to every one of ours we lose if we want to keep on top," he added. "We're doing it—as much as five to one, and we'll keep on bettering that ratio if we can. Our big problem is supply. The Japs can fly their bombers *and fighters* direct from the factories to the Pacific war zones. But there are no stepping stones between Australia and America as there are between New Guinea and Tokyo. Our fighters have to be crated to Australia."

Among his pilots Kenney is trying hard to destroy the myth of "invincibility of the Zero."

"If you want to sacrifice weight you can always get altitude," he says. "That's what the Japs have done with the Zero. They have sacrificed the safety of the pilot and the gas tanks. If one gets a good burst it almost always comes down in flames or the wings come off. It's true that the Japs get certain results, but they lose an awful lot of planes. And they lose an awful lot of pilots because they sacrifice things like armor protection—things that we intend to keep."

It's undeniable that the Japs have lost a great number of Zeros and equally true that many of their best pilots have gone. The quality of the Jap fighter pilot has deteriorated amazingly in recent weeks. They are still using Zeros of the type that gave us many headaches in New Guinea two and three months ago, that won tactical superiority against our best fighters—and held it for many weeks. But the planes are now being flown by pilots of the Japanese army of completely different calibre from their navy pilots. That's why they are becoming increasingly easy to bring down.

"Anyway," Kenney added, "I've yet to meet the Australian or American fighter pilot who will trade his Kittyhawk for a Zero!" The general, by the way, has the greatest regard for the two Australian Kittyhawk squadrons which have just carried out such a grand job at Milne Bay. "The pilots in those squadrons have no superior in the world. I would back 'em in competition against Germans, American, British, Japanese or any other airmen in the world. They have got the guts and determination to tackle anything put up against 'em."

Kenney is quite confident about the war in New Guinea, and his confidence is contagious. "We're burning up Hirohito's planes on the ground as fast as he can put 'em there. For five days we haven't had a single plane intercepted. Our job is to pump holes in the enemy's air umbrella, and at the same time throw an umbrella over our own forces. That's how we'll win this war—upstairs and downstairs."

General Sir Thomas Blamey, Commander-in-Chief of Allied Land Forces in the southwest Pacific, has been visiting his troops in New Guinea and he is equally confident about the outcome of a campaign which, at the moment, admittedly looks grave. But, as he took care to explain, every man in New Guinea, from senior officers down to privates, was quite confident that the Japs would never take Moresby. The gloomy view taken of the Japanese advance—so widespread on the mainland that it was occasionally not far removed from panic—petered out as he moved northward. On the fighting front there was a complete absence of gloom and pessimism.

"The Japs are already feeling the difficulties of supply," he added. "They have a few light mountain guns but they have no chance of getting heavy supplies along that terrible track, with its precipices and jagged ridges and awful river crossings and great stretches of track that are merely moving streams of black mud. Moresby is in no danger, and I think we shall find that the Japs will be beaten by their own advance, with its attendant problems of supply. It will be a Japanese advance to disaster, an Australian retreat to victory."

I was glad to find, when he was speaking to us, that General Blamey paid a tribute to the work of the Papuan native carriers. Our good treatment of the natives in the past has earned us rich rewards. "These natives can't be given too much praise," he said. "They've carried stretchers through feet deep mud with the Australian wounded, down slimy defiles, through terrible jungles. They were almost at the point of exhaustion, but they always kept two men awake at night to take care of the patients, to wash their muddy limbs, to attend to their bandages and to give them their meals. The work of these natives has been astounding. We owe them a lasting debt."

General Blamey intends to return to New Guinea to establish his headquarters in the field. There is a widespread rumor that General MacArthur, the Commander-in-Chief, as well as General Kenney, will also move northward to Moresby. It will stimulate morale on the island if these stories are true—not that morale seems to need much stimulating at the moment.

While we are on the subject of the Higher Command, it might be interesting to set down a speech that General MacArthur has just given to the United States infantry who will go into action for the first time soon against the Japs. This particular division is being flown into New Guinea, and MacArthur's talk is an almost classical summing-up of the answer to that question which is asked so often these days: "How can we beat the Jap?"

"The Japanese soldier is no easy enemy," said the General. "He is a hard fighter, and one who fights courageously and intelligently. He gives no quarter. He asks for no quarter. His tactics are to disperse along his enemy's lines rapidly in groups of never more than 1000, and often half that number, and keep pushing in until he finds where his enemy is and then hit him. The Japanese are the greatest exploiters of inefficient and incompetent troops the world has ever seen. When the Jap contacts this sort of troops nothing can stop him.

"Never let the Jap attack you. Make it a fundamental rule, whatever your position might be, to be prepared for an attack. When the Japanese soldier has a co-ordinated plan of attack he works smoothly. When he is attacked—when he doesn't know what is coming—it isn't the same.

"The Japanese soldier has an extraordinary capacity to fight on to the end. He never stops. He believes that if he surrenders his enemy will kill him, or that if the enemy doesn't kill him he will be executed when he returns to Japan. He has no use for a quitter. Some soldiers have shown a tendency when they get into a tough spot or when it looks hopeless in front of them to fall back. That is the end.

"All I ask of you men when you go into action is that each of you shall kill one Japanese. If you do you will win. But if, when you are hard pressed, you begin to look for a position in the rear, or begin to think it beyond human endurance to continue the fight, you will not only be destroyed physically but you will lose your reputation in the eyes of your friends and your country.

"The psychological factor is three times the material factors, which, translated, simply means that if a man has the fighting courage, even if he has poor equipment and poor training, and if he has the fighting spirit, he will win. Always, the fellow wins who fights to the end, whose nerves don't go back on him, who never thinks of anything but the will to victory. That's what I want of you men—and that's what I expect."

A good many things have been happening on the fighting fronts. Most important, of course, is the fact that the "impassable" barrier of the Owen Stanley's hasn't held up the Japs. They are through the pass and advancing through the dripping trees and muddy tracks somewhere between Menari and Ioribaiwa Ridge, well into the southern flanks of the range. You hear a bit of talk these days— and it's highly dangerous talk—about the "invincibility" of the Japs as jungle fighters. It isn't that the Japs are invincible. It's merely that they happen to outnumber our men by three to one. Moreover, they are better equipped than our fellows for this sort of fighting. They are still employing their well-tested tactics of flank attack and infiltration synchronized with heavy frontal assault. Their object always seems to be to try to cut large bodies of Australians into small sections and then annihilate those sections one by one. Our troops have countered many of these moves with the point of the bayonet—which the Japs dislike more than any other weapon—and many of our patrols have been engaged in desperate hand-to-hand clashes in the shadowy wilderness of the range. Both Australians and Japs are using heavy mortar barrages extensively.

Along tangled tracks in the jungle-choked ravines, and across the terrible sawtooth ridges of slate and limestone thousands of men are waging the bloodiest battle of the New Guinea war. Casualties on both sides have been very heavy. The front line now is only ten minutes' flying time from our airfields. Airacobras and Havoc attack planes are shuttling backward and forward to harass the Japanese positions. This is tough, anxious flying. Today our planes began their attacks in clear weather, diving down the steep face of a mountain to rake the huts in the squalid little village of Efogi which the Japs are using as a forward supply base. For a few minutes Japanese machine-gunners fought back at the plummeting planes, but eventually they were all silenced and our planes left every hut in flames. Within a few hours the clouds had closed in, but our fighters courageously went through the gray blanket and hedge-hopped along the narrow, twisting mountain track to machine gun the enemy supply points and troop concentrations.

I am confident that the jungle, with its attendant problems of supply, will lick the Japs. They are now facing the difficulties which caused our retreat from Kokoda, when we could not maintain almost impossible supply lines across a scarcely negotiable goat-track. The Japs are having the same trouble. And they are advancing ahead of themselves. They don't stop to establish large, well-concealed supply dumps that might be immune from our air attacks. They don't even stop to establish hygiene and sanitation facilities which would help them to cut their sickness casualties. We hear persistent reports of fever and dysentery raging through the enemy lines.

The Japs covered the first 60 miles of their advance from Buna in five days. To push ahead another 30 miles, however, has taken them fifty days, and the speed of their advance slackens every day. Meanwhile we are building up a powerful, well-supplied jungle force on Imita Ridge. Field artillery—25-pounders—has been lugged up by sheer miracle. When the time comes to hit back we shall be able to hit back hard. That time is not far away. When we start to advance the enemy, weakened by his drive through a country of unbelievable difficulty, will be pushed right out of the Owen Stanley's.

One of the reasons why we have had almost complete immunity from the Japanese air arm is the fact that the enemy has been trying desperately to recapture Guadalcanal from the U. S. marines. Their attempts have cost them many aircraft and many ships. It's true that we have lost another aircraft carrier, the *Wasp,* but the Japs have lost the carrier *Ryujo,* as well as transports, cruisers and destroyers. Aircraft losses have been tremendous, and we've been able to contribute quite a share to the nice round total that is building up. The Japs failed yesterday in another attempt to establish Buna as an advanced fighter base, leaving 17 burnt-out Zeros as souvenirs on the ground when our Fortresses, Marauders, Havocs and Airacobras had finished with them.

The expected attack by the Japs from Mubo toward the Bulolo Valley hasn't come off. The three-pronged drive on Moresby isn't working out the way it was planned. Two of the prongs have lopped off, and the third shows signs of bending.

### *End of a Retreat*

The Japs, less than a week ago, were down to Ioribaiwa Ridge, only 32 miles from Port Moresby. They had only two more ridges to cross before they would have been clear of the southern foothills of the Owen Stanley's and on the motor road leading to the garrison. When the wind was in the right direction you could faintly hear the rumble of battle from Moresby itself.

From the rearmost garrison camp to the front line was only a few hours' walking in a green and sodden hell of forest and mountain, where the track switchbacks under rich and riotous foliage festooned with crimson parasites. A greenish light filters through the trees. The track is a tunnel floored with stinking mud. It never seems to stop raining. Everybody is soaked to the skin. It is unsafe to light fires near the "front," so everybody will stay soaked. "What the hell," someone says. "It's raining on the Japs, too, isn't it?"

The seriously wounded were being carried down. Others had to fend for themselves. One man who had been wounded in both arms was laboriously sliding down a slope on his tail, working himself forward with his feet. "I never thought I'd be crawling away from the Nips," he grinned. Acts of great gallantry up there were passing almost unnoticed. One of the bravest men has been a liaison officer who has become almost a legend with the men. Each day he sets out to look for information, equipped with two revolvers, two bandoliers, a sniping rifle, a pocketful of grenades, and two sticks. With this armory he has bagged a Japanese soldier a day, besides collecting his information.

The Jap advance ceased on September 16. Now the Australian retreat has ended. Today our forward troops began to advance from Imita Ridge back along the track to Kokoda. Their progress didn't amount to much more than a couple of miles, but it's a refreshing change from the constant story of retreat and withdrawal.

In the occasional gaps in the jungle our green-clad infantrymen can see a heavy column of golden smoke hanging in the still air above Ioribaiwa. The American bombers have been busy against the Jap positions at Nauro Creek. Pilots coming in report little sign of movement on the track, but air observation in this sort of country is almost valueless, and we have now reached the conclusion that strafing or bombing in the jungle, unless aimed at supply points, doesn't amount to much more than a waste of bombs and ammunition. Troops cannot—and do not—expect close air support in this sort of country. It's been worked out now that the best plan is to strike at known supply points and rear bases because you can kill an enemy more certainly in the Owen Stanley's by choking off his supplies than by hunting for him with a gun. That policy is bearing fruit now.

Scouting patrols are now well forward of Ua-ule Creek. One patrol came back today after having pushed several miles behind the Japanese lines in search of the 75-millimetre gun that has been sending over a few shells lately in answer to the salvos from our 25-pounders. They sighted it perched on a high knoll, which they couldn't reach. They could see the crew lolling around waiting orders from an officer standing with binoculars to his eyes. The Australians took careful aim and killed the officer and half the crew before they were forced to withdraw to escape a strong enemy patrol sent out to get them. Another patrol ambushed a Jap patrol on the southern slopes of Ioribaiwa and killed six of them.

These patrols of ours are bringing in a heap of valuable information and we don't lose any time in exploiting our knowledge. Some of our fellows went out last night and found the Japs frantically digging new trenches and weapon pits on the southern slopes of the Ioribaiwa spur. Behind them coolies—the Japs have brought in a number of Tamils from Malay, who are working with the impressed "chain gang" from Rabaul—were working on a network of new tracks through the flanks and widening the old main track.

The information was sent back to our 25-pounders and within a few minutes shells were whistling through the driving rain across two mountain ridges and bursting nicely dead in the centre of the new enemy positions. All activity ceased and the Japs scuttled back across the protecting spur.

Behind Imita new Australian forces are assembling. There's a constant procession of hard-faced, green-uniformed Australians moving northward along the slimy mountain track. Hundreds of muscular natives are slithering through the rain with great loads of machine-gun ammunition and mortar bombs and grenades. The Japs certainly won't get any closer to Moresby. And if our advance goes as it's planned they might be many miles farther away before this week is out.

# V. THE CLEANSING

*September 28, 1942—January 23, 1943*

---

*The Jungle Won*

**B**LASTED by the shells of our 25-pounders firing across Ua-ule Valley, the mountain ridge and village of Ioribaiwa, limit of the Japanese advance toward Port Moresby, was captured today, Sept. 28, by the A.I.F. and our troops are pushing ahead through a heavy rainstorm toward Nauro Creek, Menari, Efogi and the rest of the scattered villages that line the "Kokoda Trail."

The Japs offered little resistance, although they had built up a high timber palisade across the top of the ridge in front of an involved system of weapon pits and trenches. The 25-pounders blew great holes in the palisade and the Australians went in with the bayonets and grenades. The Japs didn't wait for any more. They scuttled northward through the jungle, abandoning a stack of unburied dead, a great dump of equipment and ammunition, and leaving to us the steep ridge down which we retreated only a couple of weeks ago with the Japs rolling stones and grenades down on us and plastering our rearguard with fierce mortar and machine-gun fire.

The Japs have left a lot of graves on Ioribaiwa Ridge, and trampled in the mud between the bodies of the dead is an elaborate shirt of scarlet silk with a black dragon embroidered on it. Most of the corpses are emaciated. Blamey was right about letting the jungle beat the Japs. The evidence scattered everywhere along the track and through the jungle is that this Japanese army was at the point of starvation and riddled with scrub typhus and dysentery. The stench of the dead and the rotting vegetation and the foetid mud is almost overpowering. One of our doctors carried out a couple of autopsies. Many of the Japs, he said, had died because hunger had forced them to eat the poisonous fruits and roots of the jungle. It's clear now that the enemy stopped at Ioribaiwa Ridge because he was humanly incapable of thrusting ahead any farther. Our progress will profit by these grim reminders of an advance that went too fast. The Australians are pushing ahead very cautiously, building up store dumps and medical posts as they go, taking meticulous care about sanitation and hygiene, advancing in three prongs that are exploring every side track and cleansing every yard of jungle as they go.

In this dense terrain of matted vegetation and half-hidden native *pad-pads* and steep gorges there are the ever present threats of ambush, counter-infiltration and outflanking. But the Australians are climbing slowly and grimly up the southern flanks of the Owen Stanley's with the knowledge that the only Japanese behind their thrusting spearheads are dead ones.

### Coal-Black Killer

Today, squat, broad-shouldered, well-muscled, fierce-eyed Sergeant Katue, coal-black warrior of the all-native Papuan Infantry Battalion—a force which has done magnificent work on jungle patrols since the Japanese landing ten weeks ago—walked into an Australian post with a scared-looking Japanese prisoner. Katue created a profound impression. Apparently he intended to, because stitched to his standard khaki tunic was a mass of stripes, badges and regimental insignia which Katue had taken from 26 Japanese soldiers and marines, all of whom had been killed by this tough Papuan native during a spectacular two months' patrol inside the Japanese-occupied areas north of the range.

Gunmen of the Wild West cut a notch in their revolver butts to signify each victim. Katue merely cut off their sergeants or corporals' stripes, or marines' insignia, or lieutenants' badges, and stitched them on around his own three red sergeants' stripes until his jacket outshone the uniform of a Patagonian grand admiral.

When I spoke to him today he grinned widely, showing an expanse of broken teeth, blackened by betel nut, and in pidgin English carefully explained the rank and fate of each former owner of each piece of enemy insignia. Several of his victims were privates, with no badges to take, although Katue made it clear that he had tried to concentrate on the top men, and he shrugged his shoulders lugubriously as he explained why he didn't have more stripes on his already resplendent uniform.

"Some Japanese, he no good. He wear nothing worth taking."

So just to keep the records straight Katue brought back a cloth cap, bearing the anchor insignia of the Japanese marines, which one of his victims had been wearing.

Katue is aged about thirty-five, and before joining the army in June, 1940, he had a Papua-wide reputation for valor as a police boy. On one occasion he swam a flooded river with a rope round his waist to save three white officers from certain death. He is believed to have saved the lives of more white men than any other native in the territory.

Katue's amazing saga of adventure against the Japanese began after they landed at Gona Mission. It ended seventy-three days later. He had been left by his patrol in a native village to recover from muscular pains brought on by incessant mountain patrols. As he was resting he saw 10 Japanese soldiers walking towards him. He was unable to raise his rifle to his shoulder, so he crawled from the village and hid in the scrub. He decided to wage a deadly and stealthy private jungle war against the Japanese. Picking up two native boys from his patrol he set out, and three days later three Japanese were seen riding bicycles. The two natives raised their rifles, but Katue restrained them.

"If you miss, plenty trouble," he said. "If Katue shoot, no miss."

And Katue promptly killed the three Japanese with three bullets.

The fighting sergeant moved like a black phantom through the dripping jungles, recruiting men as he went, until eventually his little private army numbered fourteen. Next day they saw a Japanese soldier climbing an orange tree. Katue picked him off from long range with a bullet through the brain. The noise of the shot brought sixteen Japanese running from a hut near by. Katue's men met them with withering fire, and four Japanese fell dead and the rest fled.

Some time later they came to a storehouse filled with food. So as to prevent its falling into Japanese hands Katue burnt it to the ground. A party of six Japanese soldiers with two native guides came trotting along to investigate the fire. Katue shot and killed the eight of them. By this time the little native force was out of ammunition, and they trekked for days through terrible country to an Australian base, where they obtained additional weapons and ammunition, and set out on their self-imposed job again. They went back into the country which was being terrorized by the wild Orokaivas—a tribe which has been helping the Japs ever since the landing (of which more later)—and the little native army patrolled the jungles, organizing villages to guard bridges and key points, training them to refuse to give the Japanese any cooperation. Some of the villagers didn't need prompting. Some did—and Katue was just the man to do it. He would stand no nonsense!

In one village the head man came out wearing long pants, a frock coat, a Japanese helmet, six stripes and a huge tin medal—all gifts from the Japanese—and refused to cooperate with Katue. A few minutes later, after Katue had very effectively demonstrated his intention, the quaking headman was completely pro-ally. He scaled a coconut palm and pointed out to Katue three Japanese soldiers walking along the track toward the village. Katue strolled out to meet them, killed two and captured the third. That was the captive he brought in today, together with a great bundle of captured Japanese equipment, including a couple of tommy guns. In his seventy-three-day jungle war in miniature Katue never had one man wounded or even sick. They lived entirely on indigenous fruits and what native food they could get from villages, and they traveled hundreds of miles.

When I asked Katue what he intended to do next he grinned at me. "Go out again quicktime," he said. "This time I bring back stripes of Japanese general!" And he ambled off into the bush roaring with laughter.*

In addition to the "escape" stories this war in New Guinea has started an avalanche of what might be termed "general human interest" stories. One of the strangest and most moving of these was the drama of Anton Ringel, eighty-two-year-old Czech gold-miner, which has just ended after forty-five years.

It ended when an unkempt figure in torn gray trousers and a stained felt hat barely covering a great mane of uncut silver hair walked barefooted into Port Moresby to board a ship that would take him out of the land that had given him nothing but hardship and sorrow for almost half a century.

* Katue was later decorated with the Military Medal.

War had done what personal tragedy, uncivilized natives, hunger, and disease had failed to do—drive the old man away from the primitive shack on the top of New Guinea's towering mountains.

Ringel first came to New Guinea in 1897 after having failed to find gold in the Louisiade Islands. Alone, except for native carriers, he fought his way through hostile tribes to the top slopes of 13,000-foot Mount Albert Edward, where he set up his prospecting plant and made his home. He made one fortune and lost the gold on the trip to the coast. He made a second fortune, and this time went on a visit to Austria. But the Great War broke out. Ringel lost all his money, and was conscripted for an Austrian labor gang. He was married soon after arriving in Austria, and raised a family, but the call of New Guinea was too strong. In 1924, with his fourteen-year-old son, he returned to the island and to his tumbledown shack up in the mists and rains of Mount Albert Edward. The field was almost worked out, but Ringel would not leave. The old man and his son stayed on in that awful solitude, with only native laborers for companions.

It was too much for the youngster, who went insane. Old Ringel sent him to an asylum in Queensland, where for years he paid for his treatment out of meagre earnings. What little was left over after his laborers had been paid went to his wife in Austria. The son died six years ago. Ringel stayed on in his mountain eyrie. When he needed stores he walked barefooted through mountain jungles to Ioma, 40 miles away.

The Japanese landed at Gona and moved up the Kokoda track; the old miner was cut off. At first he refused to leave, but eventually he was persuaded to come to safety. Traveling barefooted over the mountain summit and through jungle, he reached a coastal village, where he immediately marched up to the military officer in charge to ask permission to return to his mine. His request was refused gently, and he was advised to go to the mainland for a while. Ringel quietly accepted the decision, lifted his few belongings wrapped in soiled calico on to his thin shoulders and marched up the wharf with the sunshine gleaming on his great mop of silver hair. Then he turned round and called out: "I'll be back soon."

And Anton Ringel left the territory. Those who watched him go wondered whether he *would* come back again.

*Valley of Silence*

From the crest of Imita Ridge the vast valley of Ua-ule Creek lay like a bowl of tumbled green jungle held between the jagged purple peaks of the lower Owen Stanley's. The three-toothed ridge of Ioribaiwa guarded the other side of the valley with an almost unbroken wall of jungle, clear in the tropical light. Beyond the afternoon thunderheads were massing above and between the rising peaks of the range. The rolling clouds had beheaded the great bulk of Mount Urawa and scattered tufts and wisps of cotton-wool across the flanks of distant Maguli.

The valley below was silent. The only sound was the soft hiss and drip of rain among the great jungle trees of Imita Ridge. But no sound came from Ua-ule Valley for no man lived there—not even a native—and the only movement was the play of shadows across the matted trees. In all that great waste of dark green the only relief was a tiny square clearing of kunai grass splodged an unbelievable emerald by the patchy sun.

Behind us was the soft murmur of voices and the sucking slither of many feet moving through the muddy clay . . . occasionally a sudden shout that echoed through the trees. The carrier line stopped only for a moment on the crest of the ridge. There was a yabbering of Motu and the hill dialects, a few softly spoken orders in pidgin from a stocky A.I.F. supply corporal.

Biscuit tins clanged metallically together as the carriers lurched splayfootedly down the steep, muddy trail that snaked through the green tunnel of the jungle, sweat shining on dark muscles, mud stains smearing the vivid red, green and yellow of lap-laps. The brilliant splashes of color drained away as the serpentine column of natives moved slowly into the deepening shadows of the trees. The slap-slap of native feet had ceased before the last frizzy head had disappeared into the green depths below. Once or twice, very faintly, the clanging of the biscuit tins came up to us . . . and then all sound was swallowed by the utter silence of the Ua-ule Valley.

By the time the sun had gone from the kunai patch the carriers probably were laboriously seeking footholds on the stepping-stones along Ua-ule Creek where the mountain torrent snarled around polished rocks and tree trunks that had the appearance of weathered iron and the solidity of sponge cake.

From the slippery crest of the Imita Ridge we looked down on this strange, silent valley. From the native point of view it was rich and fertile. According to the age-old standards of Papuan husbandry it was the place for a village. But no village had ever been there. Ioribaiwa's few squalid grass huts straddling tumbling Orvi Creek were over the crest of the range that blotted out half the sky ahead of us. Behind us, beneath the bastion of Imita Ridge, were two tumbledown villages—one bearing the utterly incongruous name of Maritana, the other shouldering the cumbersome syllables of Gagabitano with all the unconcern of a Papuan carrier. Some said the valley was haunted. Perhaps it was the weird noise the hornbills made.

But generations of natives had shunned the deep silences of Ua-ule Valley: why nobody, not even the natives could tell. It had taken war to shatter that age-old loneliness with the shrill whistle of shells and the chatter of machine guns and the thud-thud-thud of mortars . . . and the cry of wounded and dying men. But the tide of war had flowed and ebbed and silence had come back to the valley. The few soldiers and the silent carrier trains that moved along the narrow, muddy ribbon that made no scar in the face of the jungle created only a whisper in that great green emptiness.

For war had moved on . . . and its legacy to the silent valley were a scene and a name and a handful of graves on the sloping flanks of Ioribaiwa Ridge. It was war's legacy to the valley and war's legacy to the history of a nation. For a nation's history is written, not in Hansard nor in the tabulated columns of a manufacturer's ledger, but in the quiet graves of that nation's people. Australia might never remember Imita Ridge and Ioribaiwa and the valley of Ua-ule as it remembers Gallipoli and it will remember Tobruk. But Ua-ule Valley is as much a part of Australia's history . . .

Down the north wall of this valley came the Japanese one day last month. For three bitter weeks they had driven everything before them. They had fought courageously, fanatically, mercilessly. Ragged, exhausted, hungry Australians straggled through the silent valley on their retreat to Imita Ridge, while the rearguard fought to stem the yellow tide on the crest of Ioribaiwa. Just as the enemy was hidden by that silent blanket of jungle so were the countless deeds of heroism.

In one tiny clearing a young Australian lay wounded by a sniper's bullet. His patrol was coming up behind him unaware of the hidden ambush. He could have feigned death and escaped when darkness came. Instead he shouted warnings and directions to his comrades. The enraged Japanese pumped more bullets into him but the Australian continued to direct his patrol. He was dead when his comrades returned after having wiped out the Japanese.

In the little patch of kunai grass that scarred the unbroken dark-green foam of the jungle young Australians had halted their withdrawal to try once more to check the inexorable Japanese advance. Three times the roar of machine guns echoed in the valley, three times the Japanese were mown down like corn ripe for the sickle. The Australians claimed 95 dead. They were officially credited with 50. But they broke the spear-point of the Japanese advance and the enemy retreated back to Ioribaiwa's ragged crest to lick his wounds.

On this same terrible slope six Victorians had squirmed to within six yards of the Japanese positions to silence a troublesome enemy gunpit and had killed every man in it. Across this mysterious valley had shrieked the 25-pounder shells from the Australian guns that held the Japanese and blasted them out of Ioribaiwa. For the Japanese never reached the foot of that valley of silence, never climbed the southern wall of Imita. Across this valley last week went the grim-faced green-uniformed Australians on the terrible march back to the crest of the path through the Owen Stanley's—and beyond.

The silence of centuries returned to the valley of Ua-ule. It was just as it had always been as we looked across to jagged Ioribaiwa, its edges softened by the veil of falling rain. That rain would be falling gently on those few crude crosses. Some would bear the crudely penciled names of Australians . . . one or two the simple words: "Unknown Australian Soldier."

No man can give more than life itself. These men had given that to the valley of silence that somehow seemed part of Australia itself. Their sacrifice was a heritage to their country's history.

By some freak of the valley and the lowering shroud of rain-clouds a thin sound tinkled up from the silent green depths—the sound of biscuit tins clanking together. . . .

*Wanigela Operation*

The biggest air transport operation of the southwest Pacific War —involving enormous organization and the handling of thousands of troops with all their supplies—was supposed to have been completed by noon today. It ended at 12:30 P.M., half an hour behind schedule, without the loss of a single soldier or a solitary piece of equipment. It's called the "Wanigela operation" and it's a magnificent tribute to the ability of General Kenney to get things done.

A whole United States striking force of thousands of men with all their equipment has been flown from the mainland of Australia to Port Moresby and then over the Owen Stanley Range to Wanigela, an improvised airfield on the north coast of Papua about 100 miles east of Buna. This force is to be the second arm of a gigantic pincer movement against the Japanese garrisons at Buna and Gona. Our troops now advancing into the pass through the mountains— with the Japs still in full retreat and not yet ready to make a determined stand—will form the first arm of the pincer when they break through the Owen Stanley's and reach the flat coastal plains north of Kokoda.

Every spare bomber and transport plane that Kenney could lay his hands on is being used for this enormous troop movement. The Americans were first flown 1000 miles from their training camps in Queensland to Moresby. Over on the other side of the range Australian officers were busy in a patch of kunai grass at Wanigela Mission area, where one of our Lockheed Hudsons had made a successful emergency landing months ago.

Willing natives, with missionaries helping, cut and flayed through the heat of the burning day at the head-high, saw-toothed kunai grass (they call it *lalong* grass on the north coast) until a crude strip had been carved out of the wilderness. It was good enough for a few planes to land, bringing in a company of A.I.F. engineers. After hours of back-breaking work with machetes, cane knives, and even bayonets, the Australian engineers had slashed out a runway, which from the air was a long straight swathe through the high grass, and flanked on either side by dense trees and jungle undergrowth. By nightfall the field was ready. The weary engineers slept, despite the attentions of innumerable weird and ferocious insects and the constant march of incredible thousands of scarlet soldier and spider crabs.

Heavy rain fell during the night, and the pickets on duty anxiously discussed the possibility of flooding, the fear that no planes would be able to land next morning on an emergency strip that by midnight was flowing with a torrent of water.

At dawn yesterday a reconnaissance bomber came over, cautiously circled a few times. The Australians watched anxiously. Landing wheels came down, flaps were lowered and the bomber came thundering in over the tree-tops and was put down in a perfect three-point landing. Australian slouch hats flew into the air, natives danced up and down with the contagious excitement, and the Japs at Buna should have been able to hear the cheering. A portable radio transmitter crackled details of the test landing.

It seemed only a few minutes before a sleek Douglas, first of the great air transport armada, crowded with green-uniformed American infantrymen and with every inch of space crowded with fighting equipment, thumped in over the trees and taxied down the strip. The American occupation of the north Papuan coast began even as nine other huge Douglases were circling round awaiting their turn to come in, and more were tiny specks coming down over the great ramparts of the range. Willing hands unloaded the great planes and swung them round to take off again to bring back other loads. By dusk more than 50 landings and take offs had been made without a hitch. Overhead patrolled swarms of allied fighters —at one time it was said we had "120 fighters up as top cover including a squadron of Lockheed Lightnings doing slow rolls at 35,000 feet!"—to ensure that if the Zeros did find out what was happening they wouldn't be able to do much about it.

As each plane landed Americans, Australians and natives rushed forward to unload and drag the precious freight hurriedly into the bushes. Fighter cover or not, they did not intend to give anything away to any casual Jap reconnaissance plane that might come over.

Each plane was loaded with mathematical care, every load calculated to the last pound. One pilot told me that weights had been checked to the last round of small arms ammunition. Everything was worked to a system whereby each plane carried exactly the number of troops needed to unload the entire freight in ninety seconds!

The average time each plane spent in landing, unloading and taking off was three and a half minutes. The last plane for the day left just as darkness was spreading over the jungle. Below, except for the dark wheel tracks made on the grass strip by the constant procession of planes, there was no sign of occupation. Yet down there, where a handful of Australian engineers, a couple of missionaries and a few natives had eaten breakfast that morning, a whole allied combat force numbering many hundreds of men was lining up for evening "chow" and cursing the mosquitoes and crabs and sandflies.

Moreover, in that one day of incredible activity the troops had dug in, established trenches, manned machine-gun and anti-aircraft positions, stacked their stores and equipment under cover, and prepared their quarters.

This morning the transport planes went in again in scores. Troops who had manhandled tons of heavy equipment by sheer sweat and muscle cheered and cheered again as the big Douglases unloaded U. S. army jeeps. Every three minutes a plane landed. While an R.A.A.F. sergeant-pilot supervised the running of the airfield with split second efficiency, Australian and American anti-aircraft gunners kept a close guard on the skies, and the Australian engineers, with native labor, looked after the maintenance of the strip. Australian-American-Papuan cooperation was perfect.

The main movement was completed half an hour after midday today. Planes will be going in for weeks, of course, with supplies and reinforcements. Australian commandos—the 6th A.I.F. Independent Company—are even now pushing westward through the swamps to blaze the trail for the infantry advance on Buna. From now on the net will tighten round the Japs.

The whole of this operation, from the Queensland mainland to the sago swamps of Wanigela, has been made without a single mishap. Every man has safely reached his destination. Every bullet and every pound of food has been moved hundreds of miles to the point in Papua where it is most needed. We are using aircraft to overcome the supply problem that defeated the Japanese.

One curious thing is that, of all days, the Japs had to pick yesterday to bring their Zeros back to the Papuan skies after a complete absence of several weeks. Fifteen Zeros tackled our bombers over Buna—we lost two bombers and the Japs lost five fighters—but the enemy was completely ignorant of the enormous and vitally important air movement which was being carried out right under his very nose. The job was continued today, also, with the Japs still in complete ignorance of the threat to their hold on Papua which is being built up at Wanigela.

NOTE: Later, several other air bases were established under almost identical circumstances at various points in a ring round Buna and very much closer to the enemy's central Papuan base. Some of these fields were less than 20 miles from Buna, and to them were flown hundreds of transport planes with reinforcements, supplies, food and ammunition for American and Australian troops. The total amount of equipment carried to forward positions by these air transports exceeded 1,000,000 tons!

### *"Miniature Coventry"*

Last night and the night before Rabaul has taken the heaviest hammering yet from Australian Catalinas and the strongest force of American Flying Fortresses ever sent out on one mission in the southwest Pacific. On a darkened airfield at midnight on the night before last I stood and watched thirty of the huge, heavily laden fortresses go into the air one after the other by the light of their own head lamps. Other planes were taking off after I had gone away, and the night was pulsing with the roar of many engines overhead. The noise increased and I went outside to see the force leaving. Overhead thundered the great four-engined planes, a huge lozenge-shaped mass of scarlet and emerald green navigation lights and occasional orange jets of sparks from throbbing motors. The same scene was repeated last night, on each occasion with support from other heavy bombers from different bases. The object of the raids has been to hit Rabaul town and nullify it, at least temporarily, as a supply base.

The men flying these bombers have done the job very capably indeed. More than 1000 high-explosive bombs—including many 2000-pounders—and innumerable incendiaries were dropped square in the heart of Rabaul. In the first raid a bomb fell in the target area every twelve seconds for ninety-five minutes. Pilots said that the whole target area was a sea of flames and explosions, and the Fortresses, attacking from various altitudes, were rolled about like ships in a gale by the fierce upcurrents of hot air from explosions.

The first wave of planes went in and dropped flares, but after that the fires provided sufficient light for every other plane to see his allotted target almost as clearly as in daylight.

Japanese searchlights and ground defenses were in full blast but most of these planes were piloted by veterans who have fought the Japs all the way from the Philippines to Java and on to New Guinea. When they had dropped their bombs they dived down and poured thousands of rounds of heavy machine-gun fire into the searchlight and anti-aircraft positions.

Bombs dropped by the second wave carved vivid strips through the docks and warehouse area, and the Chinatown section of the town—where the Japanese officers keep their Geisha girls—became a spreading mass of flame. "Business won't be very good in that area for quite a time," said one bombardier.

The final wave of planes went in to find every searchlight extinguished and not a single anti-aircraft gun in action. "It was like looking down on a miniature Coventry," one R.A.A.F. co-pilot said.

Five hours later Spud Johnson took a Fortress over to get some photographs of the damage, but found the town still covered by a huge pall of smoke broken by the lurid glare of fires still burning.

Last night the Fortresses followed up with a second attack almost as heavy. When the first planes dropped their flares they could see long lines of Japanese automobiles racing through the streets, desperately trying to get people out of the town area. One big fire was still blazing from the night before. Within a few minutes more great fires were raging in the stores and workshops areas and in the central administration district. A ship near the wharf was hit and burst into flames.

The Japs must have been more jittery than usual last night. They opened with their heavy anti-aircraft barrage when the first of our planes were still ten miles off the target, but their fire, although intense, was completely ragged for the hour that our bombers remained over the town.

The flames of Rabaul were visible from our bombers when they were 100 miles away on their homeward journey. In twenty-four hours more than 100 tons of bombs have fallen on Japan's main base in the southwest Pacific. In both attacks we did not lose a single plane. It's good, indeed, as one pilot said fervently to me this morning, to be dishing it out now instead of taking it. . . .

### They Fought Uphill

I may be wrong, for I am no soothsayer, but I have an idea that the name of the "Kokoda Trail" is going to live in the minds of Australians for generations, just as another name, Gallipoli, lives on as freshly today, twenty-seven years after it first gained significance in Australian minds. For thousands of Australians who have walked the weary, sodden miles of this dreadful footpath—and these Australians are the fathers of the next generation—it will be the one memory more unforgettable than any other that life will give them.

Five days ago the Japanese began their resistance again—on the wide shallow plateau of the Gap, the pass through the forbidding spurs of the main range. The weather is bad, the terrain unbelievably terrible, and the enemy is resisting with a stubborn fury that is costing us many men and much time. Against the machine gun nests and mortar pits established on the ragged spurs and steep limestone ridges our advance each day now is measured in yards. Our troops are fighting in the cold mists of an altitude of 6700 feet, fighting viciously because they have only a mile or two to go before they reach the peak of the pass and will be able to attack downhill —down the *north* flank of the Owen Stanley's. That means a lot to troops who have climbed every inch of that agonizing track, who have buried so many of their cobbers and who have seen so many more going back, weak with sickness or mauled by the mortar bombs and bullets and grenades of the enemy, men gone from their ranks simply to win back a few more hundred yards of this wild, unfriendly, and utterly untamed mountain. Tiny villages which were under Japanese domination a few weeks ago are back in our hands—Ioribaiwa, Nauro Creek, Menari, Efogi, Kagi, Myola—and we are fighting now for Templeton's Crossing.

Fresh troops are going up the track, behind on the slimy trail from which the tide of war has ebbed and in ebbing has scattered the debris of death and destruction all the way along the green walls that flank the snaking ribbon of rotten mud. The men are bearded to the eyes. Their uniforms are hotch-potches of anything that fits or is warm or affords some protection from the insects. I remember years ago how we used to laugh at newsreels showing the motley troops of China when they were fighting the Japanese in the days when the men of Tokyo could do no wrong in the eyes of the western world. These men on the Kokoda track look more unkempt, more ragged, than any of the Chinese of those old film shots.

The men coming back, sick or wounded, look worse. But you can see they are rather proud of the scraps of rag tied round their feet, the slings made of mud-cake puttees, the slouch hats that look like dish cloths. They have already fought the Jap and they are willing to give advice to newcomers.

"How are you keepin' sport?"

"Not too bad."

"What are the Japs like?"

"Stiff!"

"Wait till we get stuck into 'em!"

"Okay, sport. We're waitin'."

Already a new language is springing up on this green and slimy trail. Whenever Australians are in an area for long enough they soon invent a new slang to describe it. They adapt themselves to discomforts, give them ironical names and laugh them off. A few weeks ago these troops were still talking the language of the Middle East, which has been their home for more than two years. They talk now like the men who have been in New Guinea for months. The curses of New Guinea are varied enough to provide troops with their main subjects of conversation but, in rough order, the worst are mosquitoes, mud, mountains, malaria and monotony. The "mozzies" and malaria are worst down near the coast, but they are speedily replaced by the mud and mountains as you go inland. The monotony, of course, is everywhere, except where the fighting provides something special to think about.

They love mosquito stories, and the more fantastic they are the better they like them.

There was one about a Jap airman who was found lying on a hill. The official explanation was that he had been shot down by our fighters, but the boys in the know say that he was picked up at Lae by a mozzy, who carried him over the Owen Stanley's, looking for a nice quiet place to eat him. He saw a flight of Fortresses heading north, and, mistaking them for his wife and kids, he dropped the Jap and fell into formation.

I heard another one on the same lines about an ack-ack gunner who caught a mosquito in his sights, and, mistaking it for a Zero, opened fire with a Bofors gun. The third shell chipped one wing, and the fourth exploded right under his tail. The boys raised a cheer as they saw him come down smoking, but instead of crashing he picked up a rock and threw it at them. They can show you the rock, too.

They all grew out of the old tale about the two mosquitoes who found a good, juicy-looking staff sergeant asleep under his net one night. One of them politely lifted the net for the other to fly in, and his friend returned the compliment by turning over his identity disc to see if he belonged to the right blood group.

"Well, he's okay," one of them said. "Shall we eat him here or take him down to the beach?"

"Don't be silly. If we take him down to the beach the big chaps will grab him."

I can't vouch for that one. I never met the staff sergeant.

Moresby's best mosquito joke, I think, is a perfectly authentic signboard that stands alongside a shallow pool on the main road in the garrison. It was erected by an anti-malaria squad which forgot to paint in the hyphen. The pool was filled with gamboesia, the little imported minnow that eats mosquito larvae, and the sign reads:

WARNING. DO NOT SPRAY. MOSQUITO EATING FISH.

And everybody who passes always makes the customary remark of awe that tradition dictates: " 'Struth, are they *that* big?"

On the Kokoda track, however, after you've been walking a few hours, you soon get above the mosquito country. As the troops toiled and grunted up they would often stop and gasp with amazement at the enormous butterflies that drifted to and fro, or alighted on their arms to drink the sweat. The insect life, from scorpions to butterflies, is impressive.

Only for a time though. You eventually reach a stage when flora and fauna, and even the Japs, gradually lose interest. Your mental processes allow you to be conscious of only one thing—"The Track," or, more usually, "The Bloody Track." You listen to your legs creaking and stare at the ground and think of the next stretch of mud, and you wonder if the hills will ever end. Up one almost perpendic ular mountain face more than 2000 steps have been cut out of the mud and built up with felled saplings inside which the packed earth has long since become black glue. Each step is two feet high. You slip on one in three. There are no resting places. Climbing it is the supreme agony of mind and spirit. The troops, with fine irony, have christened it "The Golden Staircase!"

Worn out and sodden with sweat—notebook and cigarettes were just soggy pulp—we stared up the endless steps which twisted up into the tree-tops. There was a long pause.

"Think I'll wait for a lift," somebody murmured reflectively.

A longer pause broken only by the labored gasp of breathing. We waited for somebody to start the climb. A young corporal turned to me with a look of disgust.

"I suppose we'd better get cracking," he said. "But what gives me a pain in the guts is to think that I was the bloody idiot who used to go to bloody mountains for his bloody holidays!"

Near this point is a tiny jungle camp where the Japanese had their advanced headquarters only a couple of weeks ago, but the Australians have already erected a rough signpost bearing the legend "Under New Management." The whole track is studded with these humorous signposts that testify to the unquenchable humor of the Diggers. Among the anonymous cartographers and signwriters whose pastime it is to erect these notice boards there doesn't seem to be much unanimity. The track starts off with a beautifully painted board bearing the name, in mock Japanese char- acters, of "Tokyo Road." Getting up toward Imita Ridge, where the Australian withdrawal ended last month, it quite inexplicably becomes "Buna Boulevard." Less than a mile beyond stands a fingerpost bearing the neat inscription "Kokoda Highway," but by the time you have reached the next bridge the name changes again to "Rabaul Road, via Kokoda and Buna."

Near the end of the motor road, if you can use the word "road" to define a tortuous, mud-covered and unbelievably narrow switch- back that tunnels through the green forest, three signs have been erected. The first reads: "To next stopping place—By air, 3 miles; By foot, 3 months." Fifty yards on we come to "Sorry. No Taxis.

All Drivers Called Up." The final notice reads: "Get Your Travel Priority Here."

At the end of the "road," where only a thin, slimy foot track spills itself down a slippery and almost perpendicular wall of red clay, there is a crudely built cookhouse, considerably less pretentious than even the average army cookhouse in the field. This calling place, famous along the track, is the "Café de Kerbstone—Gestapo Gus, Proprietor." A small tent back along the track is labelled "All-night Diner."

The talk of the troops is almost as refreshing as the signs. Their conversation is limited. They admit they talk only about the "Three T's"—"The track, the tucker,* and Tojo." Any Japanese is automatically known as "Tojo."

"Tojo's a shrewd little devil. . . . We struck one using two machine guns, and he was 100 yards away from both of them. He worked them with a complicated system of wire leads, not shooting at anything, just smacking out a few bursts every now and then to confuse us. I think he was more confused when an Australian grenade was dropped on him."

At the moment this track is Australia's road of adventure and you must never be surprised at the people you meet or the tales you hear.

Yesterday, beneath a tangle of lawyer vines, I yarned in the drizzling rain with a British army officer who had carried the gleaming badges of the East Lancashires into a strange setting. The man was Major H. M. Ervine-Andrews, who won the Victoria Cross in the retreat to Dunkirk. And we talked—of all things—about salmon fishing in Ireland!

A United States naval officer was far away from maritime surroundings as he slipped and scrambled down a clay bank, glazed by a recent shower of rain. There was a duet in American accent when an American fighter pilot, going up the track, met the returning naval officer.

During our retreat the pilot had made many sweeps over the track, strafing the Japanese positions. "They gave me a few days' leave this week," he explained. "So I thought I'd wander up the track to see what it's like. Holy Mackerel! It certainly is a million

---

* "Tucker"—Australian slang for "food."

times tougher than I ever thought! You've certainly got to hand it to those Australian soldiers. They must have gone through hell."

It is along this track that you meet the real traditional Australian hospitality. You find it in wayside tents, in tumbledown native huts, and in rude shelters made of branches leaning against the knife-edge roots of jungle trees. The scrub is parted, and a grinning face, usually unshaven, pokes through with the invitation, "Are you in a tearin' hurry?" A grimy thumb is jerked over a suntanned shoulder with the words, "I've got a billy on now, and the tea's almost ready."

The tea is always good Australian billy tea, and the yarns you hear are always worth listening to. The talk is largely of the toughness of the little Japanese as an enemy or of experiences in Bardia, Benghazi, Greece, Lebanon, or "good old Cairo," for these men have been around. They haven't struck anything though than this jungle war, but I've yet to hear a single man complain.

At one wayside camp, while a huge-muscled Tasmanian poured me a great tin mugful of "Slushy Joe's Papuan Bitter" (made of limejuice and water fermented with yeast and raisins and infinitely more palatable and refreshing than it sounds), I first heard the story of the general's fresh meat—a story that followed me all along the track.

It appears that a certain general was up with the forward troops, and, like them, living on an endless diet of canned bully or "M. and V." A friend sympathetically ordered some fresh meat to be sent up to him from base. A provost escorted the meat to the carrier lines, but it got "lost." A Light Horse unit fed that night on fresh meat for the first time for many weeks.

In response to angry "please explains" from the consignor, another parcel of fresh meat went forward along the track, this time with an armed guard, which delivered the precious parcel to the general's camp. But it went to the wrong cookhouse, and the general still had to make do with bully while some delighted "other ranks" tasted again the flavor of crackling on roast pork.

Again the wires hummed and again a parcel of fresh meat went out from base, with armed guards watching it as if it were the Koh-i-noor diamond. This time they made sure of it. They delivered it in person to the general's cook.

But the general was away making arrangements for his troops

to clear away a nasty Japanese pocket of resistance. The meat was still there when he came back, but the steamy jungle climate had been too much for it. It had gone bad.

The general had curried M. and V., which, for the benefit of laymen, is tinned army stew.

A tumbledown native hut somewhere in New Guinea is the centre of all betting activity concerning the Melbourne Cup. It carries the sign "Quotations for Melbourne Cup. Best Odds Given. No Credit." The bookie told me Skipton was favorite, but I could get 5 to 1 "if I jumped in early."

His book for the last two Melbourne Cups had been in the Middle East, but business was good here, though, and bets had come down the track from Myola Lakes, Templeton's Crossing, Efogi, Kagi, Menari, Nauro Creek, and Ioribaiwa.

Single pages torn from newspapers, showing starters, jockeys, and weights, have gone almost from hand to hand the length of the jungle track, until eventually they have disintegrated.

These grand fellows along "Tokyo Road" have a great hunger for news of the mainland, and all it means to them. I have seen the tattered remnants of a six-week-old newspaper, which has been read—advertisements and all—by an estimated number of 600 men, and has traveled 50 miles up and down the track before being written off as no longer legible.

All the way up the track you meet small, sturdy natives, who pick their way barefooted through the mud quietly and steadily, as though they could go on forever. The boys from the Middle East called them "wogs" at first, because it was their name for the Arabs. Soon they learn the New Guinea army term, which is "boong." Before they have been there long they are calling them "sport," which seems to be the second A.I.F.'s equivalent for "digger."

There is nothing more interesting to watch than the growing friendship between the Australian soldier and the Papuan. It is a good-humored, rather paternal relationship, with a lot of genuine kindliness in it. As a whole the New Guinea natives are nimble and tough, and they retain the physical fortitude and the honesty of primitive peoples unspoiled by casual contacts with the white man. It is their uncomplaining and lion-hearted endurance, and their innocence of greed and deceitfulness, which has won the hearts of the troops.

Like all other colonial races, the Papuans have learned to treat the white man with a certain amount of awe. They call him "taubada," which means something like "lord" or "master," and they do what he tells them. They are a little bewildered to hear the white man call "How are you, sport?" as they pass him, but I do not think that it is having any ill effects on their morale, and I think it is helping to develop in them a vague sense of loyalty to a cause which they can only dimly begin to understand. The only recompense they get is a few handfuls of cigarettes, and it is the only recompense they fully understand. The troops are generous with their smokes, and a cigarette means more to a Papuan than a pound note.

Life changes as you push up the track. Standards of living deteriorate, sometimes below normally accepted standards even of primitive existence. Thoughts become sombre, humor takes on a grim, almost macabre quality. When men reach the nadir of mental and physical agony there are times when sickness or injury and even death seem like things to be welcomed. Near Efogi, on a slimy section of the track that reeks with the stench of death, the remains of an enemy soldier lies on a crude stretcher, abandoned by the Japanese retreat. The flesh has gone from his bones, and a white, bony claw sticks out of a ragged uniform sleeve, stretching across the track. Every Australian who passes, plodding up the muddy rise that leads to the pass, grasps the skeleton's grisly hand, shakes it fervently and says "Good on you, sport!" before moving wearily on.

There are many Japanese graves, some crude, some elaborate, all marked with the piece of sapling bearing Japanese ideographs. There are many crudely penciled signs stuck in the bushes or nailed to the trees: "Bodies two Australians —'th Battalion, 25 yards into Bush." "Twelve Jap Bodies 50 yards northwest." "Unknown Australian Body, 150 yards down slope." In the green half-light, amid the stink of rotten mud and rotting corpses, with the long lines of green-clad Australians climbing wearily along the tunnel of the track, you have a noisome, unforgetable picture of the awful horror of this jungle war.

There are the bodies, too, of native carriers, tossed aside by the

Japs to die, discarded callously and left unburied in the jungle. These natives were recruited in Rabaul, sent to Buna, roped together in the stinking holds of Japanese freighters, and then thrown into the enemy's carrier lines. They received little food, no medical attention and payment with worthless, newly printed Japanese one shilling notes of their invasion currency. They died in their hundreds of overwork, malnutrition and sickness.

Since then the Japs have made their stand in the toughest area of the pass through the Owen Stanley's—a terrible terrain of thick mountain timber, great rocks drenched in rain, terrifying precipices and chasms. Often the troops have to make painfully slow progress by clawing with hands and feet at slippery rock faces overlooking sheer drops into the jungle. The almost constant rain or mist adds to the perils of sharp limestone ridges, narrow ledges flanked by chasms, slimy rocks, and masses of slow moving mud.

In this territory the Japanese are fighting, with a stubborn tenacity that is almost unbelievable, from an elaborate system of prepared positions along every ridge and spur. Churned up by the troops of both armies, the track itself is now knee deep in thick, black mud. For the last ten days no man's clothing has been dry and they have slept—when sleep was possible—in pouring rain under sodden blankets. Each man carries all his personal equipment, firearms, ammunition supply and five days' rations. Every hour is a nightmare.

General Allen, who had fought in the last war and who has been leading these Australians in the attack on the Kokoda Trail, says without any hesitation: "This is the toughest campaign of the A.I.F. in this or any other war."

Yet the fighting spirit of the Australians is inspirational. Today I spoke to some of the badly wounded. One man had a terrible wound caused by a bullet from a Japanese sniper which had entered his face and come out from his chest. He grinned at me and said: "We can't be worried, sport. You can't afford to lose your sense of humor in this bloody country!"

The other day I was given the copy of a letter written home by one of these young Australians—a N.S.W. private named Barney Findlay. It's worth while reprinting some of it:

"Some of the old unit are so thin now that you would be shocked to see them. This trip is a physical nightmare. We have been over loaded all the way, and all of us are carrying on our backs more than native porters do. Remember those tin-pot marches of two hours in the morning we used to grumble about? They weren't very much training for this. Yesterday we were twelve hours on the track and most of us were 'out on our feet,' but we had to keep going. It's hard to explain how gruelling these marches are, but I'll try.

"You spend four hours rising 2000 feet painfully step by step with your heart pounding in your throat, resting every 100 feet of rise. And then when you gain the top, it is only 15 feet wide, and you immediately start to descend 2000 feet. This is dangerous as well as painful, because you get 'laughing knees,' and only your prop stick in front of you keeps you from falling headlong. The farther down you go the weaker your knees become, but you don't lie down and die as you feel like doing, you keep resting and going on and on.

"At the end of the day, after, say, eight bitter hours of travelling, you have moved two miles onward, but you have surface walked eight or ten miles, and overhead you can see the planes roaring by, covering in fifteen minutes the distance it takes us five days to do. One of our chaps was a wreck at the finish.

"The first night out we tried to rest in a shelter of bushes many thousands of feet up, but none of us could manage sleep. Next day we were caught in a fierce storm, and staggered and slipped through it for two long hours. When we rested we lay out in puddles in the pouring rain, panting and steaming and wet through in the fullest sense of the words.

"But you had to keep going. Everything was wet and heavier now, and although not yet halfway we had to finish that dreadful 2000 feet climb. At nightfall we staggered into a ramshackle native grass hut. It had no sides, and the rain was driving in on us all night. One of the men sat up all night. At an altitude of 4000 feet I lay on the bare ground all night in wet clothes. It was bitterly cold. As soon as we settled down the native rats started. One of them ran across my face and scratched my nostril with his sharp claws. They kept running over my body, and when I dozed off they started nibbling at my hair. The chap next to me had a patch nibbled completely out of his hair by morning.

"He was very tired, and I kept waking up and disturbing him.

The bugs got to work then and started biting my hips and my ankles, which were itching like fire that night and all next day. By midmorning the chap I was with was in a pretty bad way, but we had a twelve-hour stage to do, and we had to keep going. It is usually half a day to climb a ridge and half a day to go down, and we had been doing a ridge a day. Now we had to go down a ridge, up a ridge, and down a ridge again. It was the cruellest day I've ever spent in my life. Each time I stopped my calves cramped, and by the time I had walked the cramp away I was too tired to go on, and I had to rest. Then I'd get cramp again.

"You might ask why I or anyone else kept going. You keep going because you have to, and because if you stop you stop nowhere, but if you keep going you might get somewhere. Everybody vows that never, never will he do it again. But there are days of this ahead of us, and the Japanese somewhere beyond. Gee, this is tough country. The farther you go the tougher it gets, but so long as a chap doesn't get sick he can hang on somehow. And Kokoda is somewhere over those ridges.

"All the water has to be carried by hand, and it is very precious. No wood will burn unless it has been roasted over a fire for many hours. So far we haven't been able to live off the country, as it would be like slow suicide. But one of these days we'll get to Kokoda . . ."

On one section of the track where the country was comparatively easy a young A.I.F. sergeant pointed out something to me in a copy of an old newspaper that had drifted around the jungle clearings. On one page was a report of the terrible fighting during the allied retreat from the Owen Stanley's in the first week of September, when men were dying in this terrible jungle, and native carriers were scaling greasy precipices with clumsy homemade stretchers bearing haggard Australian wounded. On the back of the same sheet was a column of letters to the editor.

"It doesn't worry them much," he said, pointing to the letters. I looked at them over his shoulder. There were seven letters. One was a complaint that another man in the same business had a petrol ration greater than that allotted to the writer. One condemned morals of soldiers. Two were concerned with the Government's ruling on holiday pay. One discussed the latest political controversy, and two condemned the single cuff short as a false economy.

Well, those things were probably important to the people who wrote them. Nobody had thought the Owen Stanley battle worth writing to the editor about. Or perhaps people who really think about these things don't write letters to editors. . . .

*Body Blows*

Three months ago today the Japanese landed for the first time on Papuan soil. Today they are being pushed relentlessly out of their last strongholds in the mountains. Three months have passed and in that time they have lost the south Solomons, they have suffered decisive defeat at Milne Bay, and they are losing the battle of the Owen Stanley's.

So far it has been a very costly enemy venture. In attempts to establish an air base at Buna they have now lost the best part of 100 aircraft. Their air power has been cut to ribbons in the Solomons. They have lost thousands of good troops. They have had ships sunk or beached.

On our side we, too, have suffered casualties but we have won three months in which to prepare and plan for the next move in the grim game of hide-and-seek in the islands. And, richest of all assets, we have built up something that we never had before—a formidable body of tough, well trained, well equipped and seasoned troops who have fought three months against the Japanese and still remain intact as a fighting force.

We celebrated the end of the third month of the campaign by recapturing Eora Creek, toughest Japanese stronghold of the Owen Stanley's, at the point of the bayonet after several days of bloody and bitter fighting.

There are many signs, however, that the show is not yet over. Today our reconnaissance planes counted 68 ships in Rabaul harbor, including an aircraft carrier, a battleship, 12 cruisers and 37 destroyers.

Operating on the principle that the man who punches first punches best, a big force of our Fortresses paid a visit to Rabaul. It was most successful. Major Bill Benn was able to try out his new principle of "skip bombing"—bouncing his bombs almost horizontally into the Japanese ships from only 200 feet above the water. It worked marvelously. The big bombers were below the anti-aircraft fire and searchlights. One destroyer, one cruiser, two large merchantmen and a seaplane tender were sunk and several other ships were left in flames. The Papuan sky today is swarming with aircraft—heavy bombers, medium bombers, fighters, dive-bombers, army cooperation planes, transports. And every one of them is on our side!

The significant thing now is that this little corner of the Pacific is not regarded as a "tropic sideshow" by the Japs. So far as they are concerned they apparently intend to fight the decisive battle for command of the Pacific in the few thousands of square miles of sea and reefs and islands bounded by the Bismarcks, New Guinea and the Solomons. The reckless way they are flinging their aircraft, despite disproportionate losses, against the American positions at Guadalcanal, the way they have exposed their trump card, shipping power, to our air attacks with land-based bombers, all suggest that Japan is willing to gamble almost everything on a desperate all-in attempt to gain control of these scattered islands and archipelagoes.

Japan's fighting capacity does not really depend upon the fanatical fighting ability of her ground troops as much as it does upon the strength and efficiency of her sea and air power. Yet in less than three months she has lost *for certain* 420 aircraft of all types (apart from more than 300 claimed only as probables or possibles). In the last eighteen days 120 enemy planes have been destroyed—77 by American pilots in the Solomons, and 43 by allied pilots under Kenney's command. In the same period more than 70 Japanese ships have been sunk, probably sunk, or severely damaged. The proportion is roughly 50-50 between warships and transports, and, among the warships, cruisers and destroyers have been the heaviest sufferers.

### *"But Kokoda Was Empty"*

The Australians have re-conquered the Owen Stanley Range. Today, on November 2, they marched into Kokoda unopposed, through lines of excited natives who brought them great baskets of fruit and decked them with flowers. They marched back to the little plateau where Colonel Owen had died so many weary weeks before. They marched downhill through Isurava and Deniki, where many of them had fought the bloody rearguard action of August. The Japs had fled. Patrols cautiously went ahead to scout, squirmed their way through the rubber trees to test out Kokoda's defenses. But Kokoda was empty. There was no sound but the droning of insects and the noise of the rain pattering through the trees. Kokoda, "key to the Owen Stanley's," had been abandoned by the Japanese without a fight. Their defense of Kokoda had been the pass through the range, and they had failed to hold that defense line.

Today Australian troops in ragged, mud-stained green uniforms, in charred steel helmets that had been used for cooking many a meal of bully beef on the Kokoda trail, stood in ranks round the flagpole in front of the administrative building while an Australian flag (dropped with typical courtesy, friendship and thoughtfulness by an American fighter pilot) was slowly hoisted in the still air. There was no cheering. There was no band playing. There was merely the packed lines of these hundreds of weary Australians, haggard, half-starved, dishevelled, many weary grimy, stained bandages, standing silently at attention in the rain. For weeks their muttered "Kokoda or bust!" had been the most quoted saying of the track. Well, here was Kokoda, and lost in the rain clouds behind was the great blue rampart of the Owen Stanley's, with the shaggy 13,600-foot crest of Mount Victoria hidden by the afternoon thunderheads.

The shadow of the Australian flag, hanging limply in the still, moist air, fell across the lines of Japanese graves sheltering beneath the shattered debris of what once had been the Government station buildings. Within 12 feet of the flagstaff was the tall, simple memorial erected by the Japanese "in memory of the many soldiers of Nippon who fell in the great battle for Kokoda." And near by was the grave of Colonel Owen.

Littered all over the area were discarded Japanese anti-aircraft shells, smashed boxes which had contained stores, wicker baskets in which food had been dropped by parachute. In a valley beyond was the Japanese cemetery, with its hundreds of neat graves.

Within an hour the Australian spearhead was snaking down the narrow track leading from the little plateau on to the flat, jungle-choked plain below. They were marching on to try to catch the fleeing enemy.

The campaign has been confused until today, but now it's possible to tell in some detail the epic story of the Australian conquest of the Owen Stanley's, because it is a story that will be told for many years to come.

By 16 September, fifty-six days after they had landed at Gona, the Japanese spearpoint had reached Ioribaiwa Ridge, little more than 30 airline miles from Port Moresby. It is significant that there was a feeling of optimism and confidence in New Guinea among ragged, weary, hungry troops who had tasted the bitterness of retreat, who had seen their comrades die, who had been compelled to withdraw even from positions where their mates lay buried in wet clay under crude crosses.

They knew that when they had been able to fight they had fought well, and on the straggling strip of jungle battlefield that stretched for 100 weary miles from Oivi to Ioribaiwa they had left many more Japanese graves than Australian.

Across the valley of Ua-ule Creek on Imita Ridge, the main force collected its strength, reassembled scattered forces, and organized for the long push back. There was no thought of merely holding the Japanese where they were. The job was to drive them back out of the Owen Stanley Range once and for all. As the main body assembled beneath the tall rain-soaked jungle trees, patching tattered uniforms, cleaning weapons, checking over every trifling detail, for this was a job where detail meant everything, strong fighting patrols combed the silent valley that was no-man's-land. They looked for Japanese, picked up natives, and scouted from hidden observation posts. They heard that the Japanese were short of rations, suffering badly from exhaustion and dysentery.

The Japanese had met their second great enemy, the jungle, an enemy that the Australians had already found a terrible foe. But the Japanese weren't giving up because of that. For 400 yards across the track on the Ioribaiwa Ridge they had built up an eight-foot timber barricade of felled trees. Behind they were digging a great system of defenses and weapon pits. Silent allied patrols could see them hacking new tracks out of the terrible jungles. The Japanese were going back to the defensive.

Behind Imita Ridge our troops and Papuan natives, all equally covered with mud, strained sinews and muscles as they hauled 25-pounder field guns along a slimy mountain track glazed by rain, up which a few months before a mountain goat would have thought twice about traveling. Beyond the ridge allied patrols probed forward more and more aggressively.

Once a militia patrol met some Japanese and killed them all. This was a jungle war, where you didn't give quarter because you didn't expect it. The Japanese had fanned out on the southern slopes of jagged Ioribaiwa. An A.I.F. patrol smashed into a forward Japanese nest and destroyed its occupants with grenades. A nicely camouflaged enemy listening post was raided by night and destroyed.

And then the roaring bark of Australian 25-pounders and the whine of shells across the Ua-ule Valley. The brown explosions of dust and smoke tufted the crest of Ioribaiwa. A Japanese mountain gun replied. Down below long columns of green-clad troops moved in single file along the jungle-covered track. It was 24 September, and the advance had really begun.

In the brief gaps between the trees the Australians could see great columns of smoke spiralling above the ranges. American Havoc bombers were smacking Japanese positions at Nauro Creek. Overhead roared American and Australian fighter planes on their way to strafe Buna and scour the track back to Kokoda. Through mist and driving rain our scouts could see the Japanese retreating back to the crest of Ioribaiwa Ridge and feverishly establishing their forward defenses. That night the red flashes of artillery fire carved ruddy strips from the darkness on both sides of the valley.

Next day Australian troops sloshed forward through driving rain, climbed toward the crest of the range that was hidden beneath a dense blanket of mist. Forward patrols almost on the crest could see the Japanese—short, stocky fellows, about five feet two inches in height—moving about, their khaki uniforms darkened by the downpour. There were a great many of them.

The battle seemed to be developing, but it was still at the stage of patrol, ambush, and skirmishing on an increasing scale. By the 27th of the month Queensland infantrymen were storming the ridge with fixed bayonets and wild shouts, while Australian 25-pounder shells smashed into the timber palisade, hurling shattered tree trunks in all directions. Three hundred yards from the exploding shells a young A.I.F. artillery captain directed the fire from his guns thousands of yards behind him, and hidden by two intervening ridges.

Soon after daybreak the following day the Australians topped the ridge where the Japanese advance had ended, scrambled cautiously down the slimy slope to the little village of Ioribaiwa. The Japanese had gone. Few of the scattered grass huts remained undamaged. Along the sides of the track were the Japanese slit trenches, ambush trenches in various shapes—semi-circular, T-shaped, or L-shaped—mortar and machine gun pits, snipers' posts, the pit where the mountain gun had been.

Equipment was scattered in the mud. In a battered hut mess dishes were overturned on a rough timber table, cutlery was embedded in the mud near a pile of torn up papers. Under the trees were unburied Japanese bodies. They were gaunt and thin. These men had been hungry when they died.

The Diggers marched on, weary, rain-soaked, but eager to get to grips with the enemy. One day was much like another—the sheer physical agony of the track, the changeless jungle scenery broken by the little clearings as village after village was retaken—Nauro Creek on 30 September, Menari two day later, Efogi the next day.

Everybody feared a trap, but everybody was guarding against one. Near Efogi a sick Japanese was found and taken prisoner. He seemed amazed when he was given food, water, and medicine. Rabaul natives were picked up in the jungle still wide-eyed with terror of the Japanese, who had impressed them for their carrier lines, treated them like beasts, and left the sick and injured to die in the mud.

The twin tracks of Kagi and Myola were covered by the cautiously advancing troops, now on an iron ration of two meals a day, bully beef and hard biscuits. By 7 October both villages had been recaptured.

The attackers were in the pass through the Owen Stanley's. When the clouds and mist cleared great jungle peaks could be seen all round them. Two days later scouting patrols struck the Japanese. The silent hills echoed again to the crack and rattle of rifle fire, the thud of grenades. Everybody asked the question: Are these Japanese stragglers or is this the beginning of a rearguard fight? Within three days they had their answer. The Japanese were entrenched in force across both tracks leading to Templeton's Crossing. The Allies fanned out and moved forward. The battle for the pass through the Owen Stanley's had begun.

Rumors that had buzzed up and down the track for days, "The

Japanese have withdrawn all the way to Kokoda," "They tell me the Japanese are evacuating from Buna," were dispelled in that first withering hail of machine gun fire, but came from the Japanese positions across Myola track, in that first blast of mortar bombs bursting in front of the jagged limestone spur astride the Kagi trail.

Scattered patrol skirmishes of the last few days had gradually developed into what was evidently a stubborn Japanese attempt to retard or smash up our advance. Razorback after razorback extend back across the ever narrowing gap through the mountains, a gap that achieved the character, almost of a rocky defile in the wild mountains from Templeton's Crossing to beyond Eora Creek. This was the country, the worst at any point through the Owen Stanley's from Moresby to Buna, that the Japanese had carefully picked to contest our challenge to command of the Owen Stanley's.

On these spurs a handful of men with mortars, grenades, and machine guns could hold up a whole battalion indefinitely if that battalion attempted to crush the resistance in a frontal attack. And there was not one but many of these Japanese strongposts dug into every commanding ridge and spur all the way back to Alola.

By 13 October the push forward had become a bitter struggle for every inch of progress. As our troops attacked frontally beyond Myola and Kagi, while patrols felt out for an opening in the flank, the Japanese attempted their old tricks calling to the attackers in perfect English to cease fire. One Japanese sniper yelled out: "Where are you, Digger?" A concealed Australian was watching him. He dropped a grenade, which killed the Japanese, and then called out: "I'm here, Tojo, where are you?"

Most of the fighting was with mortars, grenades, and automatic weapons, but often the Australians had to squirm to within five or six yards of the Japanese trenches and gunpits before they were able to charge with fixed bayonets. On this second day of bitter fighting one patrol routed out a Japanese post with the bayonet, killing 30 before they were forced to withdraw before a hail of mortar bombs. Our casualties were heavy; Japanese casualties were considerably heavier. On 22 October, with Eora Creek village behind them, the Australians attacked another strong Japanese defense line, which was systematically hammered by American bombers and fighters.

After a stubborn resistance the Japanese retired again. Rain was incessant. The advance slowed down in the slimy quagmires, but our pressure was steady, and the Japanese could leave only pockets to stem our advance, and isolated parties of snipers who were shot out of the trees systematically. Once the Japanese attempted a counter-attack, but they were hurled back with severe losses, and they didn't try again.

Gradually we advanced on Alola to close the net around the enemy. If our troops could capture Alola they felt that "they had the game sewn up."

Most troublesome obstacle was a Japanese strongpost of 100 men of a squad left behind astride a precipitous spur between Eora and Alola. For three days our patrols squirmed through the jungles to get around it. At dusk on 28 October, in a drenching downpour, the trap closed. Australian troops, who had crawled to within a few feet of the Japanese gunpits, hurled in a shower of grenades. From the opposite side another party jumped over the ridge with bayonets flashing. In the wild, desperate, twilight battle 30 Japanese fell dead, 20 more were wounded. The remainder fled in panic.

Japanese resistance in the pass through the range had ended. For a few moments the Diggers, fearing another "stand," attempted to pursue the fleeing Japanese, but there was no hope of finding them in the darkening jungle. They weren't to see the Japanese again until they had progressed through Isurava, Deniki, Abuari, and bomb-shattered Kokoda.

At Kokoda the Australians were welcomed by flower-garlanded natives, overjoyed at their release from three months of Japanese rule that had been harsh, tyrannical, and unscrupulous. Thirty-six days after they had stormed Ioribaiwa Ridge our troops had recaptured the Owen Stanley Range.

### "Death Valley Massacre"

The two natural defense barriers that stand athwart the Moresby-Buna track are the range of the Owen Stanley's and the gorge of the wide Kumusi River. The Japs have failed to hold either.

For almost two weeks they tried to stem our advance on this side of the river swollen by torrential rains to a width of 400 feet. The tiny village of Oivi was selected for the stand, where an elaborate system of covered weapon pits, trenches and timber barricades had been erected. One some ridges the Japanese had plaited vines and lawyer canes to form fences. Behind their main positions were some 60-millimetre mountain guns which constantly shelled the track from Kokoda. In the heavy foliage the enemy could not be seen, although in some areas front line positions were so close together that the Australians could hear the chatter of Japanese voices, the clicking of mortar pins, the clatter of new clips of ammunition being fed into guns.

One infantry sergeant crawled to within 10 yards of the enemy lines with a small field telephone, and remained there for forty-five minutes, within earshot of the Japs, whispering instructions through the telephone to the Australian mortar crews. He obtained ample evidence of the accuracy of the Australian fire, although he himself was often endangered. Eventually wounded by a Japanese sniper sent out to investigate the curious whispering noise from the bushes not far ahead of the forward posts, he was rescued by a stretcher-bearer who went in under heavy fire seven times to pull out Australian wounded. On his last trip he heard a voice call out in good English, "Come here, I'm wounded." He squirmed across to investigate but the caller was a Japanese sniper who shot and wounded the Australian six times.

After a heavy clash on Thursday night the Japs retreated from the Oivi positions, and the climax of the battle came on the following day when an Australian force, which had climbed round the mountains in a tough outflanking movement, cut the main track behind an enemy line and surrounded the Japanese advanced headquarters at Gorari.

The Australians refer to that little show as the "Death Valley Massacre." Which is exactly what it was. In one furious twenty-minute assault the Australians ripped the startled headquarters garrison to pieces, completely dissipated all resistance, and left more than 500 Japanese dead piled high in the tiny clearing. The few survivors fled in panic, abandoning 75-mm. and 60-mm. artillery, machine guns, mortars, packhorses and more than 300 terrified Rabaul carriers.

Under cover of night the defeated Japanese crossed the flooded Kumsui in canoes and rafts and by swimming. Many were drowned. One large raft was overturned in the swirling stream. The occupants, officers of the Japanese staff, were hurled into the torrent.

Among those who were drowned was Lieutenant-General Toma-tore Horii, Japan's expert in "landing and small-craft operations," who was the Commander-in-Chief of the Japanese forces in Papua.

Horii came to the south Pacific as commander of the Nankai (South Seas) detachment. He took part in the conquest of Rabaul, and planned the frontal attack on Moresby that failed during the Coral Sea battle. His second attempt at Papuan conquest "through the back door" has also failed. Perhaps it is just as well that he was drowned in the Kumsui. A Japanese general can't afford to lose face in two successive important operations.

The next Japanese defense line probably will be somewhere in front of Gona and Buna. But the Australians are out of the mountains and fighting with greater confidence than ever before. General Vasey, the Australian commander, tall, humorous and fearless, has sent back a signal to G.H.Q.: "It's Buna or bust, and we won't bloody well bust!"

*Two Men Are Sitting*

On an upturned packing case alongside an airstrip in the Kunai 20 miles behind Gona sat a blindfolded Japanese prisoner, awaiting the transport plane that would carry him back to Port Moresby. He had bitten off the end of his tongue to ensure that he wouldn't talk. He could hear the roar of powerful aircraft engines as our transports swept in with guns and ammunition and food. He could hear the fainter throbbing of our bombers and fighters streaking over toward Buna. His share of the war was over, but in the tangled swamps and Kunai patches of the Buna plain thousands of his fellow countrymen were facing up for the final battle of a tough campaign.

The allies were closing in from seven directions. The Americans had gone into action twenty-four hours before, and three columns of green-uniformed doughboys were even now assaulting the tough defense perimeter around Cape Endaiadere, Buna and Giropa Point. The Australians were pushing up the track to Sanananda Point and another force, advancing with staggering speed, had reached to within a mile of the north coast at Gona. The village of Soputa, south of Sanananda had just fallen to Australians and Americans after tough fighting.

But the surly little Jap with the bristly hair and with the dried blood caked at the corner of his mouth didn't know anything about these things.

There had been a sense of impending crisis in the events of the last few days. On Wednesday night a Japanese convoy made another attempt to reinforce the shattered remnants of Horii's force, but a light cruiser and a destroyer were blown to pieces by bombs from our Fortresses, and the remaining destroyer fled to the northward. There is a growing belief now that the Japs, thwarted in the Solomons, might swing over fighters and bombers in an attempt to smash our rapidly closing grip on the north coast. Already the American troops have been harassed by Zeros, which were given a temporary control of the air by the constant thunderstorms which prevented our fighters from crossing the range, whose mist-hidden peaks and razorbacks were responsible for the pilot's grim weather commentary: "Those clouds are full of golden rocks today."

But now the storm has cleared and the sky is throbbing with the swarms of allied aircraft smashing the Japanese last line of defense in front of the peacock-blue sea—American Fortresses, Marauders, Havocs, Mitchells, Airacobras, Kittyhawks, Lightnings, Liberators; Australian Hudsons, Wirraways, Beaufighters, Bostons. Occasionally we see some Zeros and some Mitsubishi dive-bombers, but not often. They come out at twilight when the allied planes have been forced back to their bases by gathering darkness.

It's been a tense week for the senior officers. Horii is dead, and so are some of his staff officers. General Harding, of the American 32nd Division, had to swim two miles to the shore when the lugger in which he was moving along the north coast was strafed and sunk by Zeros. Australia's General Vasey and America's General Mac-Nider have been strafed and sniped at.

Back at headquarters are the senior generals—MacArthur, Blamey and Kenney, all now established in New Guinea to direct operations on the spot. Blamey, who lives in a camouflaged tent lined with maps on which colored pins illustrate the inexorable advance of the troops under his command, is cautious, and wisely planning to meet the worst contingency that can happen.

"The last two months have been tough," he says, "but this is the critical stage. The real fight is just beginning. Don't delude yourself into thinking the Japs are going to give up this north coast without a very desperate fight. And it will be just as tough or tougher when we clean the whole coast up, because, even then, they aren't going to leave us alone."

Chunky General Kenney took time off from the job of pinning Silver Stars on the grease-stained tunics of two full Fortress crews, the boys who smashed the Japanese convoy off Buna, to look up at a formation of Airacobras arrow-heading toward the Japanese positions. "Just for a change, I think we're winning," he said. "But the Nips have planes they haven't used yet and it won't be a pushover."

The senior soldier of them all, General Douglas MacArthur, miraculously retains complete privacy in a garrison area where there has never been privacy before, where even American and Australian nurses have had to avert their eyes from the roadside spectacles of nude soldiers showering under roadside hydrants, and naked men wandering carelessly everywhere.

MacArthur is just as remote, just as mysterious as he has been ever since he reached Australia eight months ago. He lives with Kenney in a white-painted bungalow surrounded by a riotous tropical garden of frangipanni and hibiscus and flametrees. He is rarely seen. I remember how one American soldier came up to me in a state of great excitement because he had seen the great man. "I got a glimpse of him before breakfast," he said. "He was walking beneath the trees in a pink silk dressing gown with a black dragon on the back." Another man told me he had seen MacArthur in the afternoon with signal forms in one hand and a bunch of green lettuce which had been flown up from the mainland in the other. Between munches he doubtless analyzed the progress of the carefully prepared plan to take Papua back from the Japs.

That plan probably had its beginning at a special press conference in July which I had flown down to Melbourne to attend. That conference was—and unfortunately still is—off the record, but one remark of the general's can be told. "We suffer because our forces are split over many fronts," he said, "but so long as we can keep fighting on every one of those fronts we keep the enemy fighting there, too, and his forces are similarly split. We must attack, attack, attack!"

Well, that is what is happening in Papua today. The Japs, for the moment, are on the defensive everywhere. There are many problems that the three generals must overcome. The Australians call

this a "Q War"—a quartermaster's war, in which supply and movement are everything that matters, except fighting courage. Those
problems have been largely solved by the dynamic General Kenney
who has built up his air transport organization to an enormous
scale. Almost every foot of our advance from Ioribaiwa across the
Owen Stanley's and across the northern plain to Buna has been
made possible only by the endless job of innumerable young pilots—
many of them American kids from flying schools who flew the
great Douglases and Lockheeds across the Pacific and straight to
New Guinea—who have dropped or landed thousands of tons of
food, equipment, munitions and guns. Within a month the rookie
pilots had accumulated hundreds of hours of operational flying,
right up to the front line through storms and over country that
would test the courage and flying ability of the best pilots in the
world. Bully beef, blood plasma, mortars, blankets, everything the
fighting men needed, was dropped by these planes, and every day
they carried bundles of mail from home and tossed them down for
the troops in action against the Japs. Day after day they shifted 100
tons of goods between sunrise and dusk. If planes could be landed
they were put down on crude emergency strips carved out of the
kunai. Where planes could not be landed the goods were thrown
out on to specially made "dropping grounds" a mile or two behind
the firing line. Fragile goods went down in special parachutes, but
other stuff, specially packed, was kicked out of the planes' open
doors as they roared across the dropping areas at 150 miles an hour,
just above the tree-tops.

As the troops advanced into the more open country special landing strips were prepared. Batteries of artillery were flown in—
25-pounders, 3.7 inch mountain guns, 105-mm. American howitzers.
Jeeps, and tractors, and motor-rollers, and even an entire field hospital, were flown right to the front line by the "bully beef bombers."
The transport planes were unarmed. A few were shot down by
Zeros. Some disappeared in jungle storms. Many were peppered by
fire from Japanese anti-aircraft machine guns and some were holed
by shrapnel from heavier ground batteries. The immense organization was never allowed to slow down, let alone stop.

If this is a Q War we have just seen a perfect example of efficiency in fighting that sort of war. The Japs have been beaten in
the air, beaten on supply, beaten in straight-out fighting ability.

Today we can see the end of the picture in sight. The Japs have lost almost all that they have struggled so hard for during the last one hundred and twenty-one days.

And today two men are sitting. They are many miles apart. One is a blindfolded Japanese prisoner. I wonder what he is thinking? The other is the mysterious, aloof American general from the Philippines sitting beneath the frangipanni and munching Australian lettuce as he reads the reports coming in from the front, where allied troops are battering down the enemy's final Papuan resistance. Perhaps he sees in this little jungle campaign the first complete justification of his months old theory of "Attack, attack, attack!" But I'm not sure. Because, you see, I don't know what he is thinking either. . . .

### Gunfire in Arcady

I have just walked 11 miles along the road to Buna, and I doubt if I have ever been so conscious before of a feeling of such utter incongruity. It was like walking through Arcady in search of a war.

My eyes told me this could not be a site for battle even though my ears told me otherwise, for the earth was shaking to the thunder of bombs, and the air trembled faintly even from this distance to the roar of artillery fire, the boom of mortars, the irritable chatter of machine guns.

But where was the visual evidence of war? Blue hills, green plains, and grass waving in the soft breeze that came through the bottle-green banks of jungle, a stream gurgling, a band of natives carrying pandanus leaves over their heads to ward off the scorching rays of the midmorning sun (only the fool Australian trudged along, his scalp boiling beneath tin helmet), and the natives laughing and singing softly.

It was—apart from the natives—like a midsummer day in England, with the droning of insects almost deafening when one stopped to listen to them, and quite unheard when one was thinking of other things. There were other things to think of—the heat, the sweat pouring into my eyes, the leaden weight of pack and blanket roll, and the unbroken thunder of gunfire somewhere ahead. One had to keep an eye on the droning aircraft high above, too. Once a flight of American bombers thundered by, barely skimming the tree-tops. Often one could see our fighters patrolling in the unblemished cobalt of tropic sky.

Once when the sky was otherwise empty a lone Japanese Zero slid along overhead, and I had the immediate and quite stupid sensation that the pilot was looking right at me and trying to make up his mind whether I was worth wasting bullets on. He guessed the truth. I wasn't, and he made off.

There had been bitter fighting on this track, but there was scant evidence of it until I realized after a mile of walking that the square holes dug on either side of the track had been Japanese machine-gun pits. Occasionally one passed a group of graves with Japanese characters painted on square-faced slabs of timber. Once I saw a Japanese steel helmet half-buried in the sand, and there were signs in Japanese at bends and cross-tracks.

My mind was yanked away from war by the sight of a soldier 200 yards ahead, casually strolling down the track with a black toy Pomeranian dog trotting at his heels. I lengthened my stride to catch up with this strange wartime enigma of "taking the dog out for a walk" a few miles behind the Buna battlefield. The soldier was a brigadier who had brought his Pomeranian—pedigreed, by the way—from Melbourne to keep him company. And here we were moving down a dusty track shimmering with heat and flanked by 8-foot kunai grass, and the sullen mutter of guns and mortars always beating gently on our eardrums. It's a strange war. The fact that men—Australian, American, Japanese—were fighting and dying just over that low jungled hill didn't interrupt by so much as a beat the droning chant of the insects.

Down the track toward us came a long line of native carriers bearing wounded on litters. The men looked tragically ill. Over each man's face and head a native held a broad palm leaf to give protection from the burning sun. A blood-soaked bandage was round one man's head. The roar of battle ahead gained a new meaning. As we passed an abandoned Japanese workshop another party came toward us—armed Australian soldiers and five Japanese prisoners. Husky, shavenpolled, surly looking, the Japanese strode by with expressionless eyes.

I was near the end of my hike. The bark of the guns was louder now. There were craters in the ground, and great coconut palms had been torn down and shredded like carrots. It was some time later, after I had seen the sooty puffs of ack-ack fire bursting over Buna and Gona, that I was told the significance of the noise of battle that had been the grim undertone to this journey in Arcady.

For two hours our fighters and bombers have been plastering Gona, where strong Japanese positions are still holding out. Reports coming back tell us that the fiercest and most concentrated air attack of this sector has been most effective. There is a sudden jumbled roar as Australians on the right flank pour scores of mortar bombs into the battered Japanese positions. Reports come back that the Australians are now attacking, seizing strategic points.

A screen of our fighters drones overhead in the cloudless sky. It doesn't quite seem like Arcady now, and there's nothing imaginary about what's going on behind me. A Rabaul native, who showed me lacerated fingers, inflicted as punishment when he was in the enemy's carrier line, is talking in quite unintelligible pidgin as he "makes me a bed." It consists of saplings lashed together on a wooden frame built a few inches above the ground. It looks the most acutely uncomfortable contrivance—short of the inquisitor's rack—I have ever seen or heard of.

## The Wounded Come Back

The guns had been silent on the jungle track for almost an hour. I squatted beneath a shady, vine-clad jungle tree listening to the drone of aircraft high overhead and the noises of teeming insect life all about me.

Two groups of men came toward me, one from the northward black against the chrome of a kunai patch, one from the southward difficult to pick out with their green uniforms blending with the bottle-green wall of jungle.

There were three wounded—one man walking with his right arm in a bloodstained sling, his right eye hidden beneath a heavy bandage, two others lying on crude litters on the hard-muscled shoulders of native bearers.

The uniforms of the three Australians were torn and smeared with sun-dried, gray mud, and each man had grown a heavy beard. The Australians moving up, also heavily bearded, looked like modern Robin Hoods in their green uniforms, and green slouch hats pinched, torn, and battered into all sorts of weird shapes. Rifles and tommy guns were slung over their shoulders with grimly efficient nonchalance.

The stretchers were placed in the shade. The walking wounded man pushed back his net-covered tin helmet and with a grin took the cigarette I offered.

One of the Robin Hoods, whose hat looked more like a Mexican bandit's than an Australian soldier's, turned to one of the stretcher cases—a tall, rangy young Western Australian farmer with a brown, stained bandage round bare chest and shoulder.

"Well, how's it going, cobber?" he asked.

"Oh! Not bad at all, sport," the Western Australian replied with a faint grin. "Where you bound for? Gona?"

The Australian who looked like a Mexican spat out the piece of grass he was chewing. "Yeah. Gona."

He looked toward the coast where a sudden rattle of machine gun fire had begun, and then spoke again, "They tell me it's pretty tough up there."

"It's a bit willing, but not too bad," the wounded man replied. "The trouble is those blanky Japs are going to stay there till they're dead, and there are hundreds of 'em dead already. But we're getting 'em one by one." He squirmed round a little on the stretcher, and the bandage round his shoulder suddenly reddened. He explained with an air of apology, "I've got one bullet in my behind, and I can't lay on it too well." He chuckled and the others laughed with him.

There was a gap in the conversation and the silence was broken only by the drone of insects, the faint crack of "ack-ack" over Buna, and the crump of mortars behind the jungle belt ahead.

I was wondering why it should be regarded as amusing that a man had a bullet in his buttocks when the conversation was resumed again by the Mexican-hatted soldier. "How did you get yours?" he asked.

"Snipers," the Western Australian said simply.

The look of questioning on the faces of his listeners prompted him to go ahead. "There were 30 left out of our company," he said. "We'd been chopped about a bit. I got mine yesterday afternoon when we had to tackle a pretty strong Jap post through the coconut grove. It didn't look too easy, but it's no use waiting round and weighing everything in the balance up there. The post was about

70 yards away, dug down beneath the roots of a whacking big tree. Those Japs are cunning. They'd cut down the grass all the way, and we knew we'd have to run across that open area before we could get among 'em. We had a go at it with bayonets. I saw several of my cobbers go down as I galloped along, but some of us reached the post and dropped our grenades through the roots where we could, and then went at 'em with bayonets. I went round to the right hand side, and I know I killed four of 'em with the tommy gun. They didn't get me. Two of our jokers had gone to the other side, and they caught a few of the Japs trying to escape from the back of the tree. They got 'em on the run with Bren guns and brought them down.

"We got 31 Japs at that post, but we'd lost two-thirds of our strength. Twenty of ours had gone down in the charge and attack, although only two of our blokes had been killed.

"Three of our wounded decided to be in the attack on the next post—a real toughy, because they had the grass cut in front of this one for a distance of a hundred yards. They hadn't cut it so thoroughly this time, and there was a little bit of cover. We dashed forward again. I suppose I'd gone about 20 yards when I felt a sting in my side and went down. A bullet had come down through my shoulder and into my ribs.

"I lay there for a while, and then I saw a Jap squatting in the fork of a big tree on the other side of the clearing. I squirmed on my belly for a couple of feet and grabbed my tommy gun, and let him have a burst. He came toppling down head first. Next second bullets were whistling all round me. I spotted the gun flash and saw another Jap in the top of a coconut palm. I started to let him have a burst, and the gun jammed after two shots. A Jap bullet had hit right in the magazine, so I put a new one on and let him have it. He came down spread-eagled, and I heard his body crash in the undergrowth.

"Next minute a bullet whizzed over my head, and then one hit the stock of the tommy gun and smashed it to pieces. I couldn't fire any more, so I decided to get out. I started to crawl away, and they shot me in the bottom. I flopped down, but the sun was pretty hot so I thought, 'Well, what's it matter if I cop another,' and I started to crawl again. A few bullets whizzed near me, but I got out all right. That's about all there was to it."

Trying not to look at the redly wet bandage, I said: "Well, it looks as if you'll be out of it for a while, anyway."

The Western Australian grinned and jerked his head toward the little party of Robin Hoods on their way up to the front.

"These blokes will probably clean up this little show, but I'll be back with my cobbers in the next one," he said. "You see, my average is improving. In the fighting at Eora Creek I was wounded by a mortar bomb, but killed four Japs. In this scrap I was wounded twice, but I killed six of the bastards. It looks as if Tojo had better look out when I come back again."

He looked towards the other stretcher case, a swarthy, stocky young clerk from Perth, and added: "Darky's coming back again with me. He had stiff luck."

Darky laughed. "It wasn't bad luck; it was my stupidity," he said. "We were having a spell before attacking a Japanese post on the beach and I suddenly felt a terrific thump on my hip. I was carrying three tins of tobacco and the bullet went through two and didn't get past the third. I pulled out the tins to show Mac how lucky I'd been, and then I went over. That ruddy Jap had got me again in exactly the same place, and this time I didn't have the tins there. You know a man ought to be shot for doing a damnfool thing like that."

His listeners nodded their heads with amused sympathy, and there was another odd gap of silence.

I looked at these three wounded men, all probably suffering considerable pain and discomfort, all grinning and joking together. From over the trees came the ponderous hammerblows of Japan's "woodpecker"—the Juki heavy machine gun. That might mean more wounded Australians. It was answered by a rattle of Bren gunfire. That might mean more dead Japs. I kept thinking how strange it was that these soldiers never complained. I had seen hundreds of wounded men, some of them with five or six ugly wounds. I had never seen a single man wince; I had never heard a word of complaint, not even the regular and expected grumbling about the heat, the insects, the interminable meals of bully and biscuits.

They complained about nothing. It seemed as if there were an unwritten law among these wounded diggers coming back from one of the bloodiest actions of this war—a law which proclaimed that no man should complain about anything, even the most trivial things, lest others should think of him as a squealer.

I have spoken to these men who had fought an incredibly agonizing war for three dreadful months, men who came back from the front line shambling through the dusty tracks with eyes closed from sheer weariness, men whose undaunted spirit and morale always rose above the crippling weight of physical agony and exhaustion.

There was only one basic answer to the query, "Well, how are things?" Always it was a grin and a laconic, "Goodo, sport, no complaints."

I think perhaps I am too soft-hearted to be a good war correspondent, for there were many times on that track when there was a lump in my throat as I talked to these quietly spoken young men with their grimy, blood-soaked bandages.

The natives lifted the heavy crudely built stretchers. The soldier who looked like a Mexican Robin Hood shouldered his pack and tommy gun and patted the Western Australian farmer on the leg.

"We'll square it for you, mate," he said with a grin. "And all the best."

"Thanks, sport," was the reply. "I'll be all right. And good luck to you blokes."

The stretchers jolted down towards the advanced dressing station. The Mexican bandit grinned at me. "Good blokes, those," he said. "Well, we'd better get stuck into it. Look after yourself, and thanks for the smokes."

The column of green-clad men filed toward the jungle belt and the hammerblows of the "woodpecker."

### Twenty-four Marched Out

Along the narrow, winding Sanananda track, flanked by swamps and thick jungle, both sides had dug in in small pockets. Little isolated battles were raging to the noise of thudding mortars, chattering machine-gun fire, and the zip and whine of bullets.

Sometimes our men advanced with blood-curdling yells to rout out Japanese nests at the bayonet point or with grenades. But the progress generally was pitifully slow.

Soon after we had smashed through the Japanese defenses at Soputa village, the enemy had brought up a 75-millimetre mountain gun, and for two days its shelling of the Allied forward positions had held up any appreciable advance.

An order was issued that the gun was to be silenced at all costs. The job was allotted to 90 men of an A.I.F. battalion which had been fighting with magnificent courage and determination in the slimy Papuan jungles for two and a half months.

Under the command of Captain Basil Catterns, of Sydney, the 90 mud-stained, heavily armed men crept into the flanking underbush at dawn one morning.

The enemy gun position was only two miles away, but the Australians had to make a wide detour to get round the deep, evilly smelling swamps.

For more than eight hours the men hacked and smashed their way through the entangling vines and rotten trees, their direction plotted and corrected by the noise of the enemy gun in action.

Just before dusk, Catterns saw ahead of him a Japanese camp with strong defenses all round, and the mountain gun firing from a pit in front of the camp and sending shells over the trees into the Australian positions two miles away.

After a few moments' consideration the Australians decided to launch their first assault on the camp to clean out the Japanese troops.

The Australians were drawn up in a wide, sweeping curve. Zero hour was fixed at sunset, and they crouched in the jungle until the order to charge was given.

The sun dropped swiftly behind the darkening trees. Catterns gave the order. Within a few seconds one of the most spectacular and bloody battles of the New Guinea war was raging in the tiny clearing.

The Australians tore their way through two barricades of plaited vines that the Japanese had erected, and swept across three lines of trenches with Bren guns and tommy guns blazing. Others lobbed showers of grenades into the Japanese posts.

The Japanese were taken completely by surprise as thousands of bullets whacked into native huts. Screaming, they came pouring from the huts, but within a few seconds every exit had been blocked by a pile of Japanese dead. More were blown to pieces by Australian grenades, and others were mown down like ripe corn as the Australians continued their terrorizing rush through the camp.

Grenades burst among the fires on which the Japanese evening meal was cooking, and in the great flash of flame some of the huts caught fire.

Some Australians had been killed and many wounded. The enemy had recovered from his surprise, and was hitting back hard. The Australians circled round their wounded with blazing guns, and slowly retreated into the jungle, carrying their wounded with them, behind the screen of gunfire. In the darkness the Australians dug defense positions as best they could while the wounded were attended to, and half the men fought a defensive action against more than a hundred Japanese, who maintained a constant night-long fire from machine guns, mortars, and grenades. Other Japanese were pouring from a second camp nearby.

By dawn the Australians were completely surrounded and there was no way of getting a message through to inform their unit of their plight.

"We were holding a sausage-shaped perimeter sixty yards long and thirty yards wide," said Captain Catterns. "We had stacked our wounded around a large tree in the centre of our position, but as the Japanese counter-attacked throughout the day the wounded were systematically picked off one by one by snipers. The Japanese sniped at the slightest movement.

"Under the protection of heavy machine-gun fire, their grenade throwers would advance and concentrate on one of our weapon pits or trenches, and plaster it until they were satisfied it was wiped out.

"Then they would turn to another Australian position. It was evidently their intention to whittle our defenses away one by one until we were exterminated."

Lieutenant Stewart Blakiston, of Geelong, one of the few officers to survive, said: "When we first occupied our little defense position we were hemmed in by jungle. When we left it looked like a sports field. Every blade of grass had been levelled and all the scrub and trees had been cut down by machine-gun fire. Even six-inch trees had been levelled to the ground by Japanese heavy machine guns.

The parapets of trenches had been blown in and flattened by the constant hail of bullets, and the sides of weapon pits were shot away. Sometimes the Japanese would circle our defenses with their gunfire like Red Indians attacking a wagon train in the old wild western films. How any of us survived throughout that day I still don't know.

"Some of us almost cried with relief when, just before sunset, we heard the rattle of musketry as an Australian battalion advanced up the track towards us. Some of the Japanese who were around us sped through the jungle to meet the new threat. There were enough of them left to keep us busy until after dark, when we were able to retire a few hundred yards to better defenses behind."

When the tide of battle had rolled on, by dawn next day, only four officers and 20 other ranks of the gallant 90 lived to march out from that terrible jungle clearing. But near the bodies of the 66 brave Australians who had not died in vain were the bodies of more than 150 Japanese.

And the Australians had done their job. They had silenced a dangerous enemy pocket; they had paved the way for an almost bloodless advance of two miles by the troops behind them.

And buried in the mud beside the tangled jungle track was the 75-millimetre gun—abandoned by the Japanese—which the Australians had been ordered to put out of action.

### Battle of the Rice Dump

The Gerua River splits this wide and tangled battlefield so effectively that when one is with the troops on the Sanananda side of the stream it is quite impossible to know anything about what is happening on the Buna side. Sometimes we can see Japanese dive-bombers plummeting down a mile away from us, we can hear the crash of the bombs bursting and feel the concussion in the air, but because the incident happens to be across the Gerua we haven't the faintest idea what it's all about.

On this particular track it's possible to watch two fronts, because the track splits just outside Soputa village, one arm traveling to Gona and the other twisting through the swamps to Sanananda Point. On this second track Australian and American infantry are in action together.* Elsewhere the campaign is divided, Americans handling certain sectors and Australians looking after others.

Up along the Sanananda track the fighting is tough and bitter. The main fight is known locally as the "Battle for the Rice Dump." It has been raging now for several days, since the Australians pushing north from Soputa saw ahead of them a huge Japanese food dump of hundreds of bags of rice and dehydrated vegetables and cases of canned onions—enough to feed a whole battalion.

That dump was like an oasis in the desert to troops who had lived on an almost unbroken diet of bully beef and hard biscuits for weeks. The Australian attack did not lack vigor, but the Japs wanted that food, too. They replied with a hail of machine gun and mortar fire. The Australians were at the southern fringe of the dump, the Japs at the northern. And then an American force came in on the eastern side. And for days now the great stack of food has been flanked on three sides by soldiers of three different nationalities, but all hungry and all fighting with unabated determination.

Three times the Japs have launched heavy counter-attacks to recover the food, and three times they have been hurled back with heavy casualties. The dump remains a no-man's-land. In daylight no man dares to cross the area where the food is stacked. From the jungle belt all around hungry men watch like hawks throughout the day and the slightest sign of a suspicious movement brings a torrent of bullets and grenades. But at night, when the fighting dies down to intermittent bursts of nervous fire, the position is different. Men squirm along the muddy ground under cover of that deep protective blackness, hurriedly grab a few bags of rice or vegetables or onions and slide back silently to their positions. They have to be careful, for the dump is the target for scores of alert sharpshooters—American, Japanese and Australian—who will belt off a few rounds at the cracking of a twig or a movement in the shadows.

The Australians have replenished their meagre rations and so have the Americans. I asked an A.I.F. captain if the Japs were also getting the food at night. "Well, I'd be bloody surprised if they aren't," he said. "After all, it's *their* food!"

---

* This position, first centre of enemy resistance in the Buna-Gona area, was the last to fall. The Japanese held out on this narrow section of track for two months!

I have a vague idea that when this war is over, from Melbourne to Milwaukee some yarns will be told at soldiers' reunions of the "Battle of the Rice Dump."

Food plays an enormous part in things up here, I suppose because there isn't much of it. One of the American units which had been down to emergency rations for days, found a large wooden cask in the jungle yesterday. On the side were Japanese characters, which one private stated "stood for Beef Extract." So the excited doughboys gathered round while the cook broached the keg. Inside was a dark, strange-smelling, treacly liquid rather like molasses. The soldiers looked at it with regret, but the burly cook offered to try it. There are some acts of great heroism carried out in wartime, and not all of them are in the firing line! The cook took a liberal helping and swallowed it with a frightening gulp.

The eyes of every man were on him. For half an hour he walked around thoughtfully, not uttering a word. Forty hungry men anxiously watched his every movement. At the end of the half hour he walked firmly up to the cask and licked his lips.

"Dish her out!" he said gruffly.

Five minutes later the cask was empty. . . .

*Sunday Night*

In a little darkened tent a few miles behind the front line, but within range of the Japanese artillery, is the advanced headquarters of the Y.M.C.A. It's a good place to go for a yarn and a cup of tea and a sing-song at night.

Last night was Sunday night and the sullen rumbling of the fighting ahead was echoing through the trees. A few infantrymen, grimy and weary, were sipping strong tea inside the tent. Another man was holding the pannikin to the lips of his cobber, lying back on a stretcher with two mangled arms strapped to his body. Outside were Australians and Americans, sitting on the warm, moist ground, and singing the songs they wanted to sing.

Behind them could be heard the roar of artillery, the crunching thud of mortars, occasionally the chatter of machine guns. But most of the time all other sounds were drowned by the songs these soldiers sang to the accompaniment of a battered concertina.

And the songs they sang were not the current hits or the usual soldiers' songs. They sang "Silent Night." And when that was finished they asked for "The Holy City."

"Jerusalem, Jerusalem! Lift up your gates and sing . . ." The magnificent song swelled to a roar that almost could have been heard by the sorely pressed Japs fighting up the track a mile or two away. It was a moving and intensely emotional scene. The men were black shapes, lighted occasionally by the flicker of a flame from the red embers of the cooking fire. Around was the warm, scented, almost solid blackness of the tropic night, spangled with the million glittering pinpoints of the dancing fireflies.

". . . Hosanna in the highest . . . Hosanna to your King!"

There was little talk about the fighting. Once, when an unusually heavy crash of artillery shattered the peace of the night, one man muttered, "Somebody's gettin' it tonight." But I think everybody's thoughts were thousands of miles away, in little homes in ordinary streets far away in Australia and the United States.

I walked back through the rich darkness of the night, through the fireflies, to my rude shelter in the jungle. It was no use trying to sleep. The roar of battle had reached an almost deafening crescendo, and my mind kept turning to that sing-song at the Y.M.C.A. tent, to the reverent, confident roar of those voices singing "The Holy City" just behind the battle line. There seemed some great significance behind that strangely impressive scene. I suppose it was merely the simple conviction that men like these grimy, war-weary Australians and Americans, with their unbroken spirit and undaunted resolutions, couldn't possibly be beaten.

### "The Wildest, Maddest, Bloodiest Fighting"

The Japanese are trying desperately to reinforce their last garrison in Papua. Under cover of darkness and bad weather several destroyers have succeeded in running the allied air blockade and have landed reinforcements at Buna. Other formations of fresh enemy troops have been brought down the coast from Salamaua in small boats, landing barges and even native craft. Today they continued their plan of reinforcement with submarines, at least nineteen (including one big fellow of 3000 tons) of which were sighted heading for Buna on the surface in convoy formation. They crash-dived within sixty seconds when our planes came over.

Nevertheless our forces are closing in everywhere. At Gona the Australians have cut their way through to the beach and are now trying to silence the immensely strong pill-boxes and gun-pits that the Japanese have established near Gona Mission. At Buna the Americans have driven a wedge to within 800 yards of Buna government buildings, where the Japanese apparently have their focal positions. But it's a tough job. Deep swamps of black mud in which a man would drown limit the terrain over which we can attack. Every logical and practical line of approach is covered by a network of fortifications which the Japs have been working on for months.

Every weapon pit is a fortress in miniature. Some are strengthened by great sheets of armor and by concrete, but the majority are merely huge dug-outs—several are 150 feet long—projected from our fire and bombs by sawn logs and felled trees which form a barrier six, ten, and sometimes 15 feet thick. The logs are held in place by great metal stakes, and filled in with earth in which the natural growth of the jungle has continued, providing perfect camouflage. Many of the pits are connected by subterranean tunnels or well protected communication trenches. The pits are heavily manned and each is filled with sufficient food, water and ammunition to enable the Japs to withstand a long siege. From every trench or pit or pill-box all approaches are covered by wide fields of sweeping fire along fixed lines.

At the moment the most desperate fighting is taking place on the Gona beach sector, where the A.I.F. is gradually whittling away the enemy's grip in a series of ferocious, but costly, bayonet charges. One private describes a typical attack to me today:

"We'd been advancing for hours through stinking swamps up to our knees when we reached better country in the coconut groves, but when we pushed through the plantation to the beach we met heavy machine-gun fire from a strong Jap post on the beach. We attacked in a broad, sweeping line, charging across the sand with fixed bayonets and grenades, and stormed our way right into the position.

"It was the wildest, maddest, bloodiest fighting I have ever seen. Grenades were bursting among the Japs as we stabbed down at them with our bayonets from the parapets above. Some of our fellows were actually rolling on the sand with Japs locked against them in wrestling grips. It was all over within a few minutes. A few of the Japs had escaped, but the bodies of 30 were tangled among their captured guns.

"A bayonet charge like that is a pretty terrible business when you see your cobbers falling, when you can only see ahead of you a tree. You can't even see the Japs hidden among the roots until you're right on top of them, and they are still firing and yelling as you plunge the bayonet down. But it's the only way to clean them out. Those bastards fight to the last. They keep fighting until your bayonet sinks into them.

"That night we were forced to abandon the position because the Japs made it quite untenable with heavy enfilading fire. They reoccupied it but we attacked again at dawn and threw them out again with heavy losses. One of our officers, Lieutenant Caddy, went for a big Jap 10 yards away. The two threw their grenades together. Caddy's grenade blew the Jap to pieces, but the Japanese grenade, although it burst right on our officer's face, only gave him a superficial wound.

"Eight of the Japs ran into the water and began to swim toward a wrecked transport lying offshore. We called out to them to surrender or be shot. They took no notice, so we opened fire with the Brens and killed six of them. The other two reached the wreck, from which Japanese troops were firing heavily at our positions."

Another incident yesterday provided a typical illustration of Japanese desperation. A brawny American tommy gunner, 6 feet 3 inches tall, was patrolling alone down a track near Gona when a completely unarmed Japanese, slightly built and not much more than five feet tall, leaped out of the undergrowth, seized the big American by the throat and brought him crashing to the ground. They wrestled wildly for a few minutes, but the American broke the grip of the Jap, scrambled to his feet and brought the butt of his gun crashing down on the head of his assailant. The Jap fell to the ground, but when the American stooped over, he was grabbed by the ankle and again brought down. In the end the American was forced to strangle the Jap to death with his bare hands.

The fighting everywhere is reaching this intensity of bitterness. In most positions now Australians and Americans are facing the Japanese across a no-man's-land only 50 yards wide, and sometimes less than 50 feet. Our artillery is in action only sporadically because of the fear of lobbing shells among our own troops. Bombing is similarly restricted, and on several occasions bombs from our own planes have fallen among the Americans.

It's difficult to really know what is going on. Today I was in the front line attempting to get a picture of what was happening on the Sanananda track. The soldiers asked me how the fighting was going and I asked them, and neither party gathered very much information. In this sort of country you can see very little beyond the ten or twenty feet of black-shadowed jungle that lies immediately ahead. Going up, I met a kid who looked young enough to be suspected of playing truant from school—coming back from the Gona front for medical attention to an arm that had been badly chewed by a mortar bomb. We stopped to yarn and he handed me his water bottle.

"Taste that," he said, with a grin, and I did, and promptly spat it out.

"Salt water," he said. "That's just to show 'em that I got to the sea on the north coast—and I walked all the way!"

It was fairly quiet in this front line sector along the Sanananda track, although about two hours earlier the Japanese had staged some sort of counter-blast, using heavy mortar, machine-gun and artillery fire along the track. The Australians had replied with heavy mortar fire, and 25-pounders hurled shells into the Japanese positions to cover an attack by U. S. infantry.

When I was there the report came back that the Americans had pushed forward 400 yards and had lost contact with the enemy. Something was happening, however, because we could hear sporadic machine-gun fire and the occasional crump of a mortar. A few wounded were walking back. Cases of heavy Japanese A.A. shells littered the sides of the track. In the undergrowth lay the huddled body of a dead Japanese.

A group of grimy Australians were huddled around a cooking fire, crowing with delight at the unexpected day's ration—sausages and potatoes and an issue of cigarettes.

This was the front line, or near enough to it. Over Buna, Flying Fortresses were making their runs across the target, while the dark gray puffs of Japanese A.A. fire burst wildly nowhere near them. The Fortresses disappeared, and it was not until then that we heard the crack-crack of the A.A. fire, followed by the sullen thunder of falling bombs.

The bursts had hardly drifted away in the sky when a few of our bombers went across Buna at what seemed a leisurely speed. Again the scattered bursts of A.A. and the noise of gunfire preceded the thunder of bombs, and the smaller U. S. bombers, at low level, swept across in the other direction. This time there was no A.A. fire.

It was some time before the enemy planes put in an appearance. The explosions of bombs away on our right attracted instant attention to the Zeros plummeting down in steep power dives. They were fitted with bombs to act as dive-bombers. We could hear the bombs falling somewhere near where another U. S. force was attacking.

And then down from the cloud-spattered sky dived our fighters, with engines shrieking and guns blazing. Machine-gun fire punctuated the whine and roar of the dogfight. A Zero, pouring flame, came to earth like a spent rocket. And then it was no longer possible to tell friend from foe in the whirling thirty-minute combat. One Zero, which had been hit, went streaking over our heads like a silver flash, heading for home as fast as possible. Half an hour later our fighters were patrolling a Zero-free sky.

Along the track, which winds dustily through the jungle, there is an endless movement backward and forward. American jeeps, flown in by transport planes, speed toward the front with food and ammunition, and come back with wounded. Long lines of coal-black native carriers wind along the track toward the firing line with stores and ammunition and come back gently bearing litters on which are Australian and American wounded.

A battered 30 hundredweight truck, captured from the Japanese in this area and then found to be an Australian truck captured by the Japanese at Rabaul, jolts by at regular intervals laden with rice and bully beef and boxes of grenades.

Something is happening at Buna. There were a number of thunderous explosions, and now a huge column of gray smoke is rising slowly over the Japanese base. A long line of green-clad Australian troops marches by, heading toward Sanananda. Many Australian and American wounded are coming back for medical attention, but it is amazing how few of the wounds are serious and how great is the proportion of woundings over killings. It is a picture in reverse on the Japanese side. They usually stay in their machine-gun nests, gun-pits, and snipers' posts until the last minute. And when the allies attack they attack to kill. This is probably the most savagely fought war for centuries, but you can only beat savagery with savagery.

Steam is rising now as the blazing sun beats down on the earth and undergrowth soaked by an earlier downpour. The sun is beginning to sink more rapidly though, and soon we shall have that false ten minutes of coolness before the steaminess of the night hours. Soldiers here chuckle when in one of the rare newspapers they receive they read of the "austerity campaign" in Australia. Their lives have been the complete expression of austerity for months now.

This morning at breakfast I queued up next to a tall, thin-framed digger who was almost incoherent with delight when two greasy-looking canned sausages were slapped onto his mess tin. I understood something of his excitement when he told me that he had had 104 successive meals of bully beef.

From where I am standing I can see in every direction for perhaps 100 yards, for we are in what is more or less a clearing. Everywhere are scattered the temporary "homes" of the troops. Some have erected lean-to's, native style, with hanging fronds of palm leaves. Others have thrown their blankets on the ground and their few belongings alongside, and have rigged their ground sheets above to form tiny tents.

Between every little tent and hut there is a tangled wilderness of undergrowth in bright chrome yellow and vivid emerald green. Overhead soar giant, nameless jungle trees and feathery-topped coconut palms, draped in hanging lantana vines and lawyer canes. The palms have a ragged appearance where our machine gunners sprayed the tops in search of Japanese snipers and where Zero bullets and bombs have destroyed the delicate symmetry of the fronds. A spotter, with a tin hat and rifle, watches the skies for Zeros. Low over the trees roars a "bully beef bomber." I can see the black specks falling as the rations are pushed out over the dropping-ground.

Five men in green jungle uniforms are squatting round a little fire, over which a bully is simmering. One is playing "The Lights of London" on a mouth organ, which, I am told, proved a blessing to hundreds af troops during the terrible march across the Owen Stanley's. Others are discussing the prospect of getting Christmas hampers.

There was mail dropped this morning from one of the planes, and many of the troops are reading letters or writing answers. I'll bet every letter includes the phrase: "I can hear our guns and mortars in action against the Japanese a couple of miles away."

Most of them will be writing, too, of yesterday afternoon's Zero attack against the Australian and American casualty clearing stations, just along the track. The raids were quite deliberate. Each C.C.S. was marked clearly with huge red crosses, and the Zeros and dive-bombers came down to the tree-tops to make repeated passes. Thirty-one were killed and 56 wounded. Most of the casualties were Australians, including a number of wounded just brought in from the front lines and the two senior Australian doctors who were attending them. Those two doctors had saved hundreds of lives. For days they had been working eighteen, sometimes twenty, hours a day on the almost constant stream of wounded. They worked stripped to the waist and pouring with perspiration in the steamy heat of the Buna plain, just as they had worked night and day on the edge of marshy Myola Lake, in the pass through the Owen Stanley's more than 6000 feet above sea level.

The doctors who took over from them had no time to think that what had once happened could easily happen again. In the destruction and horrible carnage of the wrecked hospital they methodically set to work to patch up the 50 wounded men lying on the ground in long rows amid the shredded trunks of coconut palms.

And not from one of those wounded—Australians, Americans and natives alike—came a single murmur of complaint or one groan of pain. The doctors, working on the wounded until long after midnight, would not rest, would not even eat, until the last dressing had been completed.

The operating theatre was a rude native hut of saplings with a thatched roof of kunai grass. All round was the clatter of the war in the night. Steam rose from the water boiling in the sterilizer—a camp dixie over an open fire. Around the operating table men stood with torches which gleamed on the sweating, naked backs of the doctors. . . .

One of the badly wounded men was Tom Fairhall, war correspondent of the Sydney *Daily Telegraph,* one of the grandest chaps who ever tapped a typewriter. Tom will be out of circulation for a long time. Ian Morrison of the London *Times*—son of the famous "Chinese" Morrison—and Geoff Reading, of the Sydney *Daily Mirror*—who thus chalks up his second narrow escape from death at the hands of Japanese Zero pilots—were lucky to get out of it with a few scratches from tiny bomb splinters. Tom will go south to hospital with five ugly wounds, but Ian and Geoff are staying on the job.

### Buna Nocturne

The harsh white light of mid-afternoon has softened and there is a misleading hint of coolness in the light breeze that ruffles the wide waters of the Gerua River. This is the beginning of zero hour on the Buna front. Up here zero hour isn't used in its last war sense. It is the period of the day towards evening when the American fighter cover generally disappears and the Japanese Zeros can be expected to show their snub noses again, and perhaps enliven the ending day with strafing and dive-bombing. Sometimes the Zeros don't come, of course, but the air spotters are vigilant, and every man looks upward expectantly as the drone of a plane is heard over the trees.

They settle back again to their little tasks of stoking the camp fires, filling the billies and dixies, getting the night's supply of cool river water into water bottles, writing letters home while there is still sufficient light to see. The plane is only an army cooperation aircraft heading toward Sanananda Point to spot and register targets for the night's artillery shoot. The last transport plane for the day wheels overhead, its enormous wings almost brushing the tree-top and heads toward the cloud-capped Owen Stanley's.

The setting sun is daubing color into the previously dried-out whiteness of the glaring tropic day. The smoke clouds over Buna and Gona and Sanananda are tinted now with orange. There is a warmth of tone in the tree trunks, and the Hydrographers Range, which rears its craggy peaks behind us, is deep purple in the shadows and rich gold on the highlights. Naked men, white and black, are swimming in the shallow stream. The scene is no more martial than a Boy Scouts' Christmas camp. From the front, a couple of miles ahead, there has been no sound now for two hours.

A sergeant, wearing only shorts, and with his three chevrons drawn on his bare arm with indelible pencil, calls his men in the voice of a stentor—"Don Company. Here's your soap issue and cigarettes. One cake of soap and razor blade, forty cigarettes per man. And don't any of you mugs try and come the double!"

The men assemble quickly. Another voice cries: "C Company. Tucker." And there is the noise of many bare legs swishing through the undergrowth and the clatter of mess tins and pannikins. From the bushes comes a mocking voice that feigns girlish delight—"Oh, goody, goody. Isn't this a thrill! Bully beef and biscuits. Oh, what a lovely surprise!"

Chuckles ripple through the bustling bivouac area. The sky is purpling, and the shadows in the trees are mysterious black caves and chasms.

The sun drops swiftly, and there is an air of tenseness and expectancy that comes suddenly and without reason. For the first time for hours one can imagine crouching figures in the jungle, men flattening to earth and fingering triggers of automatic weapons, slant-eyed Japanese peering from loopholes in their tree trunk weapon pits, men looking at the dense wilderness all round them with that faint, uncontrollable feeling of fear that comes each evening in the jungle when the trees seem to be hiding watching eyes, when every sound is magnified by the awful hush that precedes the nightly cacophony of the insect world.

The hush is broken by the sudden frightening roar of 25-pounders just ahead of us—the curious double bang followed by the strange, rushing whistle of the shell and the distant *"fruump, frump, frump, fruuump"* of the explosions. It is the regular overture to another night of battle.

Mortars start to cough, and on the Gona track and north of Soputa there is a wild rattle of machine-gun fire. The Japanese are nervous. They have been hammered solidly for many nights now, and they are jittery at what this new night has in store for them. Their fire ripples unevenly along the wall of jungle. Occasionally, I can see the flash of a rifle, once the orange splash of a bursting grenade.

Over the east bank of the river, where Australian and American guns are supporting the infantry attacks on Buna Mission, and the airfield and the Cape Endaiadere pill-boxes, the guns begin with a full-throated roar that echoes crashingly from the dense walls of the jungle. The earth shakes and the air is filled with sound and movements. The rushing roar of the shells is like an express train plunging through a culvert. The air throbs and is still.

A suntanned digger spooning bully beef into his mouth, grins across at me. "Here they go again," he says. "Pity help the Buna boys on a night like this. No sleep again tonight, I suppose." He laughs out loud.

"I was speaking to an artillery bloke today, and he said that the guns had been in action at night to make sure the Japs didn't get any sleep. Trouble is we aren't getting any ourselves."

There was no bitterness in his remark. The troops know how wonderful it is to have that ring of guns supporting them. When the 25-pounders were first brought up by transport planes and towed into action by jeeps, the track was lined with cheering Australians, and the shouts of "You bloody beauts" must have been heard by the Japs.

It is almost dark. Crickets and strange insects are filling the night with sound. Strange birds with narrow-gutted bodies and great wings—the troops call them flying lead pencils—are rocking in the green branches and cawing like crows. Overhead is the nightly procession of giant black fruit bats, countless hundreds of them, all flying on exactly the same course from the seashore toward the jungle hills behind. The fireflies are flitting everywhere. One soldier has caught two in his hair, flickering like brilliant diamonds.

A signals sergeant whose tobacco has filled my pipe looks up to the silently flitting bats. "A man must be going troppo," he remarks quietly. "About three nights ago I was looking up at those bats heading inland from Buna and I jokingly said to a cobber, 'There go the black souls of Japs killed at Buna, heading back to that big cemetery we found at Kokoda.' Do you know that now, every time I see those blasted bats, I can't get that thought out of my mind. Those bats are evil-looking things, and I guess if the Japs have souls that's what they look like."

The brief twilight has ended and the thick tropic night has begun, a night filled with many small sounds—the murmur of voices, the crackle of cooking fires, the sharp slap of a hand on bare flesh, and the soft cursing as a man carries out a brief blitz against the mosquitoes, the distant sound of a concertina and of a man playing "Colonel Bogey" on a battered tin whistle.

Pretty soon the real battle of the darkness will begin; but all the preparations for it are hidden in the jungle. Thirty yards from a Japanese forward post an artillery officer whispers instructions into a tiny field telephone. Less than a mile behind him another man picks up his message and relays it back to the battery control post, so well camouflaged that you could never see it if you walked past it only a yard away. An operator screws his eyes as he listens at the headphones and turns to a suntanned captain: "Everett's owe pip reporting, sir." A pencil scratches on a pad and the gun crews receive their instructions.

Up forward, weary American and Australian infantry are slumped among the tangled vines and tree roots snatching sleep for an hour or two while they can. Sentries peer into the black firefly-spangled jungle toward where the Japs are chopping down trees and driving stakes into the ground. That probably means another post to be taken when this one falls. A twig cracks in the night. There is a rattle of machine-gun fire from the Japs. The Australian sentry moves away from his position, blasts off a few rounds at the point where he saw the stabs of flame from the enemy guns, and then whips back to his old position. Another spatter of fire and a couple of bullets whack the tree he has just fired from. The sentry grins.

A patrol squirms silently through a black, evil-smelling swamp on a flanking job to try to get behind the enemy positions before dawn. Almost in a whisper, a private curses the leeches clinging to his legs and arms.

The artillery has started now in its full measure. Sleep is no longer possible in the unbroken crash of sound that runs from one end of the front to another. The noise is traveling queerly tonight, and it often sounds as if the Japanese are shelling us. A soldier nearby asks his mate: "They reckon there are a couple of destroyers off Buna tonight. Sounds as if they're shelling our guns, doesn't it?"

"Dunno," the reply comes out of the darkness. "It's hard to tell tonight. But one thing's certain, somebody's at the receiving end of an awful heap of metal, and I'm glad it isn't me."

Hour after hour the firing continues. There *are* destroyers somewhere off Buna and the guns have the job of preventing any barge or small boat activity between ships and beaches. The night is an almost uninterrupted medley of noise—the double cracking bark of the 25-pounders, the deeper roar of heavy Australian mountain howitzers every now and then, the thunderous bark of big American 105-mm. howitzers. There is little break in the rushing hiss of torn air between each gunshot, and over on the northern beaches the "frump, fruuump" of falling shells marks a regular and grim anthem of destruction.

Gun flashes flicker yellowly round the entire sky line, and over on the Japanese positions the explosions. Once a great searing flash of white light splits the darkness over Buna. "Must have got a dump," suggests a man nearby. "Looks like it," I reply.

There is a great roaring drone overhead. "Bombers," somebody yells, and we all listen for the engine note. "Ours, I think," somebody says, and we accept his opinion with only slight reservations. They are ours, however, and in a few minutes the north sky is weirdly lighted by falling parachute flares, two white and one red. It's five minutes before the bombs fall with the great rolling thunder sound that seems to reach us at the same time as the shaking of the earth.

The same thing goes on hour after hour. Men sleep fitfully, if they sleep at all, tossing restlessly and muttering unintelligibly.

A half moon rises hugely over Buna, and soon afterward we hear a Zero overhead, droning round and round above the tree-tops. "Put that bloody light out," comes a roar as a man strikes a match to light a cigarette. The light goes out. But the Zero isn't looking for us. He's trying to spot the artillery positions by the gun flashes. The artillerymen don't fall for that. One battery over which the Zero is circling stays silent, but three or four miles away another battery opens up with a terrific salvo. The Zero drones across to investigate, and as soon as he's gone the other battery blasts out its shells, while the one that has been firing remains silent.

The cat-and-mouse game goes on for more than an hour. The Zero drops a red parachute flare, but apparently can't see anything, and drones away in disgust after having dropped one bomb irritably in the scrub.

A Japanese 75-mm. gun, firing at random, plonks a few shells down our way, but they fall harmlessly in the tangled trees. There is a heavy clash somewhere on the front at first light, and we can hear mortars and machine guns kicking up a terrific din. It dies away after half an hour, and firing is light and scattered all along the front.

The sun pops suddenly above the range. Aircraft drone in the pure dew-drenched light of dawn—our fighter cover over the top to begin the daylight business. An A.I.F. private looks up at the Airacobras speeding beneath the clouds, and yells out: "Good on yer, Yank."

Another night on the Buna battlefield is over.

### "I Suppose I've Been Lucky!"

I struck him on the track back from Gona, a mile or two behind the roar and chatter of the guns. I didn't know whether I should speak to him, for he looked very sick, but his mate said he wanted to speak, wanted to tell his story. Bearded and gaunt, but still smiling, twenty-two-year-old Bruce Taylor, infantry subaltern of the A.I.F., lay back on the crude stretcher made of gray army blankets lashed to logs. The bandages which swathed his body were stained with dried blood, his voice scarcely rose above a whisper, a whisper that was often drowned by the crash of artillery and mortar fire behind us. He explained painfully that his voice had just come back to him. This is the story he told me:

"It was my job to go in with a patrol of nine Australians against a troublesome Jap strongpost not far from Gona Mission. The attack had been timed for early afternoon on 22 November, but the swamps were thigh-deep in mud and took us a long time to get across. By the time we'd reached the edge of the kunai patch from which we were to launch the attack it was getting pretty late. But the job had to be done. About dusk I smashed a hole in the fence dividing the kunai patch from the coconut plantation, and we pushed through. I think we must have run into an ambush, because we were fired on heavily from the front and, I think, also from behind. I could see my men falling one by one and then I was hit by a bullet on the side of my head. I could see the blood spurting out and I said to myself: 'This is it!' Then everything went black. When I came to my head seemed to be detached and revolving slowly round my body. I must have been unconscious only for a second or two because just before I passed out again I saw the last of my men go down. He rolled over and over like a rabbit shot on the run. . . .

"It was nearly dark when I came to again. The blood from my wound seemed to have stopped flowing. I thought I might have a chance. My water bottle was full but when I tried to drink I found I couldn't swallow, as the bullet had done something to my throat. I tried to shout for help but my voice had gone and no sound came. It was a queer feeling. I decided it would be best to try to crawl away and get medical attention for myself and some stretcher-bearers to bring in the other wounded. I suppose I'd only crawled about fifteen yards when I had to stop for a rest. I must have fallen asleep because next thing I knew it was dawn and I was right in the middle of a battle between the Japs and the Australians. I could hear the crack of rifles and the noise of bullets whistling over me. And then one hit me in the shoulder. After a time the firing stopped and I lay there roasting in the sun.

"Thirst nearly drove me mad. I couldn't drink, but there had been heavy rain in the night and I knew that if I could find one of the Jap slit-trenches I'd find water in it. It must have taken me hours but eventually I found one with a foot of water in the bottom and I tumbled in. I stayed there all day, trying to absorb the cool water through my skin.

"The next few days are pretty hazy. I must have been delirious most of the time, because I found out later I'd been there a full week before the big bombardment of Gona shook a bit of sense into me. All the time I'd been only fifteen yards from the Japanese positions. I could hear them yabbering during the day and sometimes at night they walked past within a couple of feet of me. They never saw me, or if they did I must have looked like just another of the corpses packed round the area. On the Sunday morning (29 November) the Australians began a terrific bombardment of Gona as preparation for a full-scale attack. I was right in the middle of the target area. Bombs from planes, mortar bombs, and shells from the 25-pounder battery were falling all around me. The earth was rocking to the hail of high explosive and I was often lifted two or three feet off the ground. Then Flying Fortresses came over and their bombs fell all round me. A fragment hit me in the shoulder, tearing out a great piece of flesh.

"Things quieted down after an hour. Although they had had no attention for a week the bullet wounds weren't troubling me much, but the wound from the bomb splinter caused me indescribable agony. It had been pretty hard to find pools of water to soak myself in. The corpses all around me were rotting. I felt myself going mad. I couldn't stand it any longer. I could still hear the Japs chattering on my left so I decided on a good way out. I was very weak. Nothing to drink for a week, nothing to eat although a heap of abandoned emergency rations were within arm's reach of me. I staggered to my knees and began to crawl toward the Jap post, shouting: 'Shoot, you little bastards, shoot me, kill me!'

"I'd forgotten that I couldn't utter a sound, and somehow the Japs didn't see me. I must have crawled right past them, because next thing I remember I was lying in some kunai grass beyond the enemy weapon pit. The bombs must have started fires because within a few minutes the kunai grass began to burn. For the first time for a week I managed to stand up. I staggered forward until I came to a beautiful, big bomb crater. I staggered over and fell into it. It had two feet of lovely cool water in the bottom. No words of mine can describe the glorious feeling of lying in that water through the blazing heat of the day. . . ."

Taylor coughed and spat, motioning to me that he'd rest for a while. The drone of insects was all about us. Occasionally a machine gun chattered. The native carriers squatted in the dust, one holding a broad green banana leaf over the head of the wounded man. He grinned and began to speak again in the painful whisper:

"I decided it was still worth while trying to live. I kept thinking of my mother and father and my sister. I've got the best family in the world, you know. It was worth trying to see them again. When the heat had gone out of the sun I crawled out of the bomb crater and began to move toward where I thought our troops would be. Every now and then I would rinse out my mouth at any puddle of water on the ground. The pain in my shoulder had given way to a dull ache that didn't trouble me as much. I must have been moving ahead through the night, because at dawn I was astride a small ridge looking down at a track below me. There was no sign of life. I thought I must have come too far and the thought of being lost depressed me unbearably. I tumbled down the cutting and lay where I had fallen. This was the finish, I thought; I couldn't go another inch farther. There was a scraping noise above me. I looked up. Clambering down from the branches of the trees above were three Aussies of an A.I.F. observation post. They fixed me up and sent me back to safety. The doctors tell me I'll recover completely. I've got most of my voice back already." He grinned. "And they tell me I'll be going back to Brisbane. My mother lives there. I suppose I've been lucky."

Black muscles rippled as the crude stretcher was hoisted on to sturdy native shoulders. The natives went splayfootedly down the winding track toward Soputa. I headed on toward the front line, with Taylor's final sentence running through my brain: "I suppose I've been lucky!"

*Kill or Be Killed*

From a little spotter's post on the high bank of the swiftly running Gerau River I can see over the four sectors of the so-called battle for Buna. The only visible signs of war are two flat-topped pillars of smoke climbing into the still air—one from Buna and one from Gona—and American bombers weaving across the top of Buna through the sooty puffs of ack-ack fire, wildly erratic now from repeated bombing. There is nothing else but an incredibly vast sky of tropic blue above the marching plains of sun-drenched emerald-green jungle interspersed with patches of yellow man-high kunai grass. The peacefulness is deceptive.

An A.I.F. captain whom I knew well came across the river the other day from an American force attacking Buna. He had made the walk alone along a jungle track which he described as "a scenic walk of unparalleled beauty; a tropic idyll that nobody should miss seeing." The next day on that same idyllic track an American patrol of eight was ambushed by the Japanese, and seven were killed. I, too, walked alone along a track leading beyond Soputa, heading toward the front line, and did not know until I reached my destination that a Japanese patrol had been dispersed and driven off on that same track far behind our lines.

That makes it easier to understand why this strange war in the green shadows is mostly invisible. And although you can see nothing you know that in this incredibly tangled wilderness of rank vegetation and evil swamps thousands of men—Americans, Australians, and Japanese—are fighting out one of the most merciless and most primeval battles of the war. As I watched, I remembered the words of General Sir Thomas Blamey when he was talking to an A.I.F. artillery unit in a rain-drenched clearing in Port Moresby a few months before: "You are fighting a shrewd, cruel, merciless enemy, who knows how to kill and who knows how to die. Beneath the thin veneer of a few generations of civilization he is a sub-human beast, who has brought warfare back to the primeval, who fights by the jungle rule of tooth and claw, who must be beaten by the jungle rule of tooth and claw. Kill him or he will kill you."

The fighting now is even more bloody because the Japanese are defending with desperation and with bitterness. They have the desperation of men who know that only death awaits them. Fighting on this front is coldly animal. This morning I was speaking to some Australians who had been out on a mountain patrol to rescue a little party of Australian wounded who had been left in a mountain village since the retreat through the Gap in August. They found the wounded, but every man had been slaughtered by Japanese bayonets. The Japanese know the things they have done. And the slant-eyed, buck-toothed savages in the trappings of civilization who peer from their barricaded weapon pits know that they can expect nothing but death from their enemies if they do not surrender. So they fight to the death. They fight with bitterness, because they must have an inkling now that they have been left to kill and die. They hate the allied troops who are slowly closing the trap around them, and in that peaceful setting the fight goes on from day to day. For twenty terrible days now the allies have been slowly closing in, and the piles of Japanese dead are mounting higher, but many good men have died in the task.

Every day is a day of grim drama on these twisting jungle tracks, along which one sees so many of those simple wooden stakes bearing the names of Australians and Americans, but bearing many more names in the indecipherable ideographs of Japan. Back from the line where the guns are echoing, and where great American 81-millimetre mortars are thundering out their metallic bloodhounds' bay, stagger wounded men, blood still running from beneath grimy bandages, their green uniforms torn and stained gray with mud, their faces lined, insect bitten, haggard, sometimes yellowed by fever. Men with torn limbs and ugly stained bandages lie with closed eyes on the crude log stretchers borne on the stout shoulders of loyal, kindly, plodding natives. These men are silent and un-complaining, and the sunlight streaming through the great green banana leaf that wards the blazing sun from their heads paints their features with a weird undersea light.

These are the soldiers who have learned that warfare, as taught to them at the Louisiana manoeuvres or on firing ranges, is a very different thing from warfare as learned so bitterly in the steaming jungles of Papua. In this kill-or-be-killed war prisoners are rare enough to become phenomena of the track. Once a litter-borne Japanese, his shoulder swathed in a bloody bandage, is carried to the rear. Americans and Australians watch him with curiosity, but the natives move toward him with hatred in their eyes. An American hands a canteen of drinking water to a native to give to the prisoner. The native, who looks rather like Paul Robeson, glances contemptuously at the prisoner, and hurls the canteen to the ground. "Me no give water Jap pig," he says, and strides away. An Australian grins, picks up the water bottle and moves over to the Japanese.

This is a tough and bitter war. In the Cape Endaiadere and Gona areas, at Buna Mission, and on the Sanananda track a wily enemy has selected his own positions for defense. He has established con-crete gunpits and dug grenade-proof and mortar-proof nests be-neath the roots of giant jungle trees. He has put keen-eyed snipers in hundreds of tree-tops. He has mown down the grass and jungle to give lanes of sweeping fire to his many machine guns. From such positions companies can hold up battalions and battalions could resist divisions.

These pockets cannot be bypassed because of neck-deep swamps of black, sucking mud. They must be assaulted at whatever cost, and destroyed one by one. Artillery is helping tremendously—Aus-tralian 25-pounders and mountain howitzers of the type that re-duced the Abyssinian mountain stronghold of Keren, and huge American 105-millimetre howitzers which were flown into action and are now getting their first combat tests. But many of the Japa-nese foxholes are too deep and too cleverly contrived to be wiped out even by the terrific artillery and aerial bombardments which pour unbelievable tons of high explosives each day and night. It is an infantryman's war.

In this fighting war has been boiled down to simple essentials, and to simple tools for killing. It has been pruned back to the primitive fights, often hand to hand, between a man and his enemy. The elaborate impediments of war have been discarded. Engineers working on tracks use picks and shovels and often their bare hands in a land where bulldozers and graders are locked away behind the door of the Owen Stanley Range. Littered along the tracks is much of the elaborate gear, for instance, that made the American doughboy the best-equipped soldier in the world. Up here you fight light or you don't fight long. In the front lines the walky-talky radio is used only rarely, for the old-fashioned runner is still a safer and surer way of overcoming the almost unbelievably difficult task of maintaining an unbroken line of communications. Only the amazing jeep brings a new note into the age-old form of warfare, and in its ceaseless job of towing guns, running supplies and munitions to the front, and bringing back wounded, it has increased its claim to being the greatest all-purpose military discovery of the war.

Up here you will see tommy guns and Bren guns and Owen guns and elaborate mortars and machine guns and field pieces, but men have wrestled on the ground and stabbed each other to death, and men have met their end when a pair of steely, strangulating hands have closed round their windpipes. Men have been killed by having their brains bashed out with a heavy stone. The words of General Blamey came back to me again: "He has brought warfare back to the primeval. He fights by the jungle rule of tooth and claw. Kill him or he will kill you."

How many of these "sub-human beasts" we have yet to fight on this little beachhead is a question that every man asks and a question the answer to which no man knows. In the Gona sector alone the Australians have already killed 400. But the Japanese are still holding out in some of their Gona strongposts. The really staggering thing is the amount of punishment the Japanese have taken, and yet they still fought back as stubbornly as ever. How they have withstood some of those awe-inspiring bombardments I cannot understand. A few days ago I watched one of these bombardments. From dawn to dusk the earth was shuddering. When bombs were not falling in the little area that the Japanese still hold a constant barrage of artillery shells was smashing into it. For seven or eight hours the target area was a wild inferno of flame and smoke and dust and whizzing metal. Yet when the allied troops went into attack immediately after the bombardment had ended the Japanese were still there, still fighting as bitterly as ever. This might be a war on a very small scale, but it is also a war on a scale of toughness that sometimes defies the imagination, and only toughness will win it.

### Baptism for Doughboys

For more than a fortnight now American troops have been constantly in action on the Buna front, and they have learned many things that no amount of training, no textbooks, no blackboard lectures could have taught them. A few days ago I was discussing the campaign with the commander of the Australian force which has been fighting for months in the Papuan jungle. As we sat in his camouflaged tent beneath a dense overcover of thick jungle trees a small patrol of American troops filed past, heading toward the front, where intermittent machine-gun fire had been rattling all the morning. Their uniforms were ragged and mud-caked. Their faces were bearded. Only by their basin-shaped steel helmets could one identify them as Americans, and not another patrol of Australians who had been heading northward since dawn.

"Those kids are doing a darned good job," said the commander. "They are green and inexperienced, and this is the first fight they have ever been in. Doubt if a tougher baptism by fire could be imagined. But they are learning fast, because they want to learn, and they aren't afraid to ask the advice of my troops, who have learnt all the lessons at bitter cost. In a soldier's life his first battle is his most important. It doesn't matter what happens afterwards. He learns more in that first fight than he'll ever learn again in his whole military career. I think these boys expected a swift and easy capture of Buna. I was more cautious, but it's a tougher proposition than even I'd expected. But these Americans are coming through the test well, and they should be grand jungle fighters when it's over."

In actual fighting up here there are really two distinct armies opposed to the Japanese, with two distinct ways of fighting. It is rather a curious set-up. The Australians, who have been in the war now for three years, are undoubtedly the most battle-seasoned jungle fighters in the United Nations forces. They have the knowledge to beat the Japanese, but they have been bitterly fighting now for three months, twice across the terrible Owen Stanley Range, and they are tired and battered in everything but morale and spirit. The Americans are comparatively fresh—probably much fresher than the majority of the Japanese they are fighting—but this is their first battle of the war, and they are opposed to a wily, well-trained enemy, who has been fighting for a long time. One dead Japanese examined was apparently one of the reinforcements recently landed —one of the tough, seasoned, specially trained Japanese landing forces, which specialize in amphibious operations and jungle fighting.

So there it is. Freshness and battle inexperience on the one side; battle weariness and experience on the other, but no difference in the courage of each. Against these men is ranged an enemy who believes he is to die, and probably intends to take with him as many of the Allies as he can. The Americans want to take their objectives with the minimum number of casualties, not from fear but because of the desire to finish the job with a strong fighting force still intact. The Australians want to get the job over. It is significant that a great many of the Australian objectives have been gained by bayonet charges, whereas the Americans have not yet put in an attack at bayonet point.

American progress against its main objectives—the Cape En-daiadere positions, Buna airfield, Buna Mission, and Buna Village —has been a slow, relentless pressure, which is gradually closing a vice-like grip round what remains of General Horii's force, with the minimum number of casualties possible in this sort of fighting. The Australians have made more rapid progress against their ob-jectives, despite their weariness, in what is virtually a series of bloody, spectacular, slaughtering dashes, which have taken heavy toll of the Australians—a heavier toll relatively than in any other A.I.F. battle of this war.

Both forces are achieving their purpose, and the slow grip of strangulation is tightening round Japan's last Papuan garrison, now a narrow strip of coastline a few miles long and up to three quarters of a mile wide. Into these few square miles is packed all that remains of the force that landed at Gona in July and pushed all the way across the Owen Stanley's to within 32 miles of Port Moresby.

The Americans know now that they are not playing for marbles, but their spirit is splendid, their morale and discipline better than ever. They have got over the natural gun-shyness which comes to any man fighting for the first time in the jungle, when he feels that every crack of a rifle is sending a bullet straight for him. They have discovered that in jungle fighting heavy foodstocks cannot be carried, and they, like the Australians, are now fighting largely on emergency rations, concentrated food tablets, and bully beef and biscuits.

They believe in General Nathan Bedford Forrest's maxim, "Get there fustest with the mostest," but that means traveling as lightly as possible. They have found that much of the equipment that proved so magnificent in peacetime manoeuvres is a mere encumbrance in the jungle. They carry now only what they cannot do without. Most of them have abandoned even their groundsheets and mosquito nets. A few weeks ago they were carrying 50 lb. packs, besides their rifles and ammunition. You don't see many with 50 lb. packs now.

When you see these young Americans moving up toward the shattering noise of the front line, or coming back wounded, or sick with the strange jungle fever that is not malaria, not scrub typhus, not dengue, you are immediately amazed at how young they look. Many of them look like kids out of high school. I suppose the A.I.F. troops looked as young when they went abroad three years ago. They are finding now that war is not all adventure, that it is grim, bloody, callous, dangerous, hard work, in which heroes are so plentiful that heroism is no longer spectacular. And yet whenever you speak to any of them they have the same boyish grins, the same disarming candor, the same naïveté, and the universal wish: "I sure want to get me a Jap."

But "getting Japs" is a pretty tough proposition in the sectors in which the Americans are fighting. The country everywhere is difficult—at its best sandy and marshy, and at its worst a maze of slimy miasmic swamps among jungle belts, almost nauseating with the stench of vegetable matter that has been decaying for years. There has been much Allied air strafing in their area, but I think more counter-strafing by the Zeros than there has been in the areas where the Australians are pushing forward. Thanksgiving Day passed by unnoticed by some doughboys, who were entitled to think that there was nothing to give thanks about when Zeros were swooping from the sky with spitting guns.

Unlike the Australians, they have not yet become completely accustomed to the terrifying jungle nights. The jungle fighter of Nippon never abandons his little "nerve war" during nights in the jungle. He chatters disconcertingly; he fires sudden, alarming shots; he tosses over bunches of firecrackers; he keeps clicking the bolts of rifles—all little tricks designed to keep the nerves of his adversaries on edge. It still succeeds to a large extent with the Americans, as it did for a considerable time with the Australians. Now the Australian merely cocks an eye, perhaps shoots off a round to scare the Japs, and turns back to sleep with a muttered, "Aw shut up, you stupid little bastards!"

The Americans will soon learn that the Japanese is probably scared, too, and his "nerve war" might often be the equivalent of the whistling of a small boy in the dark. In most respects the Japanese defense against the American troops is based on the same basic principles of Japanese defense that has occurred throughout the Papuan campaign. There are a couple of weapons the enemy seems to have been using against the Americans, however, that have not been reported on the Australian side—weapons which might be "frighteners" rather than "killers." One is a type of small bomb, like a small, brightly polished silver ball, that explodes with a deafening roar but does not seem to scatter any fragments. The other is a type of mortar bomb which scatters a shower of metal.

Otherwise the Japanese are using their old tactics. They are still extensively using the tops of palm trees as snipers' nests and as observation posts from which mortar fire is directed on to the advancing Americans. As First class Pvt. William Haiman, of Wisconsin, said: "Sometimes you can see them in the trees, but as you move ahead they keep moving round the tree to keep the trunk between them and our fire. We've managed to bring a great many of them tumbling down, though."

Machine gun nests in pill-boxes and behind heavy log barricades have given the doughboys most trouble, however, and with the deep shelters dug by the Japanese alongside their pits they manage to survive the colossal aerial and artillery bombardments, and are able to whip back to their gun after the barrage has ended before the Americans can begin their advance.

The Yanks will come out of this fight seasoned and experienced jungle fighters. They are going through a hard school, but they are learning fast. They don't like it much. Neither do the Australians, and even less the Japanese. The one wish of the doughboys is to finish off the job and get home. Most of them will, and so will most of the Australians. But very few of the Japanese will see the islands of Japan again.

### Remember Pearl Harbor

Just to remind us that it was the anniversary of Pearl Harbor, our friends from Rabaul decided yesterday to do a little commemorating. Here's the story:

The Japanese hurled in the strongest air attacking force for months. Their gesture went wrong when the raiders ran into American fighters over the north Papuan coast, which, without loss to themselves, shot 18 enemy planes out of the sky in a few minutes.

In the devastating air attack the Japanese lost 6 medium bombers, five dive-bombers, and seven Zeros. In addition two other Zeros were destroyed at Lae, where Beaufighter pilots reported that the drome was "littered with wrecked planes," and another Zero was shot down, in flames, off Gasmata. The day's air intervention thus cost the enemy 21 planes for certain and we lost no fighters.

"Remember Pearl Harbor" had a significance for the American fighter pilots as well as for the Japanese. One Kittyhawk pilot, who shot down three Japanese planes in flames today, brought off an extraordinary double. Exactly twelve months ago during the initial attack on Pearl Harbor he also sent three Japanese planes down in flames.

How many planes the Japanese hurled into yesterday's attack is not known, but in addition to dive-bombers, which were attacking rear positions near Buna, two enemy formations were sighted—one of eighteen bombers and twelve Zeros, and the other of twelve bombers and an unspecified number of fighters. Scores of Allied fighters were swarming over the north coast—the greatest concentration of Allied fighter aircraft in the air at any one time since the beginning of the New Guinea war. It is estimated that when all types of planes—American, Australian, and Japanese—were considered, there were probably more than 250 aircraft in the air.

The enemy formation of 30 planes was first picked up five miles out to sea off Buna by patrolling Kittyhawks, which came down from medium altitude in power dives to attack the bombers head on. Other Allied fighters followed them in and saw three large, black Japanese planes crash into the sea, trailing great columns of black smoke. Two others went down in flames.

Ten minutes later another force of Kittyhawks saw twelve enemy bombers, with a fighter screen, coming in toward Buna at 17,000 feet. As the American fighters pushed in to make an attack they saw another force of Kittyhawks plummeting down on top of the Japanese formation, which was still well out to sea. One of the Japanese planes spun down into the sea in flames, and a few minutes later two columns of heavy black smoke were seen rising from the water.

Within a few minutes scores of fighters were roaring and screaming in whirling dogfights, as Allied planes pounced upon the Zeros at high altitude, while other planes attacked Zeros and dive-bombers thousands of feet below. The Allied planes had complete control, and within ten minutes seven Zeros had crashed into the sea or on to the ground, where excited Australian and American troops fighting in the swamps and jungle tracks near Buna cheered the results of the most spectacular air fight of the Papuan war.

Down almost at tree-top level Australian Beaufighters were strafing enemy ack-ack positions with thousands of rounds of machine gun fire against which the Japanese stuck to their guns and kept up an intense fire, when a Japanese dive-bomber was seen. One Beaufighter immediately began to chase it, and was overtaking it when a Zero came on to the tail of the Australian plane. Another Beaufighter roared in for a head-on attack on the Zero, and drove it off. Four enemy dive-bombers immediately came through the melee in an attempt to escape the hordes of Allied planes, but Airacobras swept down on them at nearly 400 m.p.h. Two of the dive-bombers dived straight into the sea, and another spun down trailing a great comet's tail of flame.

Other dive-bombers, which were hurling bombs on Allied positions behind the front line, were attacked fiercely, and two were destroyed. Within a few minutes eighteen enemy aeroplanes had been completely wiped out of the skies, and the remnants of the enemy force retreated.

The most spectacular day of air fighting of the whole New

Guinea campaign ended with every Allied plane safely back at its base and with the ruins of twenty-one Japanese planes in the northern jungles or at the bottom of the sea.* "Remember Pearl Harbor" was a slogan that had been given a different meaning from what the Japanese had expected.

### "Gona Gone"

A two-word signal came in last night, December 9, from the commander of the Australian unit on the left flank. It said nothing more than, "Gona Gone!" By tonight the bodies of six hundred and fifty Japanese dead had already been counted on Gona beach. It's possible at last to see the end of Japanese resistance approaching, with Gona completely in our hands again for the first time for one hundred and forty days.

For days now the fighting all the way along the enemy's "last stand" defense line has been—excepting for the tropical setting—the fighting of 1917-18 all over again. It's the same old picture of trench fighting, or dugouts and pill-boxes, of stomach-twisting bayonet charges behind lifting artillery barrages, of nerve-wracking night patrols across narrow strips of shell-torn earth lighted eerily by flares and star-shells; of deadly sniping and awful moments of suspense waiting for the zero hour that would send men scrambling across a fire-swept no-man's-land. As General Vasey said the other day: "The blasted war's gone old-fashioned on us all of a sudden!"

If it weren't for the "boongs" and the jungle and the oppressive tropical humidity it could be Paaschendaele or Château Thierry all over again.

Gradually, however, the Australians had whittled away Japanese post after Japanese post. A few days ago they had reduced organized resistance to one large pocket containing about 100 Japanese troops who were fighting on to the end, surrounded by an encircling ring of Australian steel. Japanese bodies, in advanced stages of decomposition, littered the area. The stench was almost unbearable; so bad, indeed, that the Japs wore gas-respirators most of the time, as much to ward off the evil odor of death as to protect themselves from the choking fumes of our shells.

The Australians, almost aghast at the rain of steel that had been

* On 6 February, over Wau, American Kittyhawk, Lightning and Airacobras shot down 41 Japanese bombers and Zeros without loss to themselves!

poured into the enemy pocket for days, grimly held their positions. They knew that the Japs had much ammunition and ample food in their stronghold. "But," they said, "sooner or later we'll smoke the bastards out!"

On Tuesday afternoon the final hammering began with a terrific mortar barrage from our positions, followed immediately by one of the most colossal artillery bombardments yet seen up here. Nine hundred rounds were poured into the Japanese post. Then wave after wave of American bombers came over with loads of high explosive.

The bombardment ended at dusk. It was obvious that the Japs had been severely shaken. Several seen wandering dazedly through the drifting clouds of smoke and dust, "bomb-happy," were picked off by our sharpshooters. This is a cruel war, as I've said before, and no quarter is given by either side. As night fell there was considerable movement in the Japanese positions. The story went round the Australian lines that the Japs were preparing to make a break for it. Until midnight no shot was fired, but every man was watchful and keyed up with suspense.

Rain began to fall steadily. It was not long before the Japanese began to move out cautiously, crawling in almost complete silence toward the water's edge. The Australians, watching every move, held their fire with splendid discipline. The Japs reached the water's edge and formed up to march along the coast to Sanananda. Then the Australian guns burst into chattering roar. Ruddy flashes of flame flung light into the black shadows of the jungle. Other Australians dashed forward with grenades and bayonets.

The sun came up on a scene of ghastly carnage. At the edge of the beach about 100 Japanese dead were stacked in grotesque heaps. Four badly wounded men were found and taken prisoner. They seemed astonished when a doctor carefully cleaned and bandaged their wounds.

The Australians methodically set to work to clean up the whole sector. Every tree and the remains of every hut were plastered thickly with the mud thrown up by weeks of artillery and aerial bombardment, coconut palms were uprooted or beheaded or snapped like carrots. Acres of ground were pitted with great bomb craters and water-filled shell holes.

Sprawled across one heap of dead was the body of a Japanese

officer, probably the commander of the garrison, wearing ceremonial uniform, with his ornate sword still buckled to his belt, with his white gloves covered with mud and blood. Occasionally there was the crack of a rifle or the *boop-boop-boop* of a tommy gun as the Australians dealt with isolated Japs still resisting in their foxholes. In one clearing exhausted Australians were sleeping on the ground. Scattered around them were the bodies of more than two hundred Japanese.

One Australian was searching through a patch of high kunai grass when he was suddenly confronted by five Japs. One threw his rifle with fixed bayonet, spear fashion, at the Australian. He dodged, dropped to the ground and hurled over a grenade. He waited for some minutes after the explosion and then inched forward cautiously. All five Japanese were dead.

By 4:15 P.M. every Japanese in Gona was dead or a prisoner. Many of the dead will never be found and the total number of Japanese who gave their lives to the defense of this strip of beach where the first Papuan landing was made nearly five months ago would probably exceed 1000. Many Australians have also paid the final sacrifice. Two padres are working quietly on the construction of small wooden crosses for their graves.

The news of Gona's fall has reached the Americans, still engaged in savage fighting on the fringe of Buna Village. The Yanks cheered and cheered again, and then put in a smashing drive along the east bank of Buna Creek, storming pill-box after pill-box. Five posts were taken at the point of the bayonet and in wild hand-to-hand fighting. The clearest indication I can give of the closeness of the fighting round the besieged village is to point out that that advance, involving days of preparation and an attack of savage violence, pushed our line forward exactly 50 yards!

This evening "Black Jack" Walker was flying his Beaufighter back from Lae less than two hundred feet above the sea. He saw signs of movement on Gona beach and circled back for a closer survey. Japanese bodies were massed everywhere. Beside them was a circle of Australians. The evidence strewn around indicated that they formed the burial party. Walker turned again and had a closer look. The Australians paid little or no attention to the plane skimming overhead just above the coconut palms. The pilot soon saw the reason why. They were involved in a game of two-up!

*Reform for the Orokaivas*

A few days ago I was standing at the junction of tracks leading to Gona and Sanananda. Three jeeps were unloading boxes of machine gun ammunition and grenades. Milling around the little vehicles was a crowd of coal-black natives, their lap-laps of red and purple and green splashing vivid colors across the drab background of dun-colored dust and trees.

Among the natives many tribes were represented. I saw two boys whom I had seen months before in a south coast village. As they lifted boxes of grenades on to their shining, muscular shoulders one of them grinned at me and said, "Better than mountains, taubada!" I agreed with him. The coastal plain outside Buna was a lot better than the cold, dripping jungles of the Owen Stanley's. It must have been a tough job for these laughing, sun-soaked Papuan coast boys in the carrier lines scrambling across the mighty main range.

Among the motley crowd of native carriers there were three who stood out among their fellows as much by their fierce appearance as by the fact that each wore only a G-string of bark in contrast to the calico lap-laps of the others. An Angau (Australian New Guinea Administrative Unit) sergeant, yabbering to the natives in a mixture of pidgin and Motu, saw me looking at them, and explained: "Orokaivas!"

I looked again. So these were the notorious Orokaivas! Tall, lean, wiry; fierce-eyed, heavy-browed, more negroid than the handsome Melanesians of the south coast. Two months ago the Orokaivas were notorious, hated by every Australian fighting man as traitors and murderers. And here they were back in the Australian carrier lines, looking shamefaced but eager, and showing their eagerness by working quite harmoniously with natives for whom normally they had nothing but contempt.

The story of the return of the Orokaivas was one of the many triumphs of the Angau men. The Orokaivas are traditionally fighters, with no love for the white man because he stamped out many of their cruel rites of sorcery, prevented their head-hunting, raids, and sternly crushed any tendency to return to cannibalism.

When the Japanese landed at Buna and began to push inexorably into the mountains, the Orokaivas thought that the invaders would be preferable to the Australians. They were gullible victims of the Japanese propaganda that they had come to free the natives from the "white man's yoke." And the Japanese, knowing the fame of the Orokaivas, found in them a useful weapon with which to intimidate tribes less anxious to cooperate. Wielding influence over all the Buna-Kokoda area, bands of Orokaivas began a reign of terror, killing natives who refused to cooperate with the Japanese, spying on Australian patrols, doing everything possible to hamper our already difficult defense.

That was the picture a few months ago—a picture that at one time became so serious that Allied bombers actually dropped pamphlets appealing—in pidgin and Motu—to the Orokaivas to come to their senses before it was too late.

Today the people of this wild tribe are behind our troops to the full. It is a strange contrast, and the best man to explain it is my good friend Major Elliott Smith, Angau Director of District Services, who in peacetime lived for years among the Orokaivas as a district magistrate.

He told me: "In the early days of the Japanese advance they betrayed to the Japanese the whereabouts of Australian missionaries and Allied airmen who had been forced down in the jungle. Some of the airmen were killed, some of the missionaries were massacred. Now the natives are actually helping to carry wounded and clear landing strips for our planes.

"The Orokaivas are proud, primitive fighters, and they have always resented the presence of the white man. The main thing that has helped us to bring them to heel is their own realization that the Japanese are infinitely worse masters than the Australians. They realized that long before our advance brought us into the Orokaiva country, and when we arrived, the natives were waiting to greet us. Hordes of Orokaivas came in from every village of the hills and the plains, bringing gifts of flowers and fruit, and apologizing for the poverty of the gifts because, they said, the Japanese had looted their homes and robbed their gardens until little was left. At every native village the local police boy and councillor were waiting—as they had been waiting for many days—formally to accept the return of British administrations.

"What really swung the sympathies of these Spartan people to our side was their horror at the filthy habits of the Japanese, at their wastefulness, brutality, and rough handling of native women. Soon after we returned we began to hear scores of stories of atrocities perpetrated by the Japanese against the natives. Every story was checked and counter-checked, and the total of verified incidents shows clearly the total disregard by the Japanese for normal human decencies.

"A beautiful 17-year-old native girl, daughter of an Orokaiva friend of mine, was raped in her father's hut by 24 Japanese soldiers. She died the same afternoon. The Japs regarded all native women as fair game. They killed any native who tried to prevent them interfering with them, and they killed any woman who tried to escape. Was it any wonder that the Japanese soon found that the Orokaivas were rapidly becoming dangerous enemies?

"There were one or two isolated cases of Japanese troops being attacked, and the enemy immediately took harsh steps to see that no natives carried weapons. Eleven members of the Biagi tribe, who knew nothing of this, came into Kokoda with the men in the party carrying their ordinary hunting spears. The whole party—including women and children—were herded together and all were bayoneted to death.

"The Orokaivas were also disgusted at the filthiness of the Japs, whose camps were revolting in their untidiness and lack of hygiene and sanitation. They were also aghast at Japanese wastefulness. Coconut trees were chopped down to obtain a few nuts. Gardens were uprooted and ruined just for the sake of a few yams.

"Some of the tribal chiefs told me that when the Japs first came they gave food to the natives, who helped them because they hoped that if they were friendly the Japanese would not destroy their gardens and villages. For a few days the policy succeeded. Within a week, however, the Japs were grabbing whatever they wanted.

"Now the Orokaivas are seeking to make amends for the assistance they gave to our enemy. They are working magnificently on our side."

I saw some of the work of the Orokaivas at Popendetta air strip, a few miles beyond the Buna front. When the natives were told that the Australians wanted to clear patches of kunai grass to make airfields hundreds of Orokaivas flocked along the jungle tracks to Popendetta; they brought their own primitive tools with them, and the first plane laden with supplies landed three hours after they had begun the job. Next day I arrived at Popendetta in one of the 58 planes which landed on the new strip between dawn and dusk.

The Orokaivas kept on the job of making other strips, slaving in the blazing sun from sunrise to sunset. Then, in the "cool" of the evening, scores of them would arrive at the Allied advanced casualty clearing stations just behind the Japanese lines to carry wounded back 10 or 12 miles to the waiting transport planes. And the tenderness which these huge, fierce-visaged head-hunters showed for the Australian and American wounded was the perfect expression of how much the Orokaivas had changed.

### Bottcher's Salient

Today the greatest individual act of heroism among the American forces in New Guinea came to an end when a grimy party of twelve men under the leadership of a tough sergeant who can scarcely speak English were relieved in the salient on Buna beach that they had held against an overwhelming force of Japanese for seven days and nights. The establishment of that tiny salient and the holding of it might well prove one of the vital factors in breaking the Japanese grip on the entire Buna sector. Sergeant Herman Bottcher, of "Bottcher's Salient," richly deserves the D.S.C. he's going to be awarded, and also the promotion to commissioned rank which is being rushed through the "usual channels."

Bottcher is 37 and he comes from San Francisco. He is German-born, from Landsberg, near Berlin, worked in Australia for some years in the late "twenties," and then went to the United States to try his luck. He knows modern war, because soon after he received United States citizenship he lost it when he enlisted with the International Brigade to fight against the Axis in Spain. He was a good soldier and a brave fighter for the Republicans, in whose army he rose from the rank of private to that of captain. He enlisted later with the United States Army and found himself in Papua, fighting his second war against the Axis.

Bottcher is of medium size, wears a magnificent black beard, looks at you with fierce eyes, and speaks almost unrecognizable English with a thick German accent.

On December 5 the Americans were hammering in vain at the strongly defended Japanese posts outside Buna. The enemy held the village on one side and the Government station on the other. There had been a disheartening series of failures by the Americans to breach the defenses. Bottcher was in the thick of it. He came back to get a pail of water for some of his wounded and saw two or three American officers sitting on the ground trying to work out ways and means of assaulting the enemy line. Bottcher glared at them as he filled the bucket. "If you guys would get up off your goddam tails and start fightin' maybe we'd get something done!" he snarled and strode back to the forward positions.

Bottcher decided to do something himself. He called for volunteers to drive a wedge right into the Japanese positions and through to the beach. It was a tough job. Many men volunteered and Bottcher picked twelve of them.

They squirmed through the swamps and coconut palms toward their objectives through a hail of heavy fire, but the tommy guns and grenades of Bottcher and his men cleaned up enemy machine-gun posts, and brought snipers toppling from trees. After several hours of heavy fighting the little force reached its objective, where Bottcher ordered his men to dig in on the beach and stay there.

Trenches and weapon pits were dug. At dawn the Japanese attacked from both flanks, one force rushing from the village and one from the Government station. Both attacks were repulsed by fierce machine-gun fire, and the Japanese retired, dragging some wounded with them, and leaving forty dead on the beach. A few hours later a Japanese machine-gun post brought harassing fire to bear on the American post, so Bottcher crawled out with a pocketful of grenades, squirmed across the bullet-torn sand, and blew the post to pieces with grenades. He crawled back to his little garrison.

That night the watchful doughboys saw enemy barges moving offshore, and opened up on them with heavy machine-gun fire. One barge was set on fire, and Japanese could be seen scrambling from it on to the other, which escaped at full speed to the northward.

Next day a party of Japanese was seen sneaking across a bridge over Buna Creek, and Bottcher's guns brought down six of them before the others fled.

All this time the little beachhead was constantly under fire from strong enemy positions on both sides, but the thought of retiring never occurred to the German-born sergeant who had been wounded several times. The American post was causing great concern to the Japanese, and on the night of December 9 another double attack was made from both sides. Again the Japanese were driven back in confusion.

Next morning Bottcher and a few of his men crawled out of their trenches into no-man's-land. They counted seven more Japanese dead added to the pile of corpses in front of their weapon pits, and found two abandoned Japanese machine guns with ammunition. These were dragged back to the post to increase its armament.

Once or twice Bottcher had visitors. On one occasion the American commanding officer—General Eichelberger, a brave man and a fine soldier—crawled along to Bottcher's Salient, and did a bit of useful sniping while he was there! But most of the time the thirteen men were alone, with hundreds of Japanese all round them.

Today a stronger party of fresh troops went in to relieve them. But before he came out Bottcher was able to get a final crack at the Japs. For some hours they had watched the Japanese building a heavy timber barricade leading from Buna Village toward the American post. It was obviously their intention to launch an attack from behind the barricade. Bottcher got his mortars ranged and waited until the palisade was almost completed. Then he sent over a string of bombs and blew the timber wall and all the Japanese working on it to pieces. Since then the Japanese haven't attempted to begin the job again.

By a conservative count it is believed that Bottcher and his twelve men have killed more than 120 Japs from this little salient. Now the Americans have attacked in force through the salient, and have completely cut the main enemy line, dividing the village force from that fighting from the Government station. Thanks to Sergeant Herman Bottcher, late of the International Brigade. The next time I see him, according to all reports, he will be *Captain* Herman Bottcher, D.S.C.!

### Massacre at Mambare

The Japanese lost one north coast beachhead today, with the fall of Buna Village, and gained another at tremendous cost well up the coast near the Mambare Delta, 53 miles away. Attacking in force from Bottcher's Salient, the Americans smashed right through Buna Village to the coast, completely cleaned up the area, which is littered with the bodies of hundreds of Japanese, and effectively isolated the enemy's Sanananda force from the main garrison which holds a strong line from Giropa Point to Cape Endaiadere. General Eichelberger practically led his troops into the attack. This is every man's war up here. Senior officers will be found in the trenches with the troops, and right in the front line you will see commanding generals directing machine-gun and mortar fire and blazing away with tommy guns at Japanese snipers in the tree-tops!

The Mambare landing appears to have been a very costly Japanese attempt to establish a coastal staging point for the barges which run between Salamaua and Buna carrying reinforcements down and bringing the sick and wounded back. The landing was attempted by five warships, two cruisers and three destroyers, but very few of the enemy troops reached the shore, thanks again to our overwhelming superiority in the air.

Bodies of hundreds of Japanese troops are strewn along the beaches and mangrove swamps of the Mambare Delta or floating in the sea, where they were slaughtered in scores by the blazing gunfire of Australian-manned Beaufighters and Havoc dive-bombers, and American bombers.

More than 100 Allied planes were in action against the Japanese landing force, which arrived shortly before dawn. Two big motor landing barges were already packed with stores, lowered from each warship, and were taken to the beach four miles away. At the same time floating metal drums of stores tied together in rafts of forty, with wooden cases lashed alongside, were pushed over the side from the warships, to be floated ashore.

The landing barges returned to the ships to ferry troops ashore, fifty in each barge. Ship's lifeboats were also used, but the troop movement had scarcely been started when the first of the swarms of Allied planes came roaring in with the first streaks of dawn.

About three hundred Japanese, wearing only lifebelts, had jumped over the sides of the ships, and were attempting to tow the clumsy store rafts ashore, when two Australian Beaufighters began the fierce air blitz. Almost touching the waves each of the Beaufighters swept in with ten guns blazing. Japanese troops, some of them wearing packs and tin helmets, dived out of the barges into the water. Others were killed in the boats. Five barges went to the bottom.

Japanese were seen swimming fully dressed, others completely naked. One barge carrying only a load of corpses kept circling crazily round and round, often cutting down troops frantically trying to keep afloat two miles off shore. One ship's boat drifted out to sea with dead Japanese huddled in the sternsheets. Oil from shattered fuel drums spread over the water. Four of the big supply rafts were blown up by cannon fire. By this time the Japanese had a hornet's nest around their ears. Overhead North American bombers rained down high explosives. Other Beaufighters as well as Australian Havoc dive-bombers, had joined in the attack, and a powerful force of American Boston Havoc attack planes was strafing the sea and the beaches. Dead Mangrove Island, a large jungled island in the delta, where many Japanese had made landings, was a mass of flames caused by our bombs.

Ashore at the village of Cauora, columns of smoke were rising from dumps of stores the Japanese had established with the first landings. One Beaufighter observer said that the Japanese on the Beach were like ants. They fell in rows before the hundreds of guns pouring lead from the skies. Scores of corpses were washing in the sea at the water's edge, others were floating in the water, more were huddled on the sand. Many planes made between 30 and 40 passes across the landing area. Beaufighters alone poured out about 75,000 rounds of machine-gun and cannon fire.

Many of the Japanese who had reached the beach ran frantically for the jungle belt. Some fell before they reached it, and then Havocs roared in and systematically sprayed the trees with bullets to strike at those who had reached the shelter of the jungle. A strong force of Japanese soldiers in full battle dress was caught as they were wading through the shallow, and were brought down like corn before a scythe. Three barges were seen well offshore with about 100 troops in them, and 50 more troops were struggling in the water nearby. The men and boats were strafed. One barge went up in flames, and within a few minutes the only men in the other two were dead. The remainder of the Japanese were struggling in the water.

How many of the Japanese survived the hour-after-hour air attack cannot even be estimated. Undoubtedly hundreds died. Planes that went over to attack many hours later found the beaches deserted by all except the dead, but scores of Japanese were still swimming in the water from a mile to two miles offshore. They were strafed again.

## Morale Goes Two Ways

Although I am far away from New Guinea now I can visualize the scene that the newspapers are describing—the base camp at the beginning of the Owen Stanley's, a green clearing that overlooks the valley leading down to Moresby. Ahead lies the great bulk of the main range, tier after tier of blue and violet ridges stretching away until the topmost summits are lost in the great rolling cumulus. Lines of gaunt Australian troops in green uniforms that are stained and tattered stand motionless in the clearing. Their ranks have been painfully thinned by death and casualties and illness, for these are the men who marched across the Owen Stanley's, who fought the bloody battles of Templeton's Crossing and Eora Creek and Oivi and Gorari, and then marched across the steamy northern plain to assault Gona and Sanananda and Buna and Giropa Point. In front of them stands General Sir Thomas Blamey. He speaks with a voice that often trembles with emotion, the genuine emotion of a man who has seen these troops, whom he really loves, fighting and dying in conditions of filth and hardship almost indescribable. The Australians are listening to him, but their eyes are on the great range ahead of them, and some of them must be thinking that never before was there so much truth in the adage that "distance lends enchantment to the view." The range has a grandeur of beauty that is inspiring. But these men know its cruelty, its horrors of slow starvation and quick death. The wind whispers in the trampled kunai as Commander-in-Chief of Allied Land Forces speaks: "I bring you from the Prime Minister of Australia the thanks of the nation for what you have done. In all its history the A.I.F., both the First and the Second, has never been called upon to perform a more difficult task than fell to you. No Australian force has ever accomplished their task with greater credit. You deserve and you have the very highest praise of our nation and our Army.

"Many of you have been through the desert, where all is utter desolation, but I am sure you have never encountered anything comparable to the miasmic jungles of the Owen Stanley's and round

Gona. In this defense of your country you have acquired every military virtue and have established a standard for yourself which it will be difficult for the rest of the A.I.F. and the Australian Army to live up to.

"You have taught the world that you are infinitely superior to this inhuman foe against whom you were pitted. Your enemy is a curious race—a cross between the human being and the ape. And like the ape, when he is cornered he knows how to die. But he is inferior to you, and you know it, and that knowledge will help you to victory.

"During the last war a distinguished British general once said to me, 'There's something remarkable about this A.I.F. of yours. They have more in common with the Roman legionnaires than any other soldier in history.' This was a very great tribute, because the Roman soldier has been looked up to as the hallmark for almost 2000 years.

"I have been asked many times if the new A.I.F. measures up to the old, and I say this, that the old A.I.F. never had a harder task than you have had nor did it achieve it so well. If any should doubt me—and I speak with my long experience of the Australian soldier—let him go and walk the trail to Kokoda.

"What we have before us is so very far away that I cannot see the end of it, but I know that you and our nation will face it with courage. You have lost many comrades, but you have learnt that it is the highest and sweetest achievement of us all that we should die for our country. We all reverence their memory, for they gave all they had to give so that our freedom should continue.

"You know that we have to destroy these vermin if we and our families are to live. We must go on to the end if civilization is to survive. We must exterminate the Japanese."

I would like to have seen that parade. But I am in Melbourne, 3000 miles away. It is good to be home again. It is good to sit down before good food and clean linen. It is good to be home even if all these things mean that disillusionment comes, too. Because since my return from New Guinea I have formed some definite opinions. One is that there are remarkably few people who have even the most remote idea of what the young Australian and American troops went through to drive the Japanese 100 miles farther away from Port Moresby—and from Australia. Many people fret about the morale and discipline of the troops. They don't want me to tell them stories of the valor and morale of our fighting men. They would prefer me to substantiate the cruel, lying rumors that they have picked up—"Is it true that our chaps ran when the Japs attacked?" . . . "They tell me the Militia let the A.I.F. down!" . . . "They say the Yanks were no good." . . . Yet the A.I.F. fought and died in New Guinea, so did the Militia, so did the Americans. They died in hundreds and they died gallantly. It is a pity that these mainland scandalmongers—it is true they are few in number—didn't look to their own spirit and morale and discipline.

And these victories, which have been won at such bitter cost, are tending again to build up the same old spirit of complacency and disinterestedness (expressed to me so often by the glib comment: "Oh, well, the war will soon be over now!") that was widespread throughout the country until the Japanese advance to within 30 miles of Moresby swept public opinion out of the frying pan of complacency into the fire of pessimism, even defeatism and, in some cases, plain, unadulterated panic.

I should be glad to listen to anyone who can give me one sound factual reason—quite apart from wishful thinking—as a basis for any theory that the war is nearing its end. In my opinion the end of the war, at this moment, is quite unpredictable, and probably it will remain unpredictable until, quite suddenly and astonishingly, it comes to an end. It is true that that day might only be six months or a year away. It is equally true that it might be five years. And we should work on the belief that the latter is more likely. I do not believe that if Germany and Italy were knocked out Japan could be accounted for swiftly and easily. If the reconquest of the Pacific is to be as lengthy, in comparison, as the reconquest of Papua, it would take us many years to clear the countless islands which within the last twelve months have come under the banner of the Rising Sun. And how are we to know that the Japanese are not prepared to fight just as tenaciously and just as bitterly as the few thousands of ordinary Japanese infantrymen who for almost two months have clung like limpets to a narrow strip of bomb-pitted, shell-torn beach at Buna, subjected night and day to an almost endless hail of bombs and shells and bullets?

I have seen the Australians and Americans cleaning these stubborn fighters out of their foxholes and dugouts and trenches and pill-boxes. Weapons on both sides are much the same. We win only because our morale is good, our discipline is good, and because our spirit, in the final analysis of kill or be killed fighting, is better than that of the Japanese.

Australia might have reason to worry about the morale of its home front. There is no reason to worry about morale on the battlefield. This story gives what I feel is the expression of perfect morale and perfect fighting spirit.

I was just behind the front line at Gona, crouched down in the kunai grass with a party of 21 A.I.F. infantrymen from South Australia. They had been in action almost constantly for two months. They were thin, haggard, undernourished, insect-bitten, grimy, and physically near the end of their tether. They were fighting on fighting spirit alone. And because that spirit was good they were still superlative troops.

They were talking among themselves about a Japanese weapon pit which was concealed in the butt of a huge jungle tree at the end of a clearing which lay beyond the kunai patch. The pit had held them up for two hours. Two of their number had been killed and five wounded when they first pushed through the kunai and ran into a scythelike sweep of fire from the Japanese positions. A twenty-three-year-old subaltern from Glen Osmond was talking quietly to the men.

"No use sitting round, I guess. We might as well get stuck into it!"

The men grinned. The lieutenant—who wore no badges of rank and was clad in the same green jungle uniform as the troops—turned to a lanky sergeant. "How much of that grass do you reckon they've cleared away between the post and the edge of the kunai?"

"Seventy or 80 yards, I'd say," replied the sergeant. A couple of privates nodded and a lance-corporal estimated it as "nearer a hundred."

"Well, there are 21 of us now," said a stocky little private from Renmark. "Once we get up to the bloody pit it would only take about six of us to dig the little blighters out."

He tossed a hand grenade a few inches into the air and caught it nonchalantly.

"You ought to be one of the six, sport," interjected another private, lolling on his pack with his net-covered steel helmet over his eyes, and a piece of yellow grass moving up and down rhythmically to the slow champing of his jaws. "You're so bloody short, Tojo'll never be able to get a sight on yer!" A soft ripple of laughter ran round the little group.

But even that little burst of laughter was heard. From the Japanese post came the pap-pap-pap of a short machine-gun burst. The bullets zipped harmlessly high overhead. The man who was chewing grass tipped his helmet back and looked in the direction of the enemy post, invisible behind the screen of kunai. "Use 'em up, Tojo," he muttered. "You ain't got much longer to go."

The lieutenant buckled his belt and looked round at his men. They grinned and reached for their rifles and Brens and tommy guns. "According to Shorty here, this job's going to mean 15 of us won't get through," he said, as if it were a grand joke.

"Wouldn't count on that," said the lanky man, spitting out the well-chewed piece of grass. "He always was an optimist!"

Another ripple of laughter. "Well, some come back, they say," grinned the lieutenant. He motioned to the men. They took a final look at their weapons, saw the grenades were ready, and began to squirm slowly toward the edge of the long grass. As he moved past the lanky man winked at me. "Give us a good write-up," he said.

The movement of the 21 men made little movement in the grass and the occasional shaking of the thick blades might have been only the wind blowing in from the beach. They reached the edge of the kunai. A few yards out in the cleared area were the twisted bodies of their comrades killed a couple of hours before. There was a sudden flash of steel as the Australians sprang to their feet and started running. They were yelling like madmen. For a split second there was no sound from the enemy position. Then it started. The wild *brrrrrpppppppbrrrrrop* of machine guns firing with fingers tight on the triggers, the crack of grenades, once the scream of a man.

The Australians were running in a straight line. It's no use swerving or dodging when you're charging into machine-gun fire. Their bayonets were at the high port. Men were falling. One threw up his hands, stopped dead, and stumbled to one side. Another fell as he was running, rolling over and over like a rabbit hit on the run.

Another was spun around like a top before he crumpled up and slid to the ground. The little man who had predicted that six would get through had almost reached the Japanese pit when he fell. He went over backwards as if somebody had delivered a terrific uppercut.

He didn't live to find out, but his estimate was wrong. Nine of the Australians got through. They wiped out the post, killing every one of the 19 Japs inside.

That is the meaning of morale. I saw that happen. I saw many other incidents just as expressive of the fighting spirit that makes these young Australians and Americans the world's best assault troops. These men, after the endless weeks of short rations, the gruelling fight across the Owen Stanley's, the sight of their comrades killed or wounded or evacuated with the mysterious malady known generally as "jungle fever," would not have been condemned had their spirit wilted, their morale weakened in the final bitter struggle that preceded the fall of Gona and Buna. But that morale had been tempered in the flame of hardship, adversity, and peril. It did not wilt.

To fly down from the Buna front to Port Moresby and then to the mainland was to receive something of a shock. There was a holiday atmosphere everywhere—a spirit of happiness and laughter and carnival that was totally absent in the dripping jungle belts and slimy swamps of Buna. Beaches were crowded, guest houses were full, newspapers carried stories of strikes, there were complaints about the difficulty of getting hold of a few bottles of beer for Christmas celebrations. Politicians were still wrangling about oversea service for Australian troops. Nobody seemed to think about the crude graves near Buna where many hundreds of troops of the United States equivalent of our Militia had sacrificed their lives 10,000 miles from home in a campaign that was largely the defense of Australia.

There is nothing wrong with morale on the fighting front. It is a pity it isn't as good on the home front.

### *"Of Human Things"*

The show is over. It is January 23, 1943. The last Japanese soldier in Papua has been killed or captured. Buna station, Giropa Point and Cape Endaiadere, where the Japanese resisted stubbornly from their foxholes for two bitter months were crushed by Australian and American infantry charging behind Australian-manned and American-built light tanks. On the Sanananda track the last pockets, which had held out longer than any others, were crushed. Some of the Japanese gave themselves up. Others stayed in their foxholes to be killed or to die of starvation and disease. Yesterday fighting ceased.

It was on this date twelve months ago, that the war in New Guinea began when Rabaul succumbed to the furious onslaught of the men of Nippon. Much has happened since then. The 16,000 men that General Horii threw into the attempt to conquer Papua have been killed or wounded or captured. Mostly they have been killed. And General Horii himself is dead. So are many other uncounted Japanese, destroyed in their planes and destroyed in the scores of ships that have become twisted junk on the sea floor for the sake of Japanese aggression in the South Seas.

Since the first entry in this book a whole year has slipped away. It has been a year of boredom and excitement, or hardships that have made normal comforts seem like luxuries. It has been a year composed of long months of waiting and long months of fighting. Old friends have become heroes—although most of them will never be known as heroes except to a few of us, and old friends have been killed.

So much has happened that I have not written about, so much that cannot be written about, for the war in New Guinea is not yet over. We have not yet struck at a single main enemy base. The Japanese have many more bases south of the equator than they had when this diary of war in the South Seas was begun. We have fewer bases. But we have infinitely greater strength massed in each of them. That is the important thing. Port Moresby, which was given 36 hours to hold off the enemy, has survived more than 100 air attacks . . . and is incalculably stronger than ever before. Fear and anxiety have been replaced by courage and firm confidence. We have fought an army of Japan's "unbeatable" jungle fighters. And we have destroyed it. We have matched our aircraft against the Zero—the plane we all thought once was invincible—and we have wrested from the enemy the supremacy of the air and considerably more than 1000 of their vaunted aircraft are charred and mangled wrecks in the seas and jungles of the islands. We, who began the battle alone, now have staunch allies, the Americans and the Dutch, fighting gallantly shoulder to shoulder with our own men. We, who first stood in the way of a war machine at the full peak of its efficiency, in the full tide of its ruthless conquest, matched its overwhelming strength with nothing, or next to nothing, except the determination to resist. We can match its strength now—for the Japanese war machine is still immensely strong—with strength, and our strength grows daily. It is still far below the potential of the Japanese. Foreign Minister Evatt, our great fighter in the Battle for Supply, is getting ready to go to Washington again to tackle the policy of an inelastic interpretation of the "Beat Hitler First" strategy. He did a grand job for the fighting men on his first mission. We are all hoping that he will succeed again in making official America conscious of what is really happening out here, where we have been fighting for months on a dangerously narrow margin of safety and beating the enemy only because our quality is better than his quantity. To do this, many men have died. The thousands of men—very many thousands—who have died have gone, as individuals, unknown to the world, but they will be forever remembered by the men who knew them and the men who fought alongside them. Many more will die, because there is much warfare ahead of us before Japan is beaten. Even in New Guinea, the war will go on. As I write these words fierce fighting is flaring up again in the Bulolo Valley, between Mubo and Wau. Our bombers are still hammering Lae and Salamaua and Gasmata and Rabaul and the Solomons. This will go on for a long time. Sometimes I think the place to beat Japan is Asia, not these scattered islands. I think it is correct that we should defeat Germany first and then turn all the weight of the United Nations against Japan, but we must not put Japan aside to be dealt with later. It will be tough enough, God knows, even now, tougher with every day we spend in postponing the inevitable.

But as I look back over the year that has gone I don't think of matters of high strategy. I don't even worry about whether the campaign in New Guinea has been an important part of the war for civilization's survival or whether it has, in fact, been merely a spectacular tropic sideshow.

I think more of the little human things that go to make war what it is. Wars are things for men, not machines alone. Each soldier, each airman, each sailor, each native carrier, represents a lifetime, and every one of those lives has in some way been affected by the events of three hundred and sixty-five days. The effect on each has itself affected others. So that on this earth there are many thousands of people, most of them humble, some of them great, to whom the war in the islands has real meaning. For many of them—in Australia, in Great Britain, in the United States, in Papua and New Guinea and the Bismarcks and the Solomons—the campaign will be the event in their lives of supreme significance.

So I think of the men of New Guinea and the good times and the bad. But the bad times don't seem quite so terrible now and the good times are all the better in retrospect.

I remember the anxiety of the early days . . . the arrival of the first fighters . . . my first air raid . . . the simple warning that flashed around the garrison whenever the Japanese bombers were heading our way—"It's on!" . . . the death of grand men like Johnny Jackson and Peter Turnbull of Australia; of Randy Lanford and Bill Benn of the U. S. A. and countless others. I remember the talks we had by lamplight and the songs we used to sing. Seventy-five Squadron's parody on *Bless 'em All* (a song which must be the *Tipperary* of this war) will stay with me for the rest of my life:

Kittyhawks don't worry me,
No, Kittyhawks don't worry me:
Oil-burning bastards with flaps on their wings;
Jiggered-up pistons and jiggered-up rings
But we're saying goodbye to them all
As back to the workshops they crawl.
There'll be only elation and much jubilation
When we say goodbye to them all!

They say there's a Hudson just leaving Milne Bay
Bound for the Seven Mile,
Heavily laden with terrified men
Who've been there a bloody long while.
They're scared stiff and frightened and browned off and all,
Sergeants and officers, too;
For they haven't a notion in which bloody ocean
They'll be doing the breast stroke or crawl.

They say that the Japs have a jolly good kite
Of that we're no longer in doubt,
So if a Zero gets on to your tail
This is the way to get out:
Be careful, be cheerful, keep calm and sedate
And don't let your British blood boil;
But don't hesitate, ram it right through the gate
And you'll drown the poor bastard in oil!

And I think of the men sweating agonizingly up the Kokoda track, and storming the Japanese pill-boxes at Gona and Buna. Of the hot sunshine and the sweat and the smell of death and cordite. And of a great crowd of village natives dancing the Ki-tolo dance—the "Dance of Happiness"—by the light of the full moon in a village on the south coast. The drums and the chanting went on for hours. And when it was over a senior Australian officer spoke to the natives and told them that when the men of Japan had been driven back to their homes the people of New Guinea would be brought to Port Moresby for the Great Dance . . . a Ki-tolo Dance such as New Guinea had never before seen. The tribes would come, he said, from the east coast and the west coast, from the villages of Milne Bay and the villages of Buna, from Huon Gulf and the Sepik, from the Trobriands and Rabaul and the Bismarcks, from the Louisiades and the Solomons. The Great Dance would go on for days and it would mean that the days of war had gone, that the *Negana Tuari* had ended, that peace had come again to the sun-drenched plains and dripping jungles and cloud-capped mountains of New Guinea.

And that is the sight I would like to see more than any other— the Great Dance of Ki-tolo in Port Moresby. . . .


*Postscript in Connecticut*

Spring in Connecticut, with the new green foliage feathering the tops of the birches and the maples, and the rolling cumulus reflected in the still waters of Lake Wononscopomuc, is so utterly different from anything else in the last fifteen months that a great mental wrench is necessary before one can think back on New Guinea, on the sweat and the dirt, and the eye-aching glare of the tropic noon, and the smell of the jungle, and the smell of death and cordite, on

the natives sloshing through the black mud and the thunder of falling bombs. War, in this country, still seems very far away, very un-
real. This is the way all people should live. Why are sane people
forced by a few megalomaniacs to discard this way of life in ex-
change for the ugliness and squalor and bestiality of war? Simply
because the megalomaniacs have brute force behind them and
with that brute force they seek to superimpose their diseased way
of life over this scene that lies before me.

The distant hills are lilac and the green fields across the lake are
shimmering in the sunshine. Somewhere in the woods a man is
chopping timber and the thud of his axe is a sound not very different from the distant noise of the "woodpecker" in the jungle. But
could any two settings be more different than the ordered, garden-
like landscape of Connecticut and the tangled, bizarre wilderness of
New Guinea? Behind me, on the terrace, my host and hostess are
sitting in the mild late-afternoon sunshine. Janie is lounging on
the grass with her hair tousled by the wind and with her dungarees
rolled up above her calves. On the other side of the road two baby
boys, Jerry and Pepper, are playing. The wind carries their screams
of delight and their bubbling laughter. That laughter of children
is a key to why tens of thousands of young Americans are squaring
up to war on the battlefields half a world away. This little Connecticut village had, I am told, a peacetime population of little more
than 1500. Now more than 400 of its young men—all of its young
men—have marched away to war. Some of them are in New Guinea.

Out there the fight is still going on. Today dive-bombers are
plastering Wau, up in the Bulolo Valley goldfields. Yesterday the
Fortresses were hammering Rabaul. Along the great defense line
of the southwest Pacific the Japanese are still pouring in their men
and ships and aircraft, pouring them into the 67 bases that they
have established along a 2500-mile arc of islands that leads from
Timor, in the west, to the Central Solomons, in the east. It is
likely that the real war in the southwest Pacific has yet to begin.
General MacArthur, the man of mystery who has been "delivering
the goods" now for fourteen months, has been talking with tough-
faced Admiral Halsey of the south Pacific. The war is running headlong to its climacteric.

Somewhere "out there" tough little General Kenney is thinking
out new ways of using his great team of fighters of the United

States Fifth Air Force and the Royal Australian Air Force so that the Japanese can be smashed. An Australian general once said to me: "The debt we owe to the Fifth American Air Force can never be understood or repaid!" They have fought always against odds but their iron resolution and dauntless spirit have never wavered. So many of them have gone. Lovable Bill Benn, who led his Fortresses into the attack on the night of the first "skip-bombing" when Rabaul became a miniature Coventry, has gone—missing on a reconnaissance job—and most of his squadron are no longer in the fight. Ken MacCullar, hero of innumerable hazardous flights on lonehanded B-17 missions, has been killed since I crossed the Pacific. The Japs didn't get him. They tried fifty times or more with antiaircraft fire and fighters, but Ken was too smart for them. He was killed on an Australian airfield when his Fortress turned over after having collided with a small kangaroo that bounded across the landing strip!

These men—so many thousands of them—have given their lives, but they have held the fort. They have done more than that. They have driven the Jap back on his tracks, rocked him with blow after blow. It was in March of last year that I sat in a Papuan grass hut and heard a Tokyo announcer boast that Port Moresby was laid waste by Japanese bombs and that it would be under the flag of Nippon within seven days. Well, Port Moresby, after fourteen months, still hasn't been laid waste, despite 106 air raids, and the only flags that fly there today are the Australian and the American ensigns. And Port Moresby has been the clenched fist that has struck shattering blows again and again at the men of Nippon.

It was from Port Moresby that the Battle of the Bismarck Sea was directed—the most complete triumph of the war of land-based aircraft over sea power. The Japs moved their ships—10 cruisers and destroyers and 12 transports—under cover of a west-moving weather front, a great monsoonal bank of storm clouds beneath which the ships heading for Lae were completely hidden. Initially, that battle was won by an American meteorologist who sat in a grass hut and worked out the movement of a second weather front, moving in a northwesterly direction from the south coast of Papua. He calculated carefully and worked it out that at a certain position at a certain time the two weather fronts would collide. Clouds would break and he estimated there would be about two hours of clear weather in which to press home our attacks. It worked out just that way—in exactly the position and at the time he had predicted. Our bombers and fighters were all bombed up and ready, placed in strategic positions so that the blow could be struck at exactly the right moment. Altogether we used 138 aircraft in the attack. The Japanese employed 150 Zeros as a screen, and they had more than 200 other planes in reserve at Rabaul.

Australian Beaufighters went in at mast-head height to strafe the decks of warships and transports to soften up anti-aircraft fire. Behind them came American Douglas Havocs and B-25's. At 6000 feet swarmed the Flying Fortresses, with top cover of P-38's above them. The main bombing attack was delivered by the B-25's, which skip-bombed from 200 feet. One formation dropped 16 bombs for 12 direct hits and four near-misses!

None of the Japanese ships reached Lae. All 22 of them went to the bottom, carrying with them 15,000 troops, 3000 seamen. Of the Japanese "protective screen" of 150 Zeros, probably 90 were destroyed or so terribly shot up that they would have great difficulty in getting home. In two hours as much loss had been inflicted on the Japanese as in six months of nightmare jungle fighting. That is the power of courageously fought aviation.

Today the Japanese are starving in Lae and Salamaua, starving because of an air blockade imposed by men who have fought long against odds, but who have fought with such superlative courage that they have overcome them. Quality has beaten quantity and the spirit of democracy has triumphed in this small theatre of war—as it will triumph in all theatres of the Pacific war—against Bushido, or Shintoism, or anything else that Japanese like to think up.

The war out there is hard and tough. It will be hard and tough until the final blow is struck. I have put a name to this book which might sound bombastic, might seem to have been written as a catch-phrase. But I believe that the fighting out there in New Guinea has been the toughest fighting in the world. And it won't get any easier until we are at length able to hurl the full great weight of the United Nations against this common enemy of all mankind.

Out there at this very minute there are the sounds of war. The screaming whine of bombs, the strange animal cries of men dying. Over here there are other sounds, more beautiful sounds . . . the sound of a girl humming a tune, the soft whisper of the spring breezes through the new foliage of the birches, the chuckling, bubbling laughter of children with apple cheeks and eyes still wide with the wonderment of babyhood.

And in the final analysis of things the sound of a laughing baby in Connecticut is dependent on the cry of a dying man in Papua or Tunisia or Attu. For only out of the blood and sacrifice and horror and stupidity of war can come the new world for these two kids in Connecticut and for the millions of other children in the world today.

New Guinea is 12,000 miles away. The sun is yellowing the light on the trees and casting purple shadows in the lake. A white swan is gliding near the shore, breaking the reflections of the fir trees into a thousand wriggling shapes of light and shade. A tousle-haired schoolboy with a fishing rod over his shoulder is kicking stones through the dust as he walks toward his home. The pale blue smoke is snaking quietly from the chimneys. Two old men walk past, and one is telling the other about his victory garden. Lights are golden in the windows and the smell of wood smoke is in the air. From the other side of the road there is quietness now. Jerry and Pepper are being tucked into their beds. . . .

No matter what happens, it's worth it!

Made in the USA
Middletown, DE
27 August 2022